For the English-language edition:

Translator
Sheila Hardie

Consultant
Dr David S Reay
School of GeoSciences
Ecology and Resource Management
University of Edinburgh

Editor
Camilla Rockwood

Prepress
Claire Williamson

Prepress manager
Sharon McTeir

Publishing manager
Patrick White

Originally published by Larousse as *Petit atlas des mers et océans*
by Anne Lefèvre-Balleydier

© Larousse/VUEF, 2003

English-language edition
© Chambers Harrap Publishers Ltd 2004

ISBN 0550 10159 4

Typeset by Chambers Harrap Publishers Ltd, Edinburgh
Printed in France by IME, Beaume-les-Dames

Anne Lefèvre-Balleydier

Seas and Oceans

CHAMBERS
World Library

Contents

Maps

Foreword

A large proportion of mankind is directly affected by the seas and oceans. Half of the world's population lives less than 150km from the coast, and over 200 million people depend on the sea for their livelihood. Throughout history, these vast bodies of water have inspired a combination of respect, fear and irresistible fascination. Today the mechanisms that control ocean dynamics are better understood. Research has revealed their extraordinary impact on the Earth's climate, and on the distribution of plants and animals around the world.

The first living organisms appeared in the oceans over three billion years ago, and the oceans still contribute greatly to maintaining life on Earth today. Not only are they the main source of atmospheric oxygen, they are also a remarkable carbon dioxide 'pump' and a universal supply of water (the oceans contain 99% of all the water on the surface of the globe). Thus, they have a great influence on the future of all living species, including our own. Capable of storing a thousand times more heat than the atmosphere, they play a vital role in regulating our climate. The El Niño phenomenon shows just how fragile the balance is between atmosphere and ocean: when the winds off the coast of Peru weaken, the sea currents in this region change direction, and this has an enormous impact on weather patterns all over the world.

Another example of this fragile balance is the limited extent of the oceans' resources. At least one quarter of the world's marine fish stocks are currently overexploited and have no potential for further increase. They are likely to continue to decrease unless remedial action is taken to reduce or reverse overfishing. Other major problems facing our oceans include rising pollution levels and warming of the waters, a result of the general warming of the atmosphere. There is an urgent and vital need to conserve the riches of the sea, not only because of the enormous economic significance of the resources and human activities linked to them, but also because the future of the whole biosphere – including that of the human race – is at stake.

The future of fishing, the oldest human activity linked to the sea, depends on carefully planned management of catches worldwide. Although fishing techniques are constantly being improved, world fish stocks are limited.

T he Earth's oceans form a huge layer of liquid water, which lies on a 'floor' made up of shifting tectonic plates. Each year, billions of tonnes of sediment fall to the ocean floor and accumulate there. On a geological scale, the shape, size and topography of the oceans are constantly evolving. Some oceans are opening up and becoming larger, while others are closing and becoming smaller. Moreover, the water levels of the oceans are not constant. For a century, they have been rising slowly but surely. Is this simply a fluctuation, or the result of global warming?

The Mid-Atlantic Ridge runs through Iceland, and the floor of the Atlantic Ocean rises to the surface here in the form of volcanic islands.

The structure of the oceans

The ocean planet

The Earth is known as 'the blue planet' for a good reason. Oceans and seas cover 71% of its surface – a total of 361 million square kilometres.

Three large oceans, mainly in the southern hemisphere

The Earth's water reserves are very unequally distributed. The southern hemisphere has a greater expanse of water than the northern hemisphere: 81% ocean and 19% land area in the former, compared with 61% ocean and 39% land in the latter. This disparity is all the more obvious when one looks at the Earth from a satellite positioned directly above France and then from one positioned directly above New Zealand. From the first position, it is possible to clearly identify a 'continental hemisphere', with 120 million of the Earth's 149 million square kilometres of land cover; and from the second position, one can see a 'maritime hemisphere', with almost 63% of the planet's total ocean surface.

The Earth is generally considered to have three large oceans: the Pacific, the Atlantic and the Indian. They are connected to one another by the mass of water surrounding Antarctica. The main features of these oceans are their vast dimensions, both in surface area and depth, and the fact that they have coastlines on more than one continent. The Pacific Ocean is the largest, covering 180 million km^2. Next is the Atlantic Ocean (95 million km^2) and then the Indian Ocean (75 million km^2).

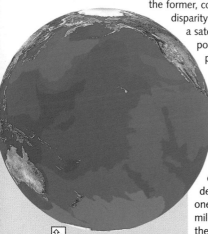

The Earth, shown here from a satellite over the Pacific, is largely covered by ocean.

Each ocean has its own seas

Most of the planet's seas are connected to these oceans. Some are linked to them directly, as in the case of the North Sea (500,000km^2) and the Mediterranean (2.5 million km^2), and some are linked indirectly, such as the Baltic Sea (350,000km^2) and the Black Sea (400,000km^2). Other seas are not linked to the oceans at all: for example, the Aral Sea (60,000km^2). As for the water masses at the poles, they play such a fundamental role in oceanic circulation that they too have been called oceans, although they do not strictly fit the definition, being made up of sectors of the other three: the Arctic Ocean, situated in the polar zone of

A vast reservoir

On average, the oceans are around 3,800m deep. When this figure is multiplied by their surface area, the volume obtained is enormous: 1,370 million km^3, or almost 97% of all the water on Earth. However, the oceans only represent a small layer on the surface of the planet and so account for only 1/800 of its total volume.

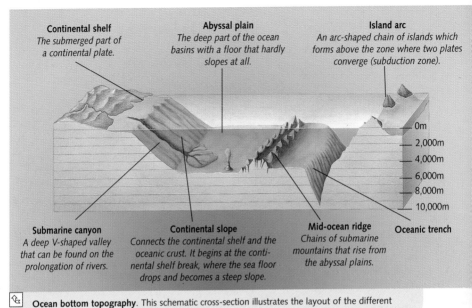

Continental shelf	Abyssal plain	Island arc
The submerged part of a continental plate.	The deep part of the ocean basins with a floor that hardly slopes at all.	An arc-shaped chain of islands which forms above the zone where two plates converge (subduction zone).

— 0m
— 2,000m
— 4,000m
— 6,000m
— 8,000m
— 10,000m

Submarine canyon	Continental slope	Mid-ocean ridge	Oceanic trench
A deep V-shaped valley that can be found on the prolongation of rivers.	Connects the continental shelf and the oceanic crust. It begins at the continental shelf break, where the sea floor drops and becomes a steep slope.	Chains of submarine mountains that rise from the abyssal plains.	

Ocean bottom topography. This schematic cross-section illustrates the layout of the different topographic units on the bottom of the ocean.

the Atlantic, covers 14 million km², while the Antarctic Ocean (or Southern Ocean), where all the oceans meet, covers around 77 million km².

The profile of the oceans

The three large oceans have the same basic profile. Starting at the shore and progressing towards the open ocean, we first encounter a zone that is a continuation of the continent: this is the continental shelf, which is generally no more than 200m deep and on average around 50km wide. This continental shelf then gives way to the steeper continental slope: the incline increases and drops to 2,000–3,000m. This slope marks the transition between the continental and the oceanic crusts. After the continental shelf we find the deep-sea zone, which is like a huge basin that reaches depths of 6,000–7,000m. The bottom of this basin contains deep trenches – such as those found along the coast of Peru or off the islands of Indonesia – and long underwater volcanic chains of seamounts, which form mid-ocean ridges. Here, magma emerges from the Earth's mantle, spreads out over the ocean floor and cools, thereby producing a new oceanic crust.

Map (following pages)

The oceans lie on a rocky floor made up of shifting lithospheric plates. The distribution of the ocean bottom relief is closely linked to that of the plates. Thus, the large abyssal plains are spread out on either side of the oceanic ridges (zones where the plates move apart), while the oceanic trenches are concentrated in zones where plates converge.

The ocean floor

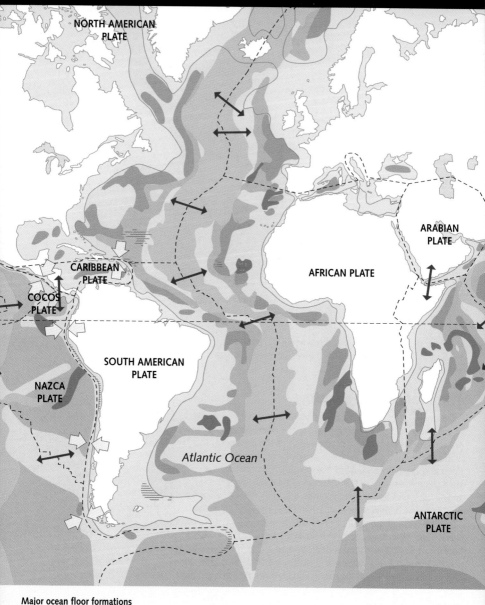

NORTH AMERICAN PLATE

ARABIAN PLATE

AFRICAN PLATE

CARIBBEAN PLATE

COCOS PLATE

SOUTH AMERICAN PLATE

NAZCA PLATE

Atlantic Ocean

ANTARCTIC PLATE

Major ocean floor formations

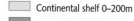

Continental shelf 0–200m

Large abyssal plain

Abyssal hills

Trenches and ocean floors over 6,000m deep

Inactive ridge

Active oceanic ridge

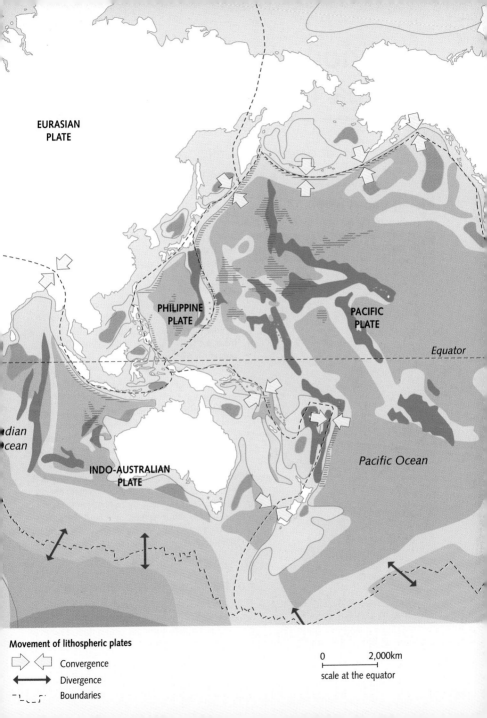

EURASIAN
PLATE

PHILIPPINE
PLATE

PACIFIC
PLATE

Equator

dian
cean

INDO-AUSTRALIAN
PLATE

Pacific Ocean

Movement of lithospheric plates

⇨ ⇦ Convergence

◄───► Divergence

⌐ ⌐ ⌐ Boundaries

0   2,000km

scale at the equator

Variations in the sea level

The sea level, used by geographers as a reference point, is not constant. It changes frequently over the centuries as a result of plate tectonics, sedimentation and glaciation.

Rising ocean levels

On a timescale equivalent to a human life span, the general level of the Earth's seas and oceans appears stable. Proof of this is that we talk about heights 'above sea level': the seas and oceans are used as points of reference to determine the heights of mountains, buildings and other landmarks. Places where the tides are weakest are chosen as zero reference levels (in England, this is at Newlyn in Cornwall). The Newlyn tide gauge, consisting of a float sheltered from the waves and the swell, constantly measures the variations – for the zero level of the sea varies, as do the levels measured by other gauges throughout the world. The statistics gathered over the last century appear to indicate an average rise in the sea level of one millimetre a year.

This variation is well known to all oceanographers, as are the reasons behind it. One cause is linked to plate tectonics, another to sedimentation, and the final (and most important) cause to the dynamics of the huge continental glaciers. Over tens of thousands of years, the combined effects of these three phenomena have caused the sea to spread over land surfaces (sea transgression) or else to recede with a dramatic drop in level (sea regression), sometimes exposing millions of square kilometres of land.

The cause of the variations

The impact of plate tectonics can be easily explained. The plates that make up the Earth's crust principally form the ocean floor. However, these plates are constantly moving towards or

The causes of the variations in sea level

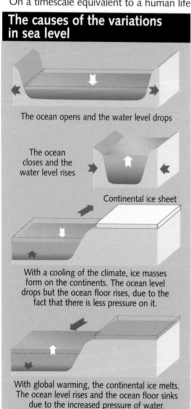

The ocean opens and the water level drops

The ocean closes and the water level rises

Continental ice sheet

With a cooling of the climate, ice masses form on the continents. The ocean level drops but the ocean floor rises, due to the fact that there is less pressure on it.

With global warming, the continental ice melts. The ocean level rises and the ocean floor sinks due to the increased pressure of water.

Antarctica. The enormous volume of water stored as ice in the polar regions helps to lower the overall level of the world's oceans.

GLOSSARY

[Plate tectonics]
Theory formulated in the 1960s to explain the movements of the plates of which the Earth's crust is composed. Types of plate movement include divergence, convergence, subduction, shearing and lateral slipping.

away from each other. When they converge, the surface of the ocean floor shrinks. If the same volume of water is contained in a smaller basin, the overall water level will rise. Conversely, when two plates diverge, the ocean floor becomes larger, leading to a drop in the water level. However, on balance, the level varies by no more than 0.5–1cm every thousand years. The effects of sedimentation on the sea level follow Archimedes' principle: when a basin with a constant volume of water is filled up with sediment, the sea level rises as a result. However, the impact is very low, because it is offset by the sinking of the ocean floor under the weight of the sedimentary deposits. The build-up of ice on the continents (known as continental ice sheets) has a very noticeable effect on the variation in global sea levels: the greater the amount of water held in the form of ice on the continents, the lower the global sea level on average. However, in the regions where the ice has accumulated, the continental shelf sinks under the weight of the ice, which means that the relative sea level in those regions is higher than elsewhere.

More than one zero

It is essential for sailors to know the depth of the sea at any one place, so that they can navigate safely without fear of running aground. They are aided in this by nautical charts, on which zero corresponds to the lowest level reached at low tide. This is different from the zero of tide gauges, which measure the variation in sea level.

The structure of the oceans **15**

A reconstruction of
the Earth as it was around
100 million years ago, during the Cretaceous period. It depicts the
Atlantic beginning to open up between the continents of America and
Africa. The position of the continents is very different from today, as is
the outline of the coasts, since the sea level was far higher.

The impact of climate change

GLOSSARY

[Storm surge]
An abnormal rise in the
coastal water level caused
by a drop in atmospheric
pressure and strong winds
blowing onshore. A storm
surge generally makes the
sea level rise by 30cm, but
in exceptional circum-
stances it can even
increase by 1m.

Today, the continental ice sheets are confined to the poles and their volume amounts to around 24 million km³. However, things have not always been like this: varying amounts of water have been trapped in the form of ice, depending on changes in climate. During cold periods, the icecaps increased in size. Thus, there was less water in the oceans and their level dropped. The ocean floors, relieved of this mass of water, tended to rise, and this helped to compensate for the drop in the water level.

At the height of the last ice age, 18,000 years ago, the continental ice sheets contained around 50 million km³ of water. North America and Eurasia were covered in ice mountains several kilometres high, while the majority of what is now Alaska and Siberia was ice-free. At that time, prehistoric man could walk from France to England without getting his feet wet: the average sea level was 120m lower than it is today.

The situation was completely different 100 million years earlier. Temperatures on Earth were rising, the ice that had accumulated during the previous cold periods had melted and water was gradually spreading over the land. The water level was 200m higher than it is today. The continent of Europe then formed part of a chain of islands, as did Australia, while part of Africa and all of western America were under water.

Fossils and minerals help to reconstruct the past

Fossils can provide proof of the Earth's turbulent past. Coral reef fossils, for example, give an indication of the old low-tide line, the area on which the reefs could form. Similarly, fossilized remains of certain kinds of oysters, winkles and calcareous (chalky) algae correspond to very specific strata. The presence in the soil of deposits rich in chlorides and alkaline sulphates, such as gypsum or rock salt, is also very revealing. Those found at the bottom of the Mediterranean Sea, for example, were deposited when the sea took on its present shape, 5 million years ago.

We know a lot less about more recent variations in sea levels. It is known that in England over the last 7,000 years the sea level, as measured in East Anglia, has been rising. However, the exact chronology is not yet clear. Apparently, the sea rose slowly in the period between 5,900 and 4,800 years ago, then accelerated until around 4,200 years ago. Later, it dropped slightly or remained stable until 3,500 years ago, before the sea began to spread over the land again, eventually reaching a level close to the one we know today.

This level is continuing to rise, partly due to the melting of the continental glaciers and the thermal expansion of water caused by global warming. It remains to be seen to what extent these two phenomena are responsible, and at what pace the sea level is going to continue to rise. Current models estimate there will be an average rise of 10–30cm per century. However, in the future it is likely that storm surges and the ensuing floods will cause more problems than a rise in the average sea level.

The landscape of Along Bay in Vietnam is the result of an erosive process typical of a continental environment, dating back to a time when the sea level was much lower than it is today.

Oceanic sediments

Each year, billions of tonnes of crushed rocks, sand that has been reduced to dust, and ash and debris from marine organisms fall to the ocean floor.

Sediments transported by air and by water

A number of different types of particles that originate on the continents are washed or blown into the oceans. Debris from eroded rocks is washed in by rivers, ice and run-off.

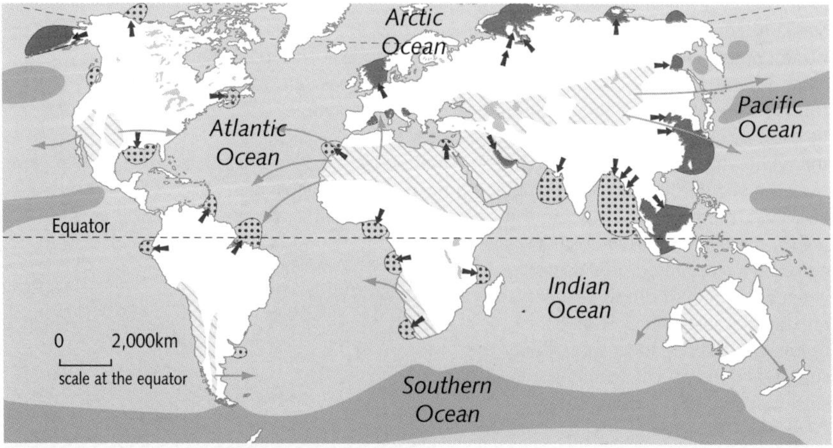

Extensive coastal and underwater detrital deposits

- Shelf deposits
- Deep-sea fans
- Desert and semi-arid regions
- Movement of aeolian (wind-blown) dust towards the ocean
- Siliceous biogenic sedimentation

Volcanic ash and dust from deserts are brought by the wind and rain. The largest particles quickly drop to the ocean floor, while the finer ones settle only after a long period in suspension. In total, these so-called terrigenous sediments amount to around 20 billion tonnes a year. In addition, large quantities of biogenic sediments derived from the remains of calcareous algae, the shells and skeletons of dead marine organisms and pieces of bone reach the ocean floor. The deposit rate of these biogenic sediments is far lower: from 1mm to 2cm every thousand years. But the majority of marine sediments are produced by the

Underwater avalanches

The sediments that build up on the edges of the continental shelf occasionally turn into real avalanches. Several tens of cubic kilometres of sediments can hurtle down the continental slope at around 100kph, and spread out over hundreds of square kilometres on the abyssal plain at the bottom of the slope.

The remains of living organisms form the largest part of ocean sediments. They cover 47% of the ocean floor. Calcareous ooze from warm waters makes up over three-quarters of the sediments and siliceous ooze from cold waters a little under a quarter.

oceans themselves. They come either from the eruption of underwater volcanoes or from the chemical precipitation of elements dissolved in seawater. The transportation and depositing of sediments varies according to the size of the particles and the speed of the current. Close to the coasts, coarse material including debris from rocks, shells, calcareous algae and corals is subjected to the action of swells, waves and tidal currents. It rolls along the ocean floor, forming ridges and dunes. During its journey, this debris is sorted out into different categories and any sharp edges are blunted.

Relief and currents sort sediments out

As a rule, the diameter of sedimentary particles decreases with increasing depth or distance from the shore. However, there are exceptions: irregularities in the relief, and the external edge of the continental shelf. In both cases, the swell is stronger and only the coarsest sand can withstand the friction of the waves. These sands and pebbles can build up until they hurtle down slopes like avalanches, sweep through submarine canyons and finally spread out on the abyssal plains in huge deep-sea fans.

The fate of the finest sediments is quite different. Measuring under 80 micrometres (µm) in diameter, they are unable to remain on the ocean floor in rough waters. Instead they are carried in suspension, and can travel around the world several times before reaching a place calm enough for them to settle.

The smaller they are, the more slowly they fall: a particle measuring 1µm in diameter takes 500 years to drop to a depth of 5,000m. Their settling creates the red clay that covers much of the deep ocean floor. Alternatively, they may combine with the rain of other planktonic organisms. If they are siliceous (silica-containing) sediments, they can fall all the way down to the abyssal plains. Calcareous (chalky) debris, on the other hand, is dissolved before it reaches the bottom. Its chemical components can precipitate and form calcareous ooze, or be fixed by other organisms and thus 'recycled'.

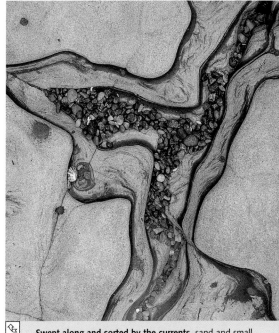

Swept along and sorted by the currents, sand and small pebbles end up on the coasts as well as out in the open sea, where they are distributed across abyssal plains.

Ocean bottom topography

The oceans are not simply flat-bottomed basins,
but contain vast submarine canyons, trenches
up to 10,000m deep and volcanoes that rise up
from the ocean floor.

From the continental shelf to the deep-ocean zone

Every sailor knows how a lead line works: a simple piece of rope weighted with lead can be used to measure the depth of the ocean. Since the end of the 18th century, people have known that the farther you go from the coast, the deeper the water becomes. The depth increases slowly at first and then suddenly drops sharply beyond depths of 200m. The shallow extension of the continent, which slopes gently, has been given the name 'continental shelf'. The name 'continental slope' has been given to the area that drops down abruptly towards the deep-ocean zone. Today we know that these shelves can lie at depths of between about 100 and 500m. Almost absent along mountainous coastlines, they are continuations of dry-land plains. Off the coasts of Siberia, they extend as far as 600km out from the coast. The average gradient of a continental shelf is 0.4%. However, this is not uniform: both underwater and on land the shelves are covered in hills and depressions.

Today, satellite measurements of altitude variations in the oceanic surface allow scientists to calculate the relief of the ocean floor fairly accurately.

Submarine canyons

The continental shelf is furrowed with deep fissures, which are sometimes extensions of existing valleys and rivers on land: these are known as submarine canyons and are found in seas such as the Mediterranean. They also occur where rivers cut into the continental shelf. The history of these canyons is linked to the movements of the sea, to strong tidal currents and to landslides caused by sand and pebbles rolling down the continental slopes. Gorges formed in this fashion can be several kilometres in length.

The canyons wind their way down until they

The ocean floor

Narrow oceanic trenches, which can reach depths of over 7,000m, represent only 0.1% of the total surface area of the ocean floor. The abyssal plains, the continental shelves and the continental slopes make up the rest. Most of the Earth's ocean floors are between 4,000m and 6,000m deep.

meet the continental slope, which connects the shelf with the abyssal plains and hills, descending to depths of around 3,000–7,000m (even deeper if there is a trench).

The flattest surfaces on Earth

Almost three-quarters of the ocean floor is made up of abyssal plains. Separated from one another by passes and channels, the abyssal plains are the flattest parts of the planet: their gradient is no greater than 0.1%. They form a chain around the continents or around archipelagos in the open sea and are never more than a few hundred kilometres in length and half that in breadth. These abyssal plains are succeeded by trenches in the zones where the ocean floor plunges beneath continents: smaller plains are then sometimes found right at the bottom. Away from landmasses, abyssal plains give way to an undulating relief made up of a mixture of hills, plateaux, seamounts and underwater volcanoes. These volcanoes sometimes rise out of the water and reefs can then build up on their sides. However, most of the relief features are underwater: the system of oceanic ridges forms a continuous chain over 65,000km long. Magma rises up in these mid-ocean ridges and creates a new oceanic crust, which becomes the floor of existing and future oceans.

GLOSSARY

[Continental shelf]
The zone bordering continents that lies under the sea between the shoreline and the continental slope. The continental shelves were formed when land was flooded by the rise of seawater during the Quaternary era.

The history of the oceans

Often created when two continents drift apart, oceans end up disappearing under the ground, leaving mountains and volcanoes behind as proof of their existence.

The life and death of the oceans

Compared with the continents, the oceans are very young. The 'life span' of the land can be anything up to two or three billion years, while that of an ocean never exceeds 400

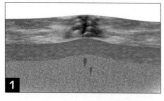

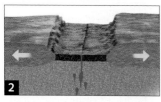

The formation of an ocean begins with a bulge in the Earth's crust (1). The crust is stretched and then breaks open, forming a rift (2), which eventually sinks beneath sea level (3).

million years. There is a simple reason for this: oceans almost always form inside the continents. The layer they form there, in the zones where the Earth's crust is fractured, acts somewhat like a constantly moving conveyor belt. After opening up and spreading out, oceans eventually close up again as their floors plunge beneath the continents.

It all begins with a bulge in the Earth's crust, the first sign that a new ocean is about to be born. This bulge, which can reach heights of up to 1,000m, is created by convection movements that, just like water boiling in a pan, cause the extremely hot magma within the underlying mantle to rise. The distended crust breaks open and collapses in a gigantic 'trench', known as a 'continental rift', which is 0.5–1.5km deep. The Great East African Rift is an example of a current continental rift.

The birth of an ocean

If the temperature of the mantle stops rising, convection currents subside and the whole process stops. Lake Baikal in Siberia is a good example of this type of scenario.

However, if the process does not stop, the edges of the rift will continue to move apart. The continental rift will become an oceanic rift. Long chains of volcanoes – the ridges – will gradually widen the rift along their axis until it turns into a valley. The duration of this phase, which scientists call 'rifting', can vary. It is thought that it lasted for 5–10 million years when the western part of the Mediterranean was formed, 10–15 million years in the case of the South Atlantic and probably quite a bit longer in the case of the North Atlantic. Continental rifting is the process that gives rise to oceans.

Evolution of the continents and oceans

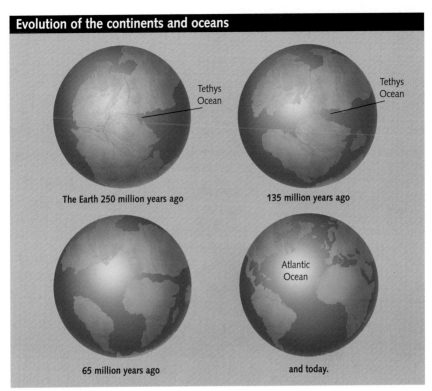

The Earth 250 million years ago

135 million years ago

65 million years ago

and today.

By dividing the continent in two, the oceanic rift allows magma to rise to the surface. The magma then starts to cool down and is flooded by seawater, thereby creating the floor of the future ocean. This oceanic crust, made up mainly of basalt, is thinner (5–8km thick) and denser than the continental crust. It spreads out across the central valley at the rate of a few centimetres a year. As the rift opens up, the crust continues to cool, becoming even denser and sinking under its own weight. The basin can now fill up with water and gradually become a young ocean like the Red Sea, which opened up around 20 million years ago.

Oceans in the ocean

Some oceans are formed inside already existing oceanic basins and not inside the continents. They can be identified by their ridges, but their initial stages are sometimes hard to reconstruct. Examples of this kind of ocean formation can be found on the Philippine Plate and near the Galapagos Islands.

Then, after intense erosion, sediment will begin to accumulate in piles around the edges of the ocean. The ocean floor will sink even deeper under the weight of this sediment: this is what is currently happening off the coast of southern Portugal. Denser and thus heavier than the continental crust, the oceanic crust finally plunges beneath one of the two original continental plates. This creates an oceanic trench.

Partially formed **25 million years ago** from the remains of Tethys, an ocean that existed between Eurasia and Africa, the Mediterranean Sea is destined to disappear one day like all the others.

Oceans disappear but traces remain

The process during which the ocean floor descends beneath a continent is known as subduction. It has several consequences for the continent in question: as a result of being compressed, the continental plate becomes distorted, folded and sheared, and sometimes piles of sediment carried along by the ocean floor are turned into mountain ranges. The friction caused by the two plates rubbing against each other can cause mild or even violent earthquakes. Lastly, subduction can create volcanoes by allowing pockets of magma from the oceanic crust to rise to the surface. The impact on the ocean is also quite considerable. The speed at which the floor disappears under the earth can be higher than that at which a new floor forms. The ocean thus contracts and closes. This phenomenon is currently underway in the Mediterranean Sea, which constitutes the last remaining traces of Tethys, a vast ocean that separated Eurasia and Africa during the Mesozoic era (around 240 million to 65 million years ago).

> **GLOSSARY**
>
> **[Spreading rate]**
> The rate at which the sea floor spreads is usually calculated for only one side of a ridge, and is often called a 'half-spreading' rate to avoid confusion. In the Atlantic and Indian Oceans, this rate has been 0.8–2.5cm per year for the last 5 million years. In the Pacific, it can be as much as 16–20cm per year.

All kinds of seas

When we are on our summer holidays, we do not mind whether we go for a swim in the sea or in the ocean. However, these two terms mean different things. 'Sea' is used to describe a much smaller body of water than 'ocean', and one that is restricted to a single climate zone. Several different types of seas can be identified. As far as their hydrology (properties, circulation and distribution of water) is concerned, they can be divided into open, enclosed or inland seas. Open seas are bounded to a large extent by an ocean: for example, the North Sea or the China Sea. Enclosed seas are linked to an ocean through sills that often only let surface water through: this is the case for the Mediterranean Sea, the Caribbean Sea or the Sea of Japan. Inland seas are basically large salt lakes, which in some cases flow into another sea (the Sea of Azov, the Black Sea or the Baltic Sea) and in other cases have no contact with any other sea (for example, the Aral Sea).

Geologically speaking, certain seas should be classified in special categories: 'epicontinental' seas (arms of the ocean sitting on top of continental lithospheres), such as the English Channel, the North Sea, the Baltic Sea and the Sunda Sea; and 'marginal' seas (formed above zones where the ocean has sunk beneath a continent), such as the Sea of Japan, the China Sea and the Caribbean Sea. In accordance with these definitions, the Bering Sea should be classified as marginal in the south and epicontinental in the north. To make things even more complicated, the terms 'bay' and 'gulf' are used indiscriminately when describing enclosed seas (for example, the Persian Gulf), open seas (the Bay of Biscay) or inland seas (the Gulf of Bothnia).

The continent of Europe is surrounded by many seas. Some seas are open, some are enclosed; some seas occupy areas that were once land, while others occupy areas that were once covered by an ocean – hence the large number of different terms that are used to name and describe them.

Seawater contains numerous chemical compounds in solution. Chlorides such as sodium chloride (cooking salt) and sulphates are particularly abundant. The total quantity of all these elements determines the salinity of the water. This varies only slightly from one ocean to the other, the average being 35‰ (35g per kilogram of water). On the other hand, the temperature can range from 28–30°C to below 0°C, depending on whether you measure it at the surface or on the ocean floor and in the tropics or at the poles. Together, temperature and salinity determine the density of the water and partially control its circulation.

An ocean's salinity varies depending on evaporation levels and the influx of fresh water through precipitation, melting snow or run-off. If there is a lack of fresh water, the salt in the ocean tends to crystallize.

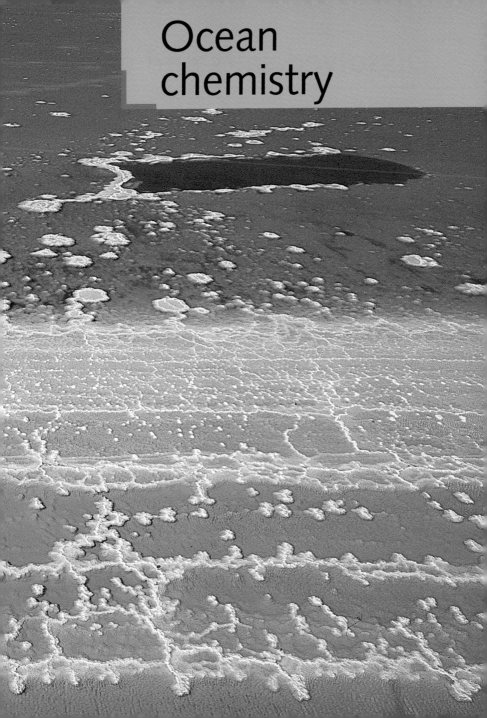

Ocean
chemistry

Dissolved salts and gases

Seawater is a complex mixture of salts and gases in solution. Certain elements are more plentiful than others, and this determines the salinity of the water.

A rich and complex cocktail

Seawater has a characteristic salty taste. However, the sodium chloride responsible for this is only one of the many compounds found in the water in our oceans. In fact, this water contains almost every naturally occurring chemical element known on Earth – if not in large quantities then in trace amounts in the form of dissolved salts and gases.

It is salt content that determines the water's salinity, which is measured in parts per thousand (also written as ppt or ‰) – that is, the number of grams of salt dissolved in one kilogram of water. The average salinity of seawater is between 30‰ and 35‰.

Some salts are found in large quantities, others are not. Sodium chloride, which in its crystallized form is the salt we cook with, falls into the first category. Just over 27g is found in a kilogram of salt water with a salinity level of 35‰; in other words, it accounts for almost 78% of the total quantity of dissolved salts. The following compounds can also be found, in decreasing order of importance: magnesium chloride (10.9%), magnesium sulphates (4.7%), calcium sulphates (3.6%) and potassium sulphates (2.5%), as well as calcium carbonate and magnesium bromide (0.5% in each case). In seawater they are present in the form

Sodium chloride – in other words, table salt – crystallizes in salt pans. It is only one of the many chemical compounds found in seawater.

GLOSSARY

[Major constituents]
These are the salts that are found in large quantities in seawater and in proportions that remain constant from one ocean to another. They are responsible for 99% of salinity.

[Minor constituents]
These are the salts that are found in extremely small concentrations and whose amounts vary depending on time and place. These minor constituents do not have much effect on the salinity of water, but they are of great importance in biological processes.

The major constituents of seawater

Element	Concentration in seawater (g/kg)	Sources	How lost
Chlorine	19	Volcanism, rivers	Sedimentation in the form of salt (NaCl)
Sodium	10.6	Rivers	Sedimentation in the form of salt (NaCl)
Sulphates	2.7	Volcanism	Deposits on the ocean floor
Magnesium	1.3	Rivers	Absorption by clayey muds
Calcium	0.4	Volcanism, rivers	It becomes locked in the skeletons of marine micro-organisms; sedimentation in the form of calcite
Potassium	0.4	Rivers	Absorption by clayey muds

of positively charged ions (cations) and negatively charged ions (anions), which can combine or separate: there are greater quantities of chlorine (Cl^-) and sodium (Na^+) than the sulphates (SO_4^{2-}), magnesium (Mg^{2+}), calcium (Ca^{2+}), potassium (K^+), the bicarbonates (HCO_3^-), bromide (Br^-), strontium (Sr^{2+}), and so on.

Salt stocks

The total quantity of salts dissolved in the ocean is calculated at 48 million billion tonnes. If these salts were spread out over the continents, they would form a layer 140m high. If all the ocean water evaporated, the salts formed would cover the ocean floor to a depth of 40m.

Compounds that are important for life

Like the major constituents, the minor constituents in seawater are dissociated in the form of ions. However, their concentrations are lower, always less than one milligram per kilogram of water.

The nitrogenous compounds (nitrites, nitrates, ammonia-based salts) and phosphoric compounds (phosphates) play a leading role: they are involved in the process of photosynthesis.

Seawater also contains silica, which diatoms (minuscule single-celled algae) use to form their skeletons, and other trace elements such as fluorine, iodine, arsenic, iron, zinc, copper, cobalt, nickel, manganese, aluminium, lead and vanadium.

Living organisms are able to concentrate these elements several thousand or million times before returning them to the ocean when they die. This could not occur if there were no oxygen or carbon dioxide dissolved in the water. Without them, there would be no photosynthesis and marine organisms would not be able to breathe. The quantities of these two gases are closely linked. Unlike nitrogen, they are found in higher concentrations in the water than in the air. Thus, the ocean plays a fundamental role: through its major geochemical cycles, it effectively regulates the oxygen and carbon dioxide levels in our atmosphere.

Map *(following pages)*

The salinity of the oceans varies very little from one part of the planet to another. Any fluctuations are mainly a result of differing evaporation and precipitation rates. In 90% of seawater the salinity is somewhere between 34‰ and 35‰. Temperature, on the other hand, varies greatly from one region to another depending on latitude. It is as low as −2ºC to 0ºC near the poles but reaches 28–30ºC in areas near the equator.

Temperature and salinity of the oceans

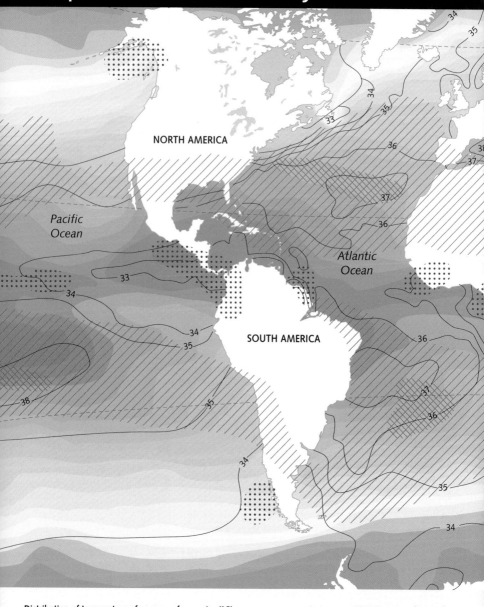

Distribution of temperature of ocean surface water (°C)

-1 0 2 4 6 8 10 12 14 16 18 20 22 23 24 26 27 28 29

Variations in salinity of
ocean surface water

34

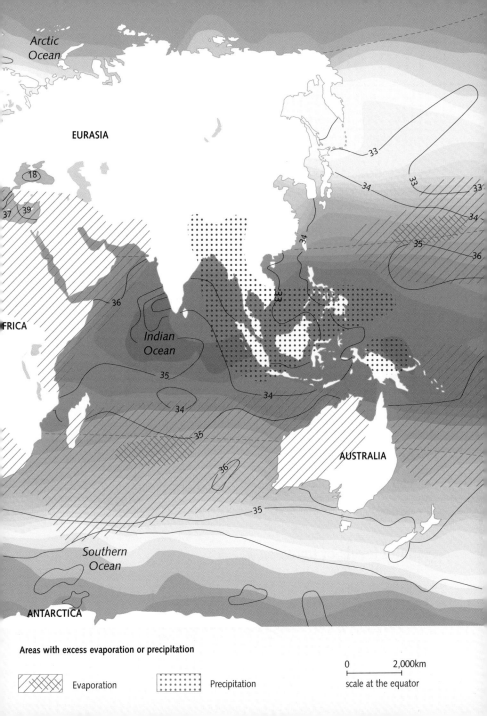

Areas with excess evaporation or precipitation

Evaporation

Precipitation

0   2,000km
scale at the equator

The salinity of the oceans

The salinity of the water – from the surface to the depths – varies very little from one ocean to the next, and is only slightly affected by the changing seasons.

Where does seawater come from?

The composition of seawater is remarkably stable. Although the concentrations of its major constituents can vary, their relative proportions remain virtually constant all over the world. What are the reasons for this? The first reason is related to the general circulation of the oceans and the fact that the water is constantly moving. Secondly, certain salts found in excess precipitate and become sediment. Thirdly, living organisms draw selectively on the stock of soluble salts, fix them and then deposit them on the ocean floor when they die.

How is such a perfectly balanced saline solution formed? Opinions as to the origins of the salts in the oceans remain divided. Some have taken up and developed the idea proposed in 1673 by the Irish chemist Robert Boyle, and consider the sea to be a vast concentration basin. According to this hypothesis, the first oceans formed 3.5 billion years ago and were filled with fresh water. In time, the Earth's soil was leached by precipitation, run-off and rivers, which brought salts into the oceans. The oceans' salinity then increased following evaporation during periods of global warming.

The problem with this theory is that the elements contained in the Earth's crust, the rivers and seawater are all very different, both qualitatively and quantitatively. This has led some people to come up with an alternative scenario. In 1903, the Swedish chemist Svante Arrhenius suggested that the waters of the oceans originated in the bowels of the Earth. As a result of volcanic eruptions, water vapour and other gases were supposedly released onto the surface of the planet as the magma cooled; when it condensed, this gas-filled water vapour formed highly acidic seas, which quickly became saline as they dissolved the surface elements in the Earth's crust.

Salinity levels of between 34‰ and 35‰

Whichever hypothesis we accept, it is clear that today the salinity of the oceans varies very little from one part of the globe to another. In around 90% of the global ocean, salinity is between 34‰ and 35‰. In the

The origin of the oceans

Over 4 billion years ago, the Earth's primitive atmosphere was made up of water vapour (80%) and carbon dioxide (15%). Upon cooling, the atmospheric water condensed into liquid water: torrential rains fell for hundreds of thousands of years. At first, the water that fell on the boiling surface of the Earth vaporized immediately. When the surface had cooled sufficiently, the water was able to stream over the relief and accumulate in hollows in the Earth's young crust, forming pools, then lakes and finally seas and oceans. Some of the water in the oceans also came from comets. Approximately 3–4 billion years ago, the Earth was subjected to intense bombardment by meteorites and comets. The latter contain phenomenal amounts of water in the form of ice.

At river mouths (here the Sambava on Madagascar), the salinity of seawater drops sharply. The influence of fresh water flowing into the sea or ocean can even be detected several dozen kilometres from the coast.

open ocean, the surface water values are somewhere between 33‰ and 37‰. This difference is a result of either an excess influx of fresh water (via rivers or rain), or a high level of evaporation.

Big rivers like the Amazon, the Niger and the Congo tend to dilute salts and reduce salinity: the salinity of the water flowing around the mouths of these rivers is less than 30‰.

Generally speaking, in regions near to the equator, where precipitation is an almost permanent feature, salt levels are near to 34‰. The opposite scenario is found in the tropics, where anticyclones produce intense evaporation, leading to salinity levels of 36–37‰. Extreme levels are reached in enclosed seas, which only exchange a very small amount of water with the ocean: the salinity of the Mediterranean Sea is around 38–39‰ and that of the Red Sea 40–41‰.

Precipitation leaves its mark on surface waters by reducing their salinity. This is particularly noticeable if there is an intense rainy season.

All oceans have the same basic composition

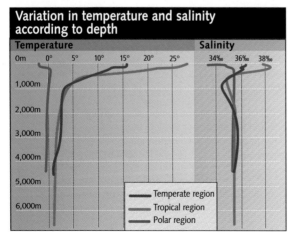

Variation in temperature and salinity according to depth

| Temperature | | | | | | | Salinity | | |

Temperature: 0m, 0°, 5°, 10°, 15°, 20°, 25°
Salinity: 34‰, 36‰, 38‰
Depths: 1,000m, 2,000m, 3,000m, 4,000m, 5,000m, 6,000m

— Temperate region
— Tropical region
— Polar region

The distribution of surface water salinity is influenced by waves and currents. In regions with temperate or tropical climates, salinity is relatively uniform for up to a few metres beneath the surface, in the so-called 'mixed' layer. It then decreases rapidly with depth until it reaches a minimum at depths of around 800–1,000m. Then it increases slightly down to depths of 2,000–2,500m, before dropping once more. In polar regions, this all

In polar regions, summer warming melts the ice, giving rise to dramatic but localized falls in the salinity level of the water.

happens in the first few metres beneath the surface: salinity increases to a value that it then maintains until the ocean floor is reached. However, below depths of 4,000m, all oceans have virtually the same salinity level, between 34.6‰ and 34.9‰. These distributions do not change from one day to the next and only vary very

Extreme cases

Some enclosed seas are not influenced by oceanic circulation. If the influx of fresh water, in particular via rivers, is greater than the amount lost through evaporation, the salinity of these seas decreases. The salinity of the Caspian Sea is around 13‰ and its waters, like those of a river, contain high levels of carbonates.

Measuring tools

Since the relative proportions of the main constituents of seawater are constant, by measuring the quantity of one of them we can work out the general salinity of the water. This is why salinity has long been defined by the water's chloride content. Today, the electrical conductivity of seawater is taken as a measure, since it is closely linked to the quantity of dissolved salts.

slightly with the changing seasons (rarely by more than 0.5‰). These variations can be very strong in places where the climate changes suddenly: for example, monsoons bring abundant rains to the north-east Pacific, reducing the salinity of the surface waters. The variations are also more marked in polar regions, where the melting and movement of ice in summer can cause quite irregular differences in salinity levels.

The oceans' temperature

Unlike salinity, the temperature of the oceans can vary consider-ably. The distribution of the temperature of surface water is an accurate indication of differing climates in various latitudes.

Water heated by solar radiation

While some solar radiation is reflected by the ocean, the rest penetrates the water and is then diffused or absorbed. All the infrared radiation that the algae and other photosynthetic organisms do not use is trapped in the first few metres beneath the surface, and helps heat up this layer of surface water. Rain and wind can also cause temperatures to rise: rain by releasing into the ocean the latent heat in its droplets, wind by transforming its energy into heat. Conversely, long-wave radiation, convection towards the atmosphere and evaporation cool the ocean down. On balance, ocean surface temperatures decrease as one moves from warm tropical waters (28–30°C) to the cold waters of the polar regions, where the minimum temperature corresponds to the freezing point of seawater, which is around −1.9°C (the figure varies according to salinity). Where there are continents or wind-created currents, there are slight variations in this distribution. The temperature gradients are thus weak in the waters on either side of the equator and at the poles, and strong in temperate zones.

The water temperature on the surface of the ocean is highest (shown in red on the map) in tropical waters, which receive the greatest amount of sunshine.

Wide variations

The variations in the temperature of ocean water between the surface and the ocean floor are similar to the temperature fluctuations registered in high and low latitudes: the temperature can vary from 28–30°C to –1°C. These variations are very weak or even non-existent at the poles, becoming pronounced as one approaches the hot regions. However, they are not evenly spread within the water column. The temperature is in fact stable in the layer closest to the surface of the ocean, which is agitated by the wind. This layer can measure up to a few dozen metres in depth. Apart from at the poles, the temperature then decreases very rapidly until around 500–1,000m below the surface: in this zone, called the thermocline, the temperature never exceeds 12°C. Its minimum value (about 2°C) occurs at around 4,000m below the surface, then rises again the further down one goes: since pressure increases with depth, the water temperature rises, even if only a little (0.15°C per 1,000m). However, this is sufficient for its effect to be felt in the ocean depths.

The effect of latitude

The temperature of the ocean surface water in polar or equatorial regions does not change much from season to season: a difference of 2°C at the most. However, in temperate zones there can be variations of around 8°C and even as much as 10–20°C in some enclosed seas such as the Mediterranean. These variations lessen with increasing depth, and disappear completely at around 200–300m below the surface. There is also a seasonal difference. When surface waters warm up in summer their density decreases, increasing the difference in density between themselves and the deepest waters. As a result, the thermocline rises and only the waters in the first 25m below the surface, which are agitated by waves, enjoy a rise in temperature. It is not until the autumn, when the thermocline tends to disappear, that the deeper waters warm up.

Separate zones

In those areas where temperatures undergo a sudden variation, two distinct water masses can be found pushing towards one another. These transition regions in the oceans are called 'convergence zones'. The best-known of these is in Antarctica, and is known as the Antarctic convergence zone – this is where cold dense surface waters descend beneath warmer ones.

GLOSSARY

[Thermocline]
The layer of water in the ocean where temperature decreases most rapidly with depth. The thermocline is usually situated at depths of between 100m and 1,000m, and tends to disappear in winter.
[Potential temperature]
Water temperature corrected to take into account the effects of pressure. This is used to compare different masses of deep water.

The great winter mixing

With the arrival of winter, the surface layers of the ocean cool down and become denser. Convection movements cause this heavier water to descend towards the ocean floor. This instability of the water favours turbulence, which causes the ocean to release some of its heat into the atmosphere. The temperature then drops rapidly, both in deep water and at the surface. Ocean water cools quickly and efficiently, and heats up only slowly and inefficiently. This is partly due to the physical characteristics of water and partly to turbulence, but the primary reason is that two-thirds of the heat provided by solar radiation is used in evaporation. The atmosphere is thus indebted to the ocean, and the ocean is in turn dependent on the vagaries of the air.

Sea ice

Icebergs help to decrease the salinity of the oceans, and the ice formed by the freezing of seawater is essential for the formation of deep ocean waters.

Ice floes (shown here on Adelie Land, Antarctica) are formed when seawater is turned into ice in the polar regions. This occurs when the temperature of the salt water reaches its freezing point of –1.9°C.

Icebergs and sea ice

In those places where the temperature drops below 0°C, water freezes. In the high latitudes, there are two types of sea ice with different origins: icebergs, which are formed by massive pieces of ice breaking away from the front of glaciers (made up of snow that has accumulated on the continents), and sea ice, which is created when seawater freezes.

Icebergs influence the oceans through the calories they draw from the water in order to melt, and through the fresh water they release. The lifespan of an iceberg is between three and four years. Swept along by the currents, they can cover large distances. In the Southern Ocean, the Antarctic Circumpolar Current ensures they never stray far from Antarctica. In the Arctic Ocean, on the other hand, the Greenland and Labrador Currents can take them down to the Atlantic Ocean – which is what happened to the iceberg that sank the *Titanic*.

Three linked parameters

Unlike fresh water, seawater becomes more dense as it cools. The density increases until it reaches a value where the water turns to ice. Fresh water is at its densest at 4°C and freezes at 0°C, while seawater – with an average salinity of 35‰ – starts to turn to ice at –1.9°C, reaching its maximum density at around 3.5°C.

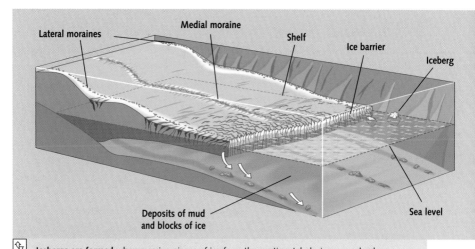

Lateral moraines
Medial moraine
Shelf
Ice barrier
Iceberg
Deposits of mud and blocks of ice
Sea level

Icebergs are formed when massive pieces of ice from the continental glaciers are calved (broken off) and then drift around the ocean for three or four years.

A key role in the formation of deep waters

Sea ice plays a very important role in the ocean. It forms in winter when the temperature of the water on the ocean surface falls below −1.9°C in water with a salinity of 35‰. This freezing is accompanied by expansion, which makes the ice lighter than water. The first ice crystals, called nilas (which form a thin elastic crust of ice in a pattern of interlocking fingers), are followed by frazil (small spikes of ice suspended in water), which is more abundant and makes the ocean look like a gigantic sorbet.

The freezing of seawater also separates the pure water from the salts. As ice crystals of pure water form, the salinity of the underlying water increases. As it becomes denser, and thus heavier, this water descends. Less salty and warmer water replaces it on the surface, before being subjected to the same process.

The water sinks down to greater and greater depths. The ice thickens until the ice floe is thick enough to form a thermal insulator. The vagaries of the climate and the turbulence of the sea can cause it to melt if it is swept out towards the open ocean in summer. The water then released is far less salty than the water the floe was created from. However, the floe may also last for several years and become covered in snow. The Arctic Ocean ice floe stretches over an area that ranges from a maximum of around 15 million km² in winter to a minimum of around 7.5 million km² in summer.

Excellent insulators

Sea ice reflects the incoming solar radiation and prevents the water from releasing its calories into the colder air. It is thus an excellent insulator. If there were no sea ice in winter, the ocean waters exposed to solar radiation would heat the lower layers of the atmosphere by up to 20–40°C.

T he water masses in the oceans are constantly moving. The combined gravitational attraction of the Sun and Moon creates bulges which spread across the ocean surface: these are what we know as tides. Irregular strong winds create waves and swells. Regular winds, on the other hand, propel the surface waters and induce sea currents. On a global scale, the surface water circulation follows large loops, or gyres, in each hemisphere. The bottom water circulation follows a more complex path, being governed by differences in temperature and salinity.

Swells and waves, created by wind blowing over the ocean surface, provide a spectacular display of ocean dynamics.

Ocean dynamics

The origin of the tides

Despite the Earth's resistance, the gravitational pull of the
Sun and the Moon affects the water on the Earth's surface,
causing a liquid bulge to form on each side of the globe.
This is how tides are created.

A universal law

The water in all oceans rises and falls at least once a day, creating the tides which make long sandy beaches so appealing. It is the combined gravitational attraction of the Moon and the Sun on the rotating Earth that produces these tides. In our solar system, all the planets are attracted by the Sun, around which they orbit. However, the law of gravitational attraction involves all the stars and planets in the universe. The influence they exert on each other depends on their mass and the distance between them.

Delayed tides

The Moon takes 29 days, 12 hours and 44 minutes to orbit the Earth. In 24 hours, the Moon's orbit shifts by an average of 13°. In theory, the Earth would have to cover this same distance with every rotation in order to maintain its original position relative to the Moon, which would take the Earth 50 minutes each day – and indeed, 50 minutes is the average interval between the same tides on successive days.

The larger an object and the nearer it is to the Earth, the more it attracts our planet. Even though the Moon is infinitely smaller than the Sun, it is much closer to the Earth than the Sun, so the Moon's gravitational pull on the Earth is 2.2 times greater than the Sun's.

The Sun and Moon

The gravitational pull of the Moon makes water bulge on the side of the Earth facing it. However, the Earth has its own role to play: a centrifugal force is generated by the rotation of the Earth-Moon system around the system's centre of mass. This force opposes the Moon's attraction and leads to another bulge appearing on the side of the Earth farthest from the Moon. Thus, there are two simultaneous high tides, one on either side of the globe. These are the result of two forces: the gravitational attraction of the Sun and Moon (which tends to pull the Earth and Sun

Spring tides occur when the gravitational effects of the Moon and Sun are combined (1 and 3). Neap tides occur when the Moon and Sun are at right angles to each other (2).

① Opposition
② Quadrature
③ Conjunction

together) and the centrifugal force (which tends to pull them apart). The sum of the gravitational and centrifugal forces is known as the 'tide-generating force'. This force is zero at the centre of the Earth, where gravitational and centrifugal forces are equal and opposite, and strongest on two locations on the surface of our planet, the points nearest and farthest away from the Moon.

As the Earth rotates, each of the two bulges (body tides) travels around the planet like a wave. It tends to follow the apparent movement of the Moon and, to a lesser degree, the Sun. However, it does not travel in a straight line. The Earth's rotation causes its path to tilt to the right in the northern hemisphere and to the left in the southern hemisphere. Moreover, continents get in the way of the wave, and the shape of the oceans can increase or decrease this body tide. Thus, in the Atlantic Ocean, which is longer than it is wide, there are tides every 12 hours (semidiurnal tides); in the Pacific and Indian oceans, which are wider, there are mixed tides of 12 and 24 hours; and in small seas such as the Gulf of Mexico, there are diurnal tides.

Variable amplitude

A tide's amplitude is greatest when the Moon and Sun are aligned, at full moon and new moon (spring tides), and weakest when they are at right angles to each other at the Moon's first or last quarter (neap tides). Semidiurnal tides are greatest at the spring and autumn equinoxes and diurnal tides are greatest at the summer and winter solstices.

Tidal ranges (or tidal amplitudes) vary from a few centimetres to several metres. The base of this unusual rock in Phang-Nga Bay (Thailand) is completely exposed at low tide.

Map (following pages)

Propelled by the wind, the surface layers of the ocean move in large loops (also known as gyres). These loops circle the high-pressure zones (anticyclonic cells) in a clockwise direction in the northern hemisphere and in an anti-clockwise direction in the southern hemisphere. They carry warm waters along the eastern coasts of continents and cool waters along the other side.

Surface circulation of the oceans

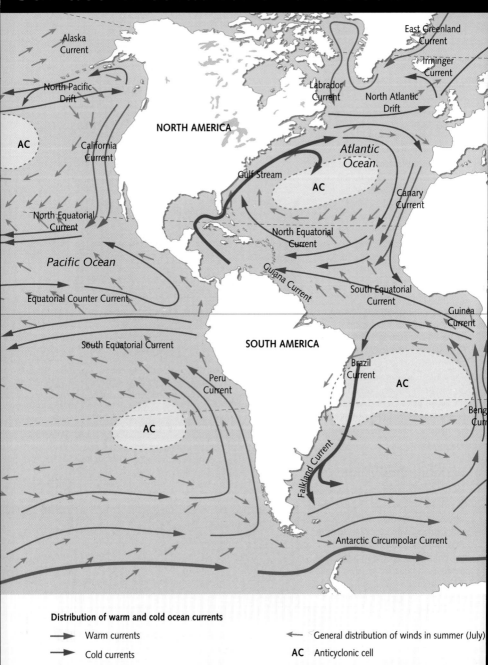

East Greenland Current

Irminger Current

Alaska Current

North Pacific Drift

Labrador Current

North Atlantic Drift

AC

NORTH AMERICA

California Current

Atlantic Ocean

AC

Gulf Stream

Canary Current

North Equatorial Current

North Equatorial Current

Pacific Ocean

Guiana Current

South Equatorial Current

Equatorial Counter Current

Guinea Current

South Equatorial Current

SOUTH AMERICA

Brazil Current

Peru Current

AC

Beng Cur

AC

Falkland Current

Antarctic Circumpolar Current

Distribution of warm and cold ocean currents

→ Warm currents

→ Cold currents

← General distribution of winds in summer (July)

AC Anticyclonic cell

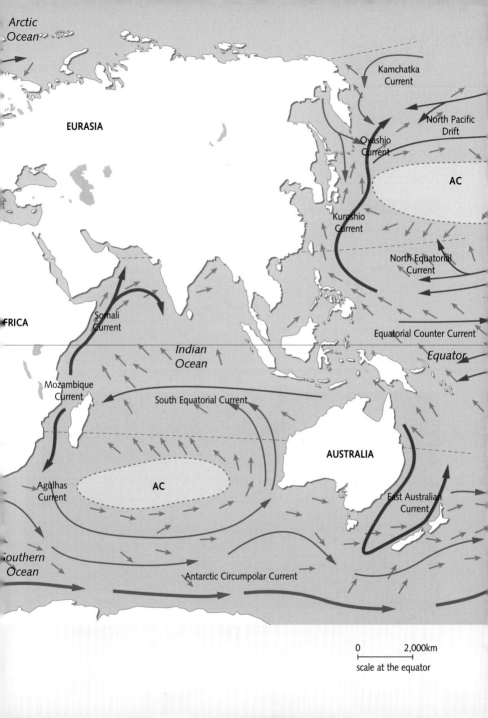

Waves on the move

When whipped up by the wind, the surface of an ocean is covered in crests and troughs. Waves form and can travel over large distances in regular undulations called swells.

A series of ripples

GLOSSARY

[Fetch]
The distance over which wind blows without changing direction.

[Chop]
A series of wind-driven waves that do not form a regular train.

If you throw a stone into a pool of still water, ripples will spread out over the surface in concentric circles. If you throw in a cork just afterwards, you will see that it rises and falls with the ripples, without moving horizontally. This is more or less the effect that wind has on the oceans. If it blows strongly enough and for long enough in the same direction, it creates a series of regular waves – in other words, a swell. The greater the strength, duration and extent of the wind, the bigger the swell will be. However, unlike a tide, a swell does not move water horizontally and so does not create any currents. In technical terms, a swell is

Endless movement

The water molecules in a swell go round and round: their movement follows an almost circular orbit whose diameter is equal to the height of the surface waves, decreasing as one goes deeper below the surface. If nothing get in its way, a swell will take a very long time to die down: a 10m-high wave can still be 4m high after three years.

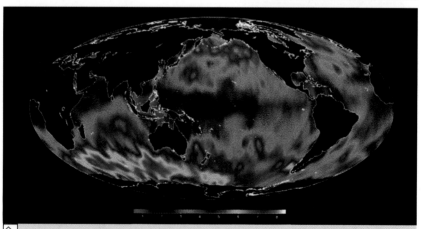

The image above, taken from the TOPEX/Poseidon satellite, shows the average height of waves. In the great Antarctic depressions south of the Indian Ocean (shown in red and yellow), waves regularly reach heights of up to 8m.

The formation of waves and swells

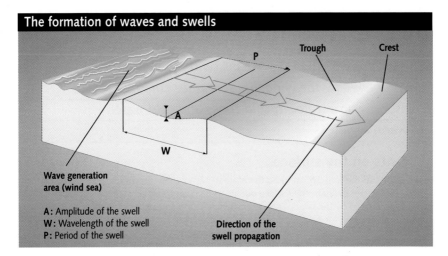

Trough | Crest | P

Wave generation area (wind sea)

A: Amplitude of the swell
W: Wavelength of the swell
P: Period of the swell

Direction of the swell propagation

characterized by its amplitude (the difference in height between the crests and troughs of its waves), its wavelength (the distance between two successive waves) and its period (the time it takes for a wave to cover the distance equivalent to the wavelength).

The speed of the swell is calculated by dividing the wavelength by the period. If this speed is too fast, the waves will break and form what are known as 'white horses' or 'whitecaps'. However, if the speed is similar to that of the wind, the swell will begin a long journey across the ocean, propelled by the airflow.

Thousands of kilometres

Swells formed in the great Antarctic depressions can cross the entire Atlantic Ocean, travelling thousands of kilometres, and at the end of their journey combine their effects with storms raging off the coast of Ireland. Swells interfere with other wave systems wherever they go, sometimes adding to the waves and on other occasions calming existing storms. This is what gives each region of the ocean its individual characteristics.

Swells are a reflection of meteorological conditions. The winds generated by the Azores anticyclone give rise to strong swells with waves over six metres high, which crash onto the western coasts of Spain and Portugal. As they travel northwards they weaken. However, the absence of anticyclones means that depressions (and thus storms) are created, and shorter-lasting but more violent swells also occur.

All in all, the state of the sea reflects a complex situation, in which swells of various origins are linked to localized chop.

High and low waves

The stronger the wind that blows over a large expanse of ocean, the higher the waves will be: a 40kph-wind sweeping across the sea for 200km generates troughs 2.5m deep, and a 100kph wind over a distance of 400km can create waves over 11m high. On average, swells have an amplitude of 1m in the English Channel, while off the south coast of Australia they normally have an amplitude of over 4m.

Sea currents

The surface waters of the oceans swirl around as they are propelled by the wind. These surface currents transport warm water to cold zones and cold water to warm regions.

Currents on the surface

The effects of the atmosphere (and therefore of air movements) on the oceans weaken rapidly the deeper beneath the surface one goes. Sea currents thus form mainly on the surface, generated by the wind. Their characteristics are very similar in all three large oceans – Atlantic, Pacific and Indian. There are, however, some slight differences: these are due to specific weather conditions and the contours of the continents.

The distribution of winds over the globe is based on the fact that they move from high-pressure zones towards low-pressure zones. However, like all large-scale movements, winds are deflected in accordance with forces generated by the Earth's rotation (towards the right in the northern hemisphere and towards the left in the southern hemisphere). This phenomenon, known as the Coriolis force, becomes increasingly strong the farther one moves away from the equator. Its effect creates various winds. In geographical order from the equator to the poles, these are: the trade winds (blowing from the north-east in the northern hemisphere and from the south-east in the southern hemisphere), the westerlies (the prevailing winds that blow from the west in the middle latitudes of both hemispheres) and the easterlies (blowing from east to west).

> **GLOSSARY**
>
> **[Anticyclonic, cyclonic]** The adjective anticyclonic describes the movement of currents around a centre of high pressure. This is a clockwise movement in the northern hemisphere and anticlockwise in the southern hemisphere. The opposite of anticyclonic is cyclonic, which describes the movement of currents around a low-pressure centre.

Huge swirls

In the lower and middle latitudes, the circulation of surface water is propelled by large wind-driven swirls of oceanic water masses called anticyclonic gyres. They transport water by swirling in a clockwise direction in the northern hemisphere and in the opposite direction in the southern hemisphere. In the western parts of the oceans, narrow, intense currents move away from the equator and make their way towards the poles. At latitudes of around 30–40° they give way to large channels of water, the drifts, which move eastwards. Finally, the return currents – moving water from the north or the south – complete the circuit.

The Indian Ocean is a special case: the monsoon regime, with its winds that sometimes

An infinite number of meanders

Maps showing ocean currents are necessarily simplified and therefore cannot give a complete image of oceanic circulation. They are based on average values and so do not reflect the infinite number of actual meanders and swirls, whose intensity fluctuates with time and place.

blow from the mountains (winter monsoon) and sometimes from the oceans (summer monsoon) – is different from that of the usual trade winds. There are also enormous continental masses to be taken into account: these descend almost as far south as the equator. Consequently, in comparison with the circulation of the Atlantic waters, the circulation of the Indian Ocean is constricted in the north, and the whole system is thus effectively pushed southwards by around 10°.

Near the poles, cyclonic gyres – moving in the opposite direction to the swirls in temperate waters – hold sway. The Norwegian, Alaskan and Labrador Currents are all related to them. They are more obvious in the northern hemisphere; in the southern hemisphere, the presence of Antarctica gives rise to other types of wind than those usually found in higher latitudes, and these modify the situation.

There are also a few cyclonic gyres in the Weddel and Ross Seas.

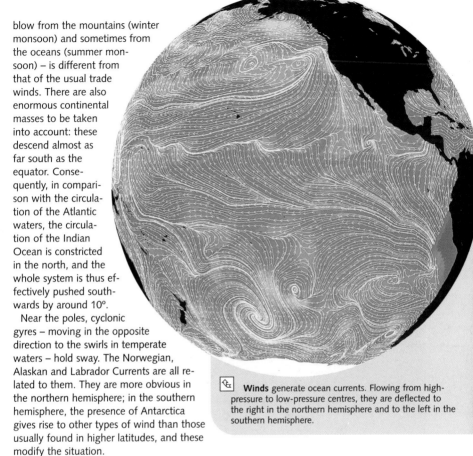

Winds generate ocean currents. Flowing from high-pressure to low-pressure centres, they are deflected to the right in the northern hemisphere and to the left in the southern hemisphere.

Troughs and mounds in the ocean

The wind regime is only partially responsible for the loops and swirls formed by the currents: ocean topography is another influential factor. In the case of the northern hemisphere, the westerly winds push enormous masses of water southwards, while the trade winds push large amounts northwards. The result is that water piles up in the centre, creating 'mounds' that can be over one metre high. Conversely, east winds in the high altitudes move water northwards, whereas the westerlies take it southwards: as a result, troughs are formed in the water. In both cases, the water flows away from the mounds or into the troughs in the same way it would flow down a plug hole, perpendicular to the slope – so creating these eddy-like currents.

The great ocean conveyor belt

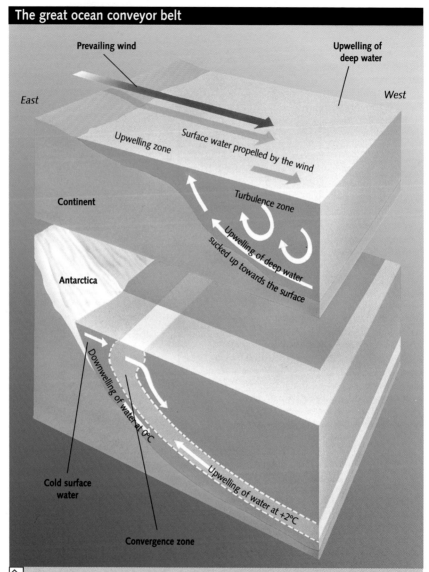

Prevailing wind

Upwelling of deep water

East

West

Upwelling zone

Surface water propelled by the wind

Continent

Turbulence zone

Upwelling of deep water sucked up towards the surface

Antarctica

Downwelling of water at 0°C

Cold surface water

Upwelling of water at +2°C

Convergence zone

Blown by the prevailing winds, warm surface water moves away from the western coasts of the continents, cools and sinks, causing deep water to rise up. The case of Antarctica is different: on the surface, the downwelling (sinking) of cold dense water is accompanied by an upwelling of deep water.

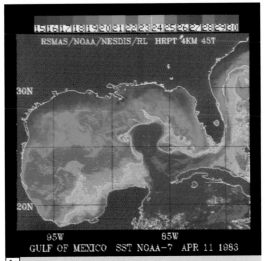

RSMAS/NOAA/NESDIS/RL HRPT 4KM 45T

30N

20N

95W   85W
GULF OF MEXICO SST NOAA-7 APR 11 1983

Like the Gulf Stream, seen here flowing along the coast of Florida, warm currents in the western parts of the oceans transport their water towards the poles.

The amplitude of the troughs and mounds is not due solely to the winds and the Earth's rotation. It is also related to the density of the water, which in turn depends on temperature and salinity. The lower this density, the more the water can expand, causing it to rise. For example, the water level is higher in the Sargasso Sea than in the northern Gulf Stream, and lower in the Mediterranean Sea than in the Atlantic Ocean.

Bulges on the western edges of oceans

The water level is also higher on the western edges of the oceans; there are two reasons for this. The first reason is the weakening of the Coriolis force near the equator: this means that water is propelled in the direction of the wind, in other words westwards. The second reason is that solar radiation is at its greatest at this latitude; the water is strongly heated and thus expands. When, after its long journey west, the water hits a continent, it accumulates against the coast, reaching a level 50cm above its level on the other side of the ocean basin. Part of this water will feed the currents travelling up towards the higher latitudes. Another part will follow the direction of the slope and form a return current near the water surface, which will move eastwards: this is known as the equatorial undercurrent.

GLOSSARY

[Undercurrent]
A current which transports water only beneath the surface.
[Sverdrup]
A unit used to measure the volume of ocean currents. Sverdrup is often abbreviated as Sv and is equivalent to 1 million cubic metres per second (m³/s).

Millions of cubic metres of water

Huge quantities of water are transported by the large sea currents. Each second the Gulf Stream moves 30 million m³ of water along the coast of Florida and over 100 million m³ off the coast of Newfoundland. These figures are far higher than the amount of water flowing through all the world's rivers combined – barely 1 million m³.

Vertical currents

All of these water movements are horizontal, but vertical currents also exist. On the eastern edges of oceans, water is pushed out towards the open ocean, causing upwelling (the rising of cold water from the depths of the ocean to the surface). Ascendant currents also occur where surface currents diverge, while water tends to sink in areas where they converge. It is this phenomenon, combined with certain conditions of temperature and salinity, which forms the deep waters of the oceans.

Weighty water

Evaporation and dropping temperatures make surface water denser, and thus heavier. This heavier water sinks to the depths of the ocean in high latitudes and then circulates around the world.

Differences in density

When winter winds cause the ocean to evaporate, or when cold weather causes it to freeze, its salinity rises and its temperature drops. These two parameters control the density of the water. As surface water becomes denser, it tends to sink to the ocean depths. The higher the salinity, the more the water sinks. Large quantities of water are formed in the polar regions and then spread out through the depths of the world's oceans. The circulation of this deep water, linked to conditions of temperature and salinity, is called thermohaline circulation.

It can be observed sporadically in the North Atlantic, mainly in the Norwegian Sea but also in the Greenland and Labrador Seas. In each case, water with a high salinity (35.25‰), which has come up from the Caribbean via the Gulf Stream, is suddenly cooled. Its density is thereby increased, making it sink. This water accumulates at the bottom of the Norwegian Basin until it has filled sufficiently to spill gradually over the submarine sill which acts as a barrier between the Atlantic and the Norwegian Sea. The water then heads south towards the Southern Ocean, where it will join other deep waters.

The importance of the Mediterranean Sea

The high salinity of the water in the Mediterranean Sea (38.5‰ in the Gibraltar outflow water) has a great impact on the salinity of the Atlantic Ocean, even though the net exchange of water is fairly small. At around 1,000m beneath the surface it forms tongues of salt water in the Atlantic Ocean, just as the Red Sea does in the Indian Ocean.

In the Ross Sea (seen here is the impressive ice shelf front bordering it) and especially in the Weddel Sea, water that has become more saline and colder in autumn and winter sinks down to the ocean depths.

The deep waters of the Southern Ocean

Sea ice builds up between Antarctica and the latitude of 60° S. During the southern autumn and winter (between April and October), this ice takes fresh water from the ocean with the result that salinity becomes higher than usual in the area surrounding the sea ice. The very low temperatures that hold sway in these latitudes then cause this high-salinity water to sink down to the ocean depths. In the Weddel Sea, and to a lesser degree in the Ross Sea, the water plunges down to 4,000m below the surface and forms the Antarctic bottom water. On the other hand, the Antarctic intermediate water slides under the warmer water, but remains above the dense water from the Atlantic. It will have taken the Atlantic water around 500 years to reach this part of the globe, its average speed being about one millimetre per second. Some of this water will rise up near continental Antarctica, where the surface currents going in the opposite direction create an upwelling. It will also slowly become enriched by the Antarctic bottom water, which abounds in nutrients and oxygen. However, the journey is far from over: this water will now head off towards the Indian Ocean and the Pacific, and will then begin a long journey around the world before finally flowing up towards the North Atlantic.

GLOSSARY

[Upwelling]
Upwelling of deep water most commonly occurs in lower latitudes on the western coastlines of the continents. It takes place when winds blow the lighter surface water away from the coast and denser, cooler water rises to replace it.

[Compensating currents]
These are layers of water that circulate on the surface or in the depths. They cancel out the excess or deficit of water in a particular region of the global ocean. The equatorial undercurrents are examples of compensating currents.

The ocean thermostat

The oceans store heat efficiently, and can redistribute it by means of their currents. They play a fundamental role in controlling the Earth's thermal balance, and thus its climate.

The first ten centimetres

In the first ten centimetres of water below the surface, the oceans are capable of absorbing all the infrared radiation they receive from the Sun and turning it into heat. As a result, the average annual temperature of the surface of the oceans is 17.5°C, compared with a little over 14°C for the average air temperature. Moreover, solids, liquids and gases do not react in the same way to solar radiation. A layer of seawater 2.60m high stores as much heat as the entire air column above it, and the average depth of the oceans is over 3,000m. The temperature of the surface water of the ocean rarely varies by more than 10°C throughout the year, whereas land temperatures can vary by up to 40°C between summer and winter months. The ocean therefore plays a fundamental role in controlling temperatures: it acts as a huge thermal regulator, storing or releasing heat as required.

Like a gigantic thermal regulator, the ocean acts in close collaboration with the atmosphere, storing or releasing heat depending on the season and the latitude.

Three control levels

Ocean temperature control operates on various levels. The ocean reflects infrared radiation back into the atmosphere, but it also releases a little of its heat by simple conduction, warming up the air when it is colder than the water. The ocean can also release energy into the air in the form of latent heat, which is almost immediately available. Water that has evaporated will return heat to the air once it condenses at a medium or high altitude and forms clouds.

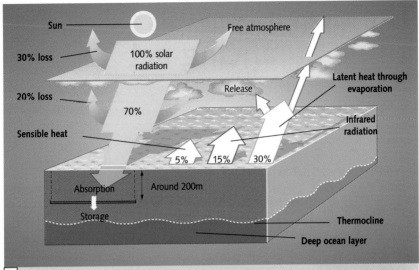

The ocean–atmosphere heat exchange. The ocean absorbs solar radiation on its surface during the hot months and stores the heat in its depths when it gets colder. It can then release the heat into the atmosphere in different ways.

This heat flux has both temporal and spatial effects. Heat stored by ocean water in the spring and summer is released into the atmosphere in the winter. This is why, in winter, it is milder near an ocean than in the middle of a continent. By taking warm water to the cold regions, the surface sea currents perform an important function, thanks to the interaction between ocean and atmosphere. Regions close to the equator are strongly heated by the Sun. Hot, light air tends to rise to the poles, where it cools, sinks back down and moves towards the equator. This phenomenon creates the winds that drive surface sea currents. These winds move tropical warm water towards the high latitudes, where it cools when it releases its heat to the atmosphere, which is in turn heated up. Now colder and denser, this water sinks beneath the surface and travels back by means of thermohaline circulation. The system has come full circle.

A question of balance

Overall, the Earth's thermal balance is more or less constant: each year, the planet receives as much heat as it loses. However, in some parts of the world there is no such balance: in the low latitudes an excess of heat is received, and in the high latitudes an excess is lost. This implies a transfer of heat between low and high latitudes, for which the oceans are partly responsible.

GLOSSARY

[Conduction]
The transfer of heat from warm to cold areas.
[Latent heat]
Heat energy that is stored and then released by a substance undergoing a change of state, such as the condensation of water vapour.
[Infrared radiation]
Electromagnetic radiation whose wavelength is between the red end of the visible spectrum and microwaves.

The ocean –
a fine balancing act

The ocean and the atmosphere play predominant roles in the four biological cycles essential for life on Earth: the water, carbon, nitrogen and oxygen cycles.

A vast reservoir of water

Within its 1,350 million km³, the ocean contains about 97% of the planet's water, making it by far the largest reservoir on the globe. Oceanic evaporation, which is intense in tropical zones where the water temperature reaches 30°C at the ocean surface, provides the atmosphere with five times more water than the amount provided by evaporation from soil surfaces and transpiration by terrestrial plants.

The atmosphere returns part of this water in the form of precipitation. The rest flows back into the oceans via watercourses and groundwater. A small amount of water (around 25 million km³) is trapped in the form of ice – when the volume of ice increases that of the oceans decreases, and when the ice melts the volume of ocean water increases.

This phenomenon is one that causes concern because of the possible repercussions of the greenhouse effect and the global warming it creates.

However, in this respect the ocean plays quite a different role: it is in fact extremely good at absorbing carbon dioxide (CO_2) from the atmosphere.

Evaporation
releases some of the heat stored in the ocean back into the atmosphere in the form of water vapour (shown in yellow). It is most intense in tropical zones.

A CO₂ sink

Produced by living organisms through respiration as well as by volcanic activity and the combustion of fossil fuels, carbon dioxide (CO_2) is used by plants in photosynthesis both on land and in the sea. However, in the oceans carbon dioxide is also absorbed and held as calcium carbonate ($CaCO_3$) in the shells of marine organisms, or else large quantities are pumped in by a gas exchange with the atmosphere. When CO_2 is at a higher pressure in the air than in the surface layer of the ocean, it is absorbed by the water. The pressure of the CO_2 dissolved in the water depends on the temperature of the ocean, biological activity and the currents. Minimal in the surface water, the pressure increases the further one descends towards the ocean floor. When it returns to the surface in the upwelling zones near to the equator, the water releases its excess carbon dioxide into the atmosphere. The biological pump works in the opposite direction in the high latitudes, amply making up for this loss.

On balance, the ocean acts as a CO_2 sink, absorbing more than it releases. Each year, around 2 billion tonnes of carbon dioxide are absorbed from the atmosphere. Since humans also produce 7 billion tonnes per year, the ocean cannot deal with it all. It does appear, however, that the ocean is able to adapt to this situation by gradually increasing its storage capacity. The CO_2 pressure measured in the surface of the ocean and in the youngest deep water rose by several per cent during the last century. It remains to be seen to what extent the ocean can continue to compensate for the carbon dioxide that humans emit into the atmosphere.

The ocean: a carbon dioxide 'pump'

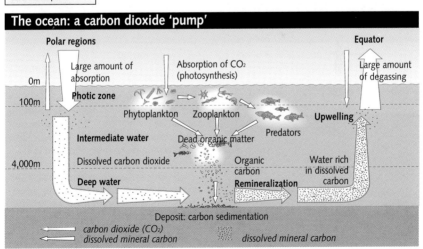

Surface water is generally poor in minerals due to the intense biological activity of plankton.

Rich in the depths, poor on the surface

The ocean depths

The ocean is not lacking in dissolved nitrogen gas, but very few species are capable of assimilating it. It is mainly used in the form of nitrates (80%) and ammonium (20%). Phytoplankton are so fond of it that the concentration of nitrates is very low, or even non-existent, in the surface water. However, dissolved inorganic nitrogen concentrations tend to increase with depth, as do those of most chemicals found in the ocean.

Like carbon, a number of chemical elements essential for life on Earth – iron, nitrogen, sulphur, phosphorous, etc – are rare in the surface water but much more abundant in the ocean depths. The fact that they are so rare near the surface is evidence of the intense biological activity that takes place in the photic layer of the ocean (that is, where sunlight penetration rates are high). Inorganic nitrogen, usually in the form of nitrate or ammonium, is taken up by the surface-living plankton and

then transported to the depths of the ocean through the chemical transformation of organic waste matter that sinks towards the ocean floor. Oxygen has the opposite distribution: its concentration is highest in the surface waters, which are tossed about by the wind, and decreases as one descends towards the depths.

The iron content of the surface waters also plays an important role. Iron is generally brought into the oceans by rivers, the leaching of coastal sediments or upwellings. Tiny iron particles are also blown from the deserts over long distances before ending up in the ocean. Where there is a lack of iron, as there is in the Southern Ocean, the eastern equatorial Pacific Ocean and the North Pacific, photosynthesis is poor, even if the surface waters are abundant in nutrients.

An inseparable couple

Periodically, the trade winds that normally drive the coastal waters of Peru towards the open ocean weaken, to the point where the habitual upwelling of nutrient-rich water does not occur. This meteorological phenomenon, which occurs around Christmas, is called 'El Niño' (Spanish for 'the Christ Child'). It has wide-ranging effects on global weather and climate, causing drought, unusual tornadoes and storms. El Niño is evidence of the close links between the ocean and the atmosphere.

A source of oxygen

Like all gases, oxygen is permanently being exchanged between the air and the water in the upper layers of the ocean. After nitrogen, it is one of the main gases in the atmosphere, where it accounts for over 20% of the total. However, it is also a by-product of photosynthesis: when algae and phytoplankton manufacture their carbohydrates using carbon dioxide, water and light, they release oxygen. This is the process that has allowed life to evolve on Earth, and today photosynthesis is responsible for producing the majority of the oxygen on our planet.

In the oceans, the colder the water is, the better the oxygen dissolves. However, this gas is rapidly used up during respiration, which explains the low concentrations of oxygen in areas where organic waste accumulates and microbial activity is high. Its vertical distribution is therefore opposite to that of other chemical elements; in other words, as the waters of the North Atlantic become rich in nitrates and carbon dioxide on their journey to the ocean floor, they lose their oxygen. Nevertheless, the ocean maintains a balance of all its elements through movement and recycling.

H ome to many species, the ocean is also the environment that contains the largest number of intermediaries between producers and consumers of organic matter. Living organisms have adapted to the conditions in the oceans – for example, some organisms drift along with the currents while others are able to swim against them, and others bury themselves in the sand or attach themselves to rocks. Some parts of the oceans, such as coral reefs, are teeming with life, while others appear to be virtually devoid of living organisms.

In the pelagic environment, dolphins share their position at the top of the ecological pyramid with other large marine mammals and sharks.

Life in the oceans

Factors that restrict life

Seemingly teeming with life, oceans are in fact restricted environments. Temperature and light vary with depth, and the availability of nutrient-rich salts is very unpredictable.

Light: the source of life

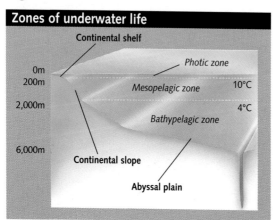

Zones of underwater life

Continental shelf
Photic zone
0m
200m
Mesopelagic zone   10°C
2,000m   4°C
Bathypelagic zone
6,000m
Continental slope
Abyssal plain

Algae manufacture their carbohydrates through photosynthesis, just as plants on dry land do. In what is known as the food chain, algae are then eaten by herbivorous animals, which are in turn eaten by carnivores, and so on. However, while there is no lack of light to enable photosynthesis on land, in water the Sun's rays are very quickly absorbed. Below the so-called compensation depth, at which the rate of photosynthesis is exactly balanced by that of respiration, there is no net gain of energy for the algae. This depth, which determines the size of the photic zone (the layer where light penetration is sufficient for photosynthesis), varies according to the time of day, the season and the clarity of the water. It is up to 40m deep in coastal waters in temperate environments but can be deeper than 100m in clear tropical waters. Animals can develop and grow below this depth, but plants cannot.

Salts essential for development

In addition to light, photosynthesis requires carbon dioxide and nutrient-rich salts. Although carbon dioxide is more abundant in cold deep water than in the sunlit surface waters, it can always be found in sufficiently large amounts for photosynthesis. This is not true of nutrient-rich salts. Nitrogen in the form of nitrate and ammonium, and phosphorous in the form of phosphates are the limiting factors here: only marine water fed by rivers or upwellings contains enough of these compounds to allow algae, the first link in the food chain, to develop.

In addition, the effect of temperatures above and below which plant activity cannot occur has to be taken into account, and the level of water oxygenation, which is greater at low temperatures, is also significant.

The distribution of marine life depends mainly on light. It is in the first 200 metres below the surface, where photosynthesis is possible, that living organisms are at their most plentiful.

Life in mid-ocean or on the bottom

Paradoxically, although they contain the largest variety of marine species, the warmest waters are those in which populations are least abundant. There is only 0.5kg of living matter per square metre in the intertropical zone, whereas there can be as much as 2kg per square metre in medium or high latitudes. The open ocean generally appears to be a desert because life is concentrated in the continental shelf zone (down to a depth of 200m on the edges of the continents).

So-called pelagic organisms live in mid-water while other organisms, known as benthic organisms, prefer to live on or near the ocean bottom. The boundary between these two worlds is not always clear. Indeed, many worms, molluscs, crustaceans and fish spend their larval life navigating between the two zones before choosing which one to remain in for their adult life.

Map (following pages)

Marine life is concentrated in coastal waters, which benefit from large amounts of nutrient-rich salts, especially off the western coasts of continents. By comparison, the zones situated in the centre of the ocean system are like biological deserts: phytoplankton (microscopic plants and bacteria), zooplankton (microscopic animals) and benthos (organisms living on or near the bottom) are rare here.

Distribution of life in the oceans

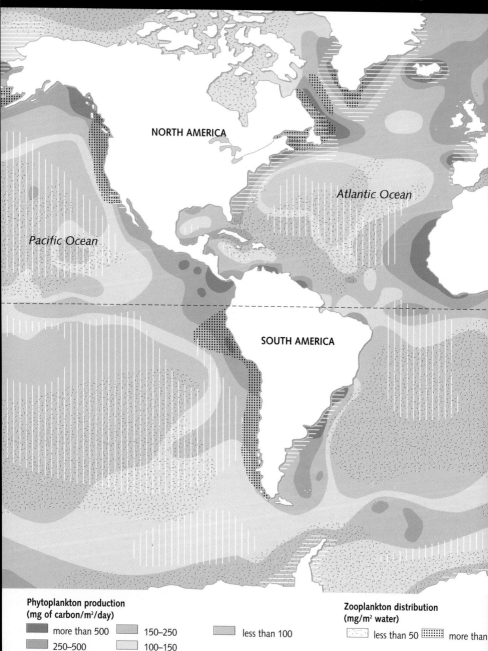

NORTH AMERICA

Atlantic Ocean

Pacific Ocean

SOUTH AMERICA

**Phytoplankton production
(mg of carbon/m²/day)**

more than 500 150–250 less than 100

250–500 100–150

**Zooplankton distribution
(mg/m² water)**

less than 50 more than

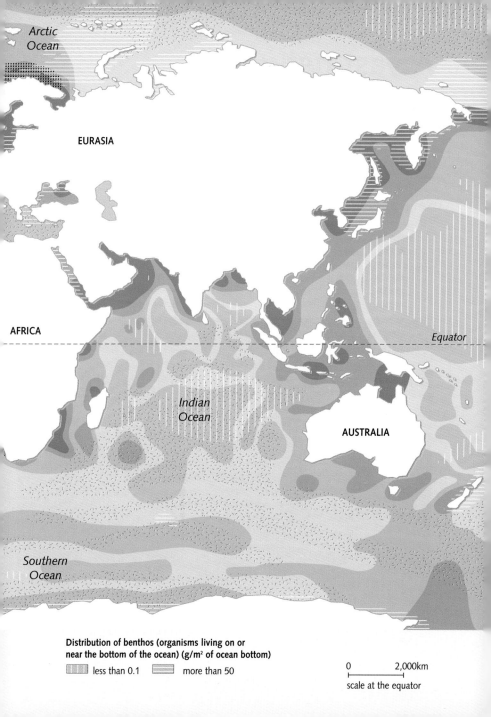

Arctic
Ocean

EURASIA

AFRICA

Equator

Indian
Ocean

AUSTRALIA

Southern
Ocean

**Distribution of benthos (organisms living on or
near the bottom of the ocean) (g/m² of ocean bottom)**

less than 0.1   more than 50

0   2,000km

scale at the equator

A vast network

Marine life can be divided into the eaters and the eaten.
The presence of algae – the first link in the food chain –
allows for the growth and development of many animals,
which are by turns producers and consumers.

Several million species

It is estimated that the oceans are home to several million different species. These species are distributed according to the resources available, in mid-water and on various kinds of ocean bottoms, and have complex relationships with regard to production and consumption. They can be compared to the links in a long chain – the food chain. Alternatively, they can be likened to layers in a pyramid: at its base, in great numbers, the smallest plants (primary producers of living matter) and at its summit the largest carnivores (tertiary or quaternary consumers depending on the length of the food chain), including man.

Tropical waters are particularly rich in species: fish, corals, sponges and a large number of other species weave a wide, complex web of ecological relationships.

Directly or indirectly, algae, diatoms and other microscopic plants provide almost all the food required for the growth, locomotion and reproduction of marine animals. The herbivores (larvae, small crustaceans) that eat them are generally found in their immediate vicinity. They in turn are eaten by other animals (larger crustaceans, small fish), known as primary carnivores or secondary consumers. These primary carnivores are then eaten by secondary carnivores, also called tertiary consumers (large fish), and they in turn are eaten by tertiary carnivores (quaternary consumers) and so on. The chain ends with the largest predators. Bacteria complete the chain – they are the decomposers of dead organic matter, which they convert into gases such as carbon dioxide and nitrogen and nutrient-rich salts. These gases and salts are then released back into the environment, where they may be reused.

GLOSSARY

[Biomass]
The total living organisms in a specific ecosystem, population or other unit area at a given moment.

A complex chain

The marine food chain is extremely complex – it is not simply a linear succession of links. There are three main reasons for its complexity. Firstly, a given species rarely has the same diet at different stages of its life: so it is hard to define its exact place in the chain. Secondly, these diets often combine several levels, combining both plants and animals. Thirdly, cannibalism is not uncommon, which complicates matters even further.

Four or five links

In general, there are four or five of these 'links' or trophic levels in the seas and oceans. Apart from plants, all species are both producers and consumers of living matter. For example, anchovies eat tiny mid-water plants and animals and at the same time are the favourite prey of larger fish, which means they are also producers. However, a large amount of energy is lost in moving between different levels of the chain: anchovies need to consume 240 million tonnes of food in order to become 24 million tonnes of fish stock. In fact, the entire secondary production is estimated to be 0.25% of the primary production: in other words, to produce the 1.25 billion tonnes of animal matter the oceans contain, no fewer than 500 billion tonnes of plant organisms are required. Given this, it is easy to understand the great impact that man can have by intervening at certain points in the chain.

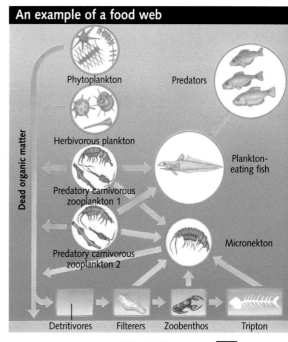

An example of a food web

Phytoplankton

Predators

Herbivorous plankton

Dead organic matter

Predatory carnivorous zooplankton 1

Plankton-eating fish

Predatory carnivorous zooplankton 2

Micronekton

Detritivores   Filterers   Zoobenthos   Tripton

Life in mid-water

Living in mid-water has its advantages and its disadvantages. There is certainly more light than on the ocean floor; however, the currents are stronger. Some organisms drift along, while others actively swim.

Drifting along ... without sinking

Pelagic organisms (those that live in the open ocean), have to adapt to currents. Some, such as nekton, actively swim; others, like plankton, drift along with the current.

Plankton is a collective term for a variety of marine organisms which are often very small and more or less transparent. They have mechanisms (floats, flagella, cilia, etc) that help them stay close to the surface.

A wealth of bacteria

Phytoplankton includes even smaller organisms: bacteria. Until recently, their role was considered to be insignificant; however, they are by far the most numerous type of plankton. Their minute size – between 0.2 and 2 thousandths of a millimetre (100 times smaller than single-celled algae) – is easily compensated for by their number: a single drop of water contains 1,000 times more bacteria than single-celled algae. Since many of these bacteria photosynthesize, they play an essential role in the production of organic matter in the oceans, thus constituting the first link in the food chain.

Plankton are often tiny (under one millimetre long) and have lightweight skeletons and floats which prevent them from sinking down to the dark and icy depths of the ocean. Some also have flagella or cilia or even fins.

Solitary or living in colonies, plankton are generally transparent. However, they can also be an intense blue colour, which makes them virtually invisible in the waters they inhabit. Other types of plankton camouflage themselves in the ocean depths by adopting a reddish-brown coloration.

Accounting for 90% of the organisms living in the oceans, plankton are classified in two categories: phytoplankton (microscopic plants and bacteria) and zooplankton (microscopic animals).

Phytoplankton

Present only in the sunlit surface waters of the ocean where sufficient light penetrates, phytoplankton are principally made up of microscopic single-celled algae, solitary or loosely grouped into colonies. The main types of phytoplankton are diatoms, which are protected by intricate shells made of silica, dinoflagellates with a cell wall often bearing two flagella and coccolithophores, which are tiny, often flagellate, algae enclosed in calcite shells. Diatoms are found everywhere, but are particularly abundant in the cold waters of the Arctic and Southern Oceans. Dinoflagellates, on the other hand, proliferate in tropical zones and

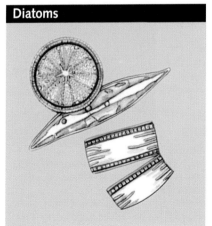

Diatoms

are responsible for the phenomena known as 'red tides'. Coccolithophores are mostly found in temperate and warm nutrient-depleted waters.

Phytoplankton use photosynthesis to manufacture the carbohydrates they need for growth. In addition to a certain amount of light, this process also requires nutrient-rich salts, brought by rivers or the mixing of water layers. This is why phytoplankton are more abundant close to coasts than in the open ocean. Over 30 million diatoms have been found in a single litre of seawater at the mouth of the River Senegal.

GLOSSARY

[Plankton]
Minute plant organisms (phytoplankton) and animal organisms (zooplankton) which are found in aquatic ecosystems. They float passively, being unable to swim against water currents.
[Nekton]
Microscopic aquatic organisms which can swim actively against water currents.

Diversity of zooplankton

1: **Foraminifer (0.4mm)**; 2 and 3: Jellyfish (15cm); 4: Ctenophore (comb jelly) (1.5cm); 5: Polychaete worm (7mm); 6: Pteropod mollusc (3cm); 7: Chaetognath (arrow worm) (3cm); 8: Deepwater prawn (6cm); 9: Copepod (2mm); 10: Lobster larva (1cm).

All major animal groups

Zooplankton comprises small, mainly microscopic animals that drift or float with the current. All major animal groups are represented in zooplankton, from protozoa – single-celled flagellate or ciliate organisms – to the larvae of crustaceans and fish. They rarely measure over one hundredth of a millimetre (a common diameter amongst phytoplankton). Size varies considerably from one organism to another, from microscopic forms to giant jellyfish like the lion's mane jellyfish (*Cyanea arctica*), whose body can be over 2m in diameter and whose tentacles can be over 10m long. These animals eat phytoplankton or other types of zooplankton, and so are not directly

dependent on light. They are found at all depths, although they are most abundant in the first 1,000m below the surface. Sometimes water masses drag them down: populations used to cold surface waters can find themselves in the depths of the ocean when these cold surface waters sink below warmer ones. However, zooplankton are also capable of vertical migration, descending during the day and rising again at night. This allows them to be less conspicuous, and therefore less vulnerable to the active swimmers that are lying in wait for them – the nekton.

A shared life

Fish, sea urchins, prawns, molluscs: many marine organisms are classed as plankton in their larval stage. The larvae, which are always tiny, sometimes drift for kilometres before falling to the bottom. Only a few set off again for the open ocean, since very often these larvae turn into sedentary benthic adults (living on the ocean bottom).

Marine predators

Unlike plankton, which drift around relatively passively with the currents, nekton are strong, active swimmers. They include prawns, cephalopods such as octopuses and squid, and various sizes of fish, as well as sea turtles and marine

Great white shark

70

⟨ **Pelagic fish** often group together in compact shoals in order to fend off predators. This behaviour can be observed, for example, in carangid fish during the daytime.

mammals. The smallest predators feed on zooplankton, as do anchovies, sprats and sardines. They are in turn the prey of larger fish like mackerel or scad, which are themselves snapped up by large marine predators such as tunas, sharks, seals, dolphins, sperm whales and killer whales. Nekton are also extremely gregarious, gathering in shoals during the breeding period. These shoals, which break up as quickly as they are created, sometimes travel from one end of an ocean to the other during long migrations.

The mobility of zooplankton

Even though they drift along with the current, planktonic organisms are not totally inert. They are able to sink down to the colder deep water in winter, where they live at a slow pace in order to use up less energy, until the good weather returns. They also move around depending on what stage of the life cycle they are at: eggs, larvae, young and adults do not have the same needs, and thus live at different depths. By moving around on a daily basis zooplankton are able to reach those places where food is most plentiful. Thus, some small crustaceans swim upwards for more than 600m, coming up to feed at night and sinking back down again during the day.

Life on the ocean floor

A number of marine organisms live on or near the ocean bottom. Most abundant in coastal areas, they have to withstand the movements of the swells and the rise and fall of the tides.

A number of marine organisms, like sea urchins, spend their larval life in mid-water and their adult life on the ocean bottom. They therefore have to adapt in order to survive in a wave-swept environment.

The importance of the substrate

After being carried along as larvae by the water, a number of adult organisms choose to live on or near the ocean bottom. These species, known as the benthos, are subjected to various constraints: if they wander too far away from the coasts they will not find enough food, but if they stay they have to adapt to local conditions like light, salinity and temperature, and the environment in general (rocky, sandy, etc). They also have to withstand tides that can convert a seemingly immobile expanse of pebbles into a substrate as unstable as sand. The nature of the ocean floor – whether loose (pebbles, sand or mud) or solid (rocks, artificial substrate, ships' hulls) – is decisive. Therefore, most large algae attach themselves to rocks with anchoring or-

Change on the ocean floor

Sandy environments sometimes house algae or encrusting sponges that secrete calcium. These secretions then aggregate and bind together substrate elements that were previously mobile. Conversely, some algae and shellfish such as shipworms (*Teredo*) are able to bore through rocks, pulverize them and gradually turn them into gravel. Or a rock might be covered in a pile of debris – pieces of algae, empty shells, and so on – which make it look like a loose ocean substrate.

gans called holdfasts, while more highly developed plants such as seagrasses or eelgrasses put down roots in the sand or mud.

Similarly, fixed animals (sea anemones, sea lilies, mussels) prefer hard substrates, whilst those that like burrowing (worms, cockles, flat fish) opt for loose sediments. Thus, the benthos can be divided into two distinct communities: organisms that live on the surface of the ocean bottom or sediment (epifauna) and those that burrow into the ocean bottom or live in the sediment (infauna).

Withstanding the onslaught of the waves

Organisms living on the ocean bottom have several options. So-called sessile organisms live permanently fixed to one spot (sea lilies, bivalve molluscs, sponges, ascidians). In order to withstand the onslaught of the waves, they cling to the ocean floor: hence the fine threads exuded by mussels, the solid holdfasts developed by algae or the sucker effect employed by limpets, which use suction adhesion and mucus to anchor themselves to rocks.

Other organisms – sedentary organisms – crawl or walk along the ocean bottom, never covering great distances. For example, on the hard floors of wave-swept environments, life forms such as winkles, sea urchins and starfish crawl along by literally sticking to the substrate.

On sand or mud, they are often replaced by good walkers such as crabs or lobsters.

A third category of organisms (including octopuses, crustaceans such as lobsters, and fish) move faster and cover larger distances: they are described as being vagile.

Both walkers and swimmers are able to migrate. Some female crustaceans cover distances of up to 200km in order to lay their eggs near a coast, before returning to the sedentary males in the deeper waters.

Holdfast

Laminaria
(brown alga)

Octopus

Life in the oceans 73

Borers and burrowers

This type of organism, which is constantly searching for shelter, is essentially made up of borers and burrowers. Boring sponges (*Cliona*) manage to encrust themselves in soft limestone rocks using a chemical technique, while boring bivalves (*Pholas*) perforate sandstone and other soft rocks in order to create a hollowed-out dwelling. Burrowers associated with loose ocean floors are far more numerous. Some do not alter the structure of the sediment: cockles, clams, razor shells or even flat fish like soles or plaice are only looking for a place to hide. Others, such as tubeworms and certain crustaceans, create a real burrow with walls consolidated by varying amounts of mucus. However, they stay in contact with the surface through vents and orifices. This allows water to circulate, providing nutrients and oxygen. Finally, many very small animals live permanently under the sediment, making use of the water it contains: tiny flatworms and minuscule crustaceans (copepods, ostracods and isopods) no bigger than 2mm, move about freely among the grains of sand.

Sand and mud make life for these creatures far easier than rocky substrates. They are not difficult to burrow into and there is plenty of room. However, for hard ocean floors – except in zones exposed by the tide or where it is totally dark – the occupation rate is often close to 100%. The populations here can create a spectacular display: individuals can pile up

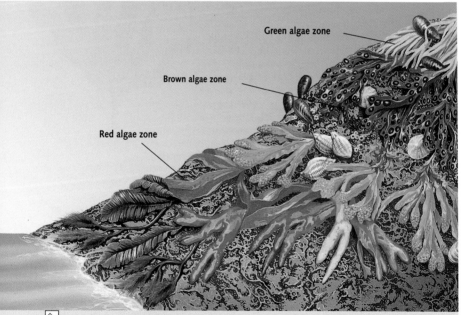

Green algae zone

Brown algae zone

Red algae zone

Observed between high and low tide, algae can be good points of reference for defining the different ecological niches of intertidal life. Their presence depends on factors including emersion time, light, and the strength of the waves.

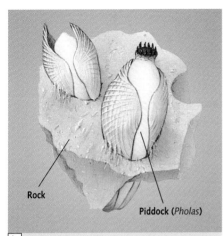

Rock

Piddock (*Pholas*)

Piddocks (*Pholas*) are bivalves that belong to the class Lamellibranchia. They can bore holes in hard rocks by twisting themselves around and using their saw-like shell as a file.

(barnacles, slipper limpets, limpets, etc), attach themselves to others already in place (polyps of bryozoans on algae, sea anemones on the shells of molluscs) or take on a vertical form, standing up or hanging down like stalks (goose barnacles).

Immobile filterers

Sessile filterers are limited in their feeding and breeding behaviour. Since they are immobile, they can only reproduce by external fertilization, releasing gametes (sperm and eggs) into the water: when these gametes meet they give rise to planktonic larvae, which have to find the right substrate to attach themselves to.

Fixed organisms resort to several different strategies for feeding. Bivalve molluscs use their gills to filter water, while tubeworms use their red gills (branchial plumes) to retain nutrition-rich particles and bacteria. Some organisms (sea lilies, sea anemones) use mobile tentacles to catch minuscule prey that ventures near them. This is nothing, however, compared to the many options open to mobile organisms, which can crawl, walk or swim, chase, trap, graze or devour carcasses left behind by other predators.

Life on different levels

Benthic life is spread out over different levels. The supralittoral or spray zone of the shore is only rarely covered by water, and its inhabitants are more terrestrial than marine. In the adjacent midlittoral zone, organisms are adapted to the rhythm of the tides: they create reserves of water to enable them to withstand exposure. The next area is the infralittoral zone, where species are found that need to be permanently covered in water. Next comes the circalittoral zone, where plants no longer dominate, followed by the bathyal zone, which corresponds to the continental slope (between 200m and 2,000m), the abyssal zone (plains below 2,000m), and finally the hadal zone in the oceanic trenches (over 6,000m deep). Living organisms are concentrated mainly in the midlittoral and circalittoral zones, above the continental shelf (0–200m).

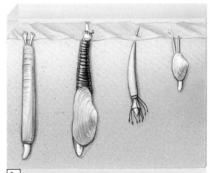

Burrowing molluscs protect their bodies and fragile gills from grains of sand. Water, containing oxygen and nutrient-rich particles, enters and leaves only through two narrow orifices, the inhalant and exhalant siphons.

Forced migration

When food is scarce or the temperature drops and threatens the future of their young, many pelagic species migrate to locations far from where they were spawned.

Thousands of kilometres

Many pelagic fish gather in shoals and travel tens of thousands of kilometres in order to reproduce or feed. For some, this is a seasonal ritual. For others, the journey is spread out over the animal's lifetime: the individual only returns to its point of departure to give birth before dying. These migrations can take fish from seawater to fresh water or vice versa. However, the whole journey can also take place entirely in the ocean. Herrings, for example, always stay in waters with a similar level of salinity. Those that breed from August to September off the coast of Scotland then head off towards the south-west coast of Norway, while others lay eggs from November to January off the French coast before spending the summer in the central and northern North Sea. Similarly, Atlantic cod in the Arctic seas move south in winter towards the Norwegian coast before going back north again in the spring. Tuna travel even greater distances: at the beginning of summer, longfin and bluefin tuna leave the waters where they were spawned (the Azores and the Mediterranean respectively) and travel to the far north, where prey is abundant. They do not return south until the winter.

From the sea to fresh water and vice versa

The upheaval is even more radical for salmons and eels. Living in the sea in high-latitude cold waters, salmon swim back to the coast in order to lay their eggs in mountain streams. They have to adapt to huge changes in the salinity of the water, and be able to swim upstream. The young salmon are then carried down to the sea, where they join the Asian and American salmon populations for three years. When they mature they go back to their native river in order to breed. Eels do the opposite, migrating from fresh water to salt water, leaving when 10–15 years old and swimming to the Sargasso Sea to lay their eggs. The spawn then turn into long, transparent, flattened

Migration lasts around 2 years
Eel
Elver
Egg
3cm
Leptocephalus (eel larva)
4.5–7.5cm

In the Atlantic Ocean, eels migrate in both directions: first towards the Sargasso Sea, where they spawn, then towards the coasts of Europe, where the elvers swim upriver to reach maturity.

The humpback whale carries out its entire migration in the ocean. Unlike the eel, it does not have to adapt to changing from a saltwater to a freshwater environment.

larvae known as leptocephali, which are carried along by the currents. These develop further, eventually becoming elvers, which gather in their millions at the mouths of rivers.

Worms, prawns, turtles, whales ...

Worms, crustaceans, sea turtles and marine mammals also migrate. Whale migrations have been very well studied. Whales spend the summer in the cold waters of the Arctic or the Southern Ocean, where they consume tonnes of prawns. With full stomachs, and the ice threatening to spread, they head towards warmer waters in winter (the Indian Ocean, the Indonesian seas, the north-west coast of Africa, the Gulf of Aden or the Bay of Bengal). There they breed and feed their young before taking them back on the return migration route. The humpback whale (*Megaptera novaeangliae*), known for its strange, melodious singing, is one of the ocean's greatest travellers. Some Pacific humpback populations feed in the icy (4°C) but nutrient-rich waters of the Southern Ocean, then swim up the western coast of South America before giving birth in the warm waters of Central America (25°C) after an incredible trip of over 8,000km.

In the darkness of the abyss

Organisms that live in the depths of the ocean must be able to withstand extremely high water pressure, as well as devise strategies to compensate for the scarcity of food.

Extreme conditions

A few hundred metres below the surface of the water, light disappears completely. At the same time, the temperature decreases until it reaches approximately 2°C at depths of around 1,000m. Living matter created on the surface only reaches the ocean bottom through the movements of large pelagic organisms, or else in the form of 'marine snow' – detritus that includes the tiny leftovers of animals, plants and non-living matter, faecal matter, dust and sand. Pressure also increases by one atmosphere every 10m, and rapidly reaches a level that is 100 times higher than on the surface. It is understandable that, in these circumstances, life is limited.

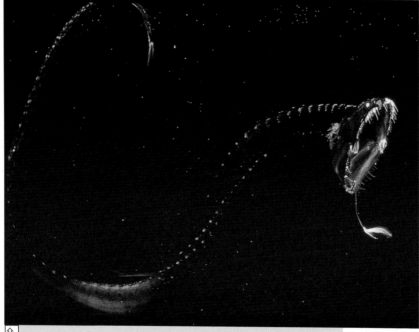

Huge jaws joined to a 'fishing line' of luminescent organs: this black dragonfish (*Idiacanthus*) is perfectly adapted to the abyssal environment.

In order to live in the abyss, organisms must adapt. Usually, fish have small air-filled swim bladders, which allow them to regulate buoyancy and thus remain in deep water. However, below 2,000m they are not equipped with this organ, and thus are able to withstand the pressure. Animals' sight also has to be modified. There is no point in being able to see in visible light if there is none. Therefore, some abyssal creatures are equipped with systems similar to military night-vision devices, which allow them to see using infrared. These organisms have also developed ingenious strategies for breeding and attracting food.

The end justifies the means

Some fish, such as the female abyssal anglerfish (*Melanocetus*), are equipped with what looks like a fishing rod on the top of their heads: a filament ending in a luminescent organ which acts as a lure. Seeing this organ moving around, prey mistake it for falling marine snow. When they pounce on this 'snow' they fall into the anglerfish's open mouth, which is equipped with long, sharp, predatory teeth. Sometimes this enormous mouth leads to an extensible stomach.

GLOSSARY

[Bioluminescence]
Light produced by living organisms by means of a chemical reaction. It is primarily a marine phenomenon.

The gulpers (*Eurypharynx*) have extremely large mouths with loosely hinged jaws, which enable them to eat fish bigger than themselves. The tactic of molluscs that swim about in the deep ocean is to produce long threads of mucus which act like 'fly paper', catching everything that comes into contact with them.

Breeding is particularly difficult in the darkness of the abyss due to the scarcity of partners. Many fish have specialized organs called photophores, which produce light, and some signal to their partners by flashing.

However, there are more radical solutions. The male of the abyssal anglerfish, once it has found a female, lives on her as a parasite and takes its food from her bloodstream. Tiny and atrophied, it is in fact no more than a provider of sperm.

The deep-ocean oases

In 1979, scientists were amazed to discover oases of life around sea-floor hot springs at depths of 2,500m on the Galapagos Rift. Colonies of large worms with red plumes, giant mussels, crabs, sea anemones, sponges and squat lobsters proliferate around basalt chimneys known as 'black smokers'. The sulphurous fluids emitted by these hydrothermal vents are responsible for this profusion of life: they allow bacteria to develop, and these find shelter inside giant worms with no mouth or digestive tract (*Riftia*). A whole living web has been able to form on the basis of these organisms. Submarine oases like those on the Galapagos Rift have subsequently been found all over the world.

Coral reefs

Warm tropical waters have low marine productivity, except in areas where coral reefs have developed. Home to thousands of species, these environments are among the richest on the planet.

Billions of polyps

Polyps are tiny rudimentary organisms related to jellyfish, living attached to rocky substrate, often on the slopes of volcanic islands. A polyp has a sac-like body inside a calcareous skeleton, with a mouth at the top crowned by a ring of tentacles. As polyps form colonies made up of billions of individuals, their calcareous structure creates spectacular formations which grow at a rate of one centimetre a year: these formations are known as coral reefs. With the passage of time, the slopes of the volcano give way beneath the weight of the coral and sink below sea level: the reef becomes an atoll,

One island, several reefs

Moving from the coast of a volcanic island toward the open ocean, it is generally possible to distinguish a fringing reef where the water is shallow and relatively calm and warm, then a lagoon, which the coral sands tend to fill up, and finally a barrier reef, situated several kilometres from the coast and facing the ocean. Bays can create openings here and there; the water then circulates in the lagoon through channels parallel to the coast.

forming a ring around a lagoon. Corals proliferate in warm waters (over 18°C) where there are only minor variations in temperature of no more than 3°C.

Corals have no need of nutrient-rich salts. Clean water and plenty of light is enough for

Structure of an atoll

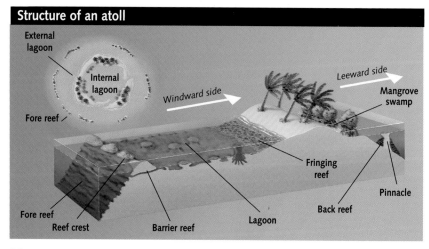

External lagoon

Internal lagoon

Windward side

Leeward side

Mangrove swamp

Fore reef

Fringing reef

Pinnacle

Fore reef

Reef crest

Barrier reef

Lagoon

Back reef

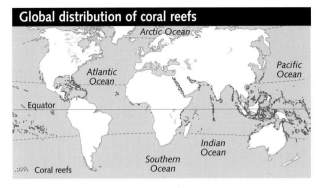

Global distribution of coral reefs

Arctic Ocean

Atlantic Ocean

Pacific Ocean

Equator

Indian Ocean

Southern Ocean

Coral reefs

them, because single-celled algae live in symbiosis in their tissues. The corals draw oxygen and food from these algae, and the algae accelerate the deposit of calcium carbonate in their skeletons.

In exchange, corals provide the algae with shelter and some of the ingredients necessary for photosynthesis – carbon dioxide, nitrogen and phosphorous – which are produced by their metabolism and immediately recycled by the algae. This close collaboration with algae means that corals do not develop in deep water.

Reefs in danger

Threats facing coral reefs include the dynamiting of reefs in fishing areas, pollution from waste water, the removal of the most beautiful pieces of coral for collectors or the jewellery trade and, in recent years, the extensive death of coral due to the global warming of the oceans.

A multitude of species

The parts of coral reefs that face the ocean are subjected to the force of swells and battered by huge waves: they accumulate blocks of dead coral, on top of which a crest of algae grows. Gaps allow water to enter the calmest (and thus the warmest) areas. Separate communities of organisms live here: encrusting algae predominate in places where

the current is strong, while sea anemones and madrepores inhabit the calm, shallow water. A large number of species find refuge in this environment, where light, currents and temperature vary. It is estimated that around 500,000 species live in the world's coral reefs.

Competition for space is severe: algae, sponges, corals, gorgonians, anemones and shellfish all have to find somewhere to attach themselves. A multitude of multicoloured fish with evocative names – parrot fish (which graze on coral), angel fish, butterfly fish – inhabit this environment. Some species such as the anemone and the clown fish have a collaborative, protective relationship, for this apparent paradise contains sharks, groupers, barracudas and a number of other predatory carnivores.

This clown fish lives in perfect harmony with the sea anemone, which protects it from predators.

Life in the oceans **81**

T he world's oceans and seas are constantly used for fishing and commercial purposes. Even though global catches have been stagnant over the last 20 years or so and several fishing grounds remain under threat, the waters of the west Pacific and the Indian Ocean are still full of fish. At the same time, aquaculture is spreading at a tremendous pace, particularly in Asian countries. And the sea contains many other resources: sand, gravel, petrol, salt and precious metals. There is a great temptation to exploit these resources freely without thinking about the consequences. Fortunately, the United Nations has regulated their use.

Fishing is carried out mainly in coastal areas, where fish are more plentiful.

Exploiting the oceans

Shipping

Competition between airlines has reduced passenger transport by ship but not freight transport. The advantages of using ships include moderate energy expenditure, the large volume of freight that can be transported and the relatively small crews needed.

People and freight

Many centuries ago, the Phoenicians already understood the importance of merchant ships, using them to trade rare fabrics, pearls, incense and oriental spices for the gold, silver, lead and sulphur offered by the peoples on the other side of the Mediterranean. In the 5th century, sailors from America reached Tahiti in simple dugout canoes, while others from Indonesia, Melanesia and even Japan turned their attentions to the islands of Micronesia. Today, liners are used mainly for cruises, carrying almost ten million passengers every year. However, the oceans are very popular for commerce, with five billion tonnes of goods carried by sea each year. The world fleet contains around 90,000 cargo ships and employs nearly 1.2 million people.

This cargo ship leaving the Canadian port of Vancouver is one of around 90,000 ships that transport freight worldwide.

Large capacity and modern equipment

Sea traffic was once very heavy in the Atlantic Ocean, but it has now largely moved to the Pacific. At the same time, ships have increased in size and are now equipped with GPS (Global Positioning System), a navigation system that uses satellite technology to pinpoint the ship's precise location. Nevertheless, the magnetic compass, the gyrocompass and the sextant are still used to check positions, especially close to war zones, where signals can be jammed or intercepted. Weather forecasts provided by satellites, radar, depth sounders, logs for measuring a ship's speed – all of these make navigation easier, but they are no substitute for a sailor's skill and experience. The crew of a modern ship generally numbers no more than around 20. Cargo handling is mechanized to ensure an optimal turnaround time.

Winches and cranes on ships allow several thousand tonnes of goods to be loaded or unloaded in just a few hours.

Specialized ships

Today's merchant ships bear little resemblance to the clippers that used to carry all kinds of cargo packed higgledy-piggledy in their holds. They are now specialized vessels: bulk carriers for transporting minerals or agricultural products in bulk, oil tankers, chemical tankers, container carriers, roll on-roll off cargo ships in which goods are loaded on pallets in lorries, and many more.

Petrol, raw materials and agricultural products (minerals, coal, cement, cereals, timber) carried in bulk by cargo ships represent 60% of global tonnage. The remainder is made up of various goods, stored in containers or on pallets in lorries, and methane and chemical products.

The total tonnage transported has quadrupled in the last 30 years.

The boom in flags of convenience

The world fleet is registered under a system of flags: the Panamanian flag is the most popular, followed (in order of popularity) by those of Liberia, Greece, Cyprus, the Bahamas, Norway, Japan, Malta and Singapore. The USA, Hong Kong and various European states prefer to sail their ships using these 'flags of convenience' in order to benefit from low or non-existent taxes, cheap labour and less restrictive regulations. Unfortunately, this situation results in dangerous ships with poor safety records being kept in circulation. Nowadays, flags of convenience are heavily criticized by seamen's and dockers' unions, and by the developing countries that this practice exploits.

GLOSSARY

[Gyrocompass]
An electrical device with a spinning disc as in a gyroscope, used to indicate true north. The gyrocompass is linked to a ship's automatic pilot.
[GPS]
The Global Positioning System (GPS) is a navigation system using the American network of satellites known as NAVSTAR.

Map *(following pages)*

The total number of ships in the global fleet may be decreasing, but the number of large freight lines has remained stable. The Pacific is now more popular than the Atlantic for fishing, since it is the only ocean in which the volume of catches continues to rise, whether it be off the Chinese coast or near to Peru. Aquaculture is most popular in Asia, which accounts for 88.5% of global production.

Exploitation of marine resources

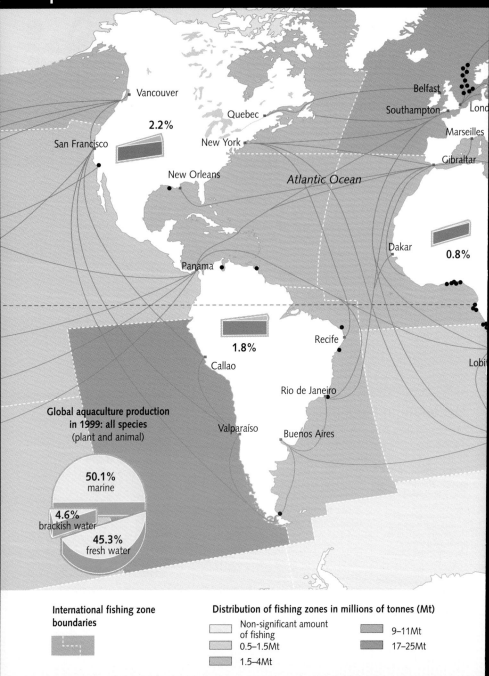

Vancouver
2.2%
San Francisco
Quebec
New York
New Orleans
Atlantic Ocean
Panama
Dakar
0.8%
1.8%
Recife
Callao
Rio de Janeiro
Valparaíso
Buenos Aires

Belfast
Southampton
Lond
Marseilles
Gibraltar
Lobi

**Global aquaculture production
in 1999: all species**
(plant and animal)

50.1%
marine

4.6%
brackish water

45.3%
fresh water

**International fishing zone
boundaries**

Distribution of fishing zones in millions of tonnes (Mt)

Non-significant amount
of fishing

0.5–1.5Mt

1.5–4Mt

9–11Mt

17–25Mt

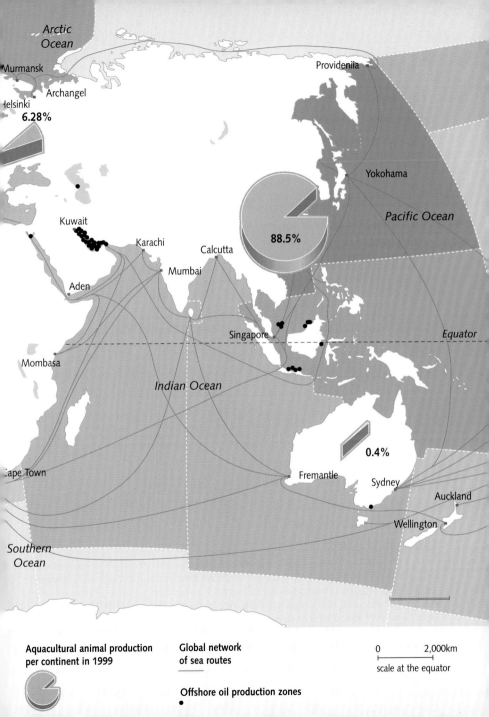

Arctic
Ocean

Murmansk

Archangel

Helsinki

6.28%

Providenila

Yokohama

Kuwait

Karachi

Calcutta

Mumbai

Aden

Pacific Ocean

88.5%

Singapore

Equator

Mombasa

Indian Ocean

Fremantle

0.4%

Sydney

Auckland

Wellington

Cape Town

Southern
Ocean

Aquacultural animal production
per continent in 1999

Global network
of sea routes

0   2,000km

scale at the equator

Offshore oil production zones

Fishing in crisis

The global catch has remained stagnant since the 1980s, especially in temperate and cold waters. Only the waters of the central-west Pacific and the eastern Indian Ocean are bucking this trend.

Fewer and fewer fish

Towards the end of the 19th century, the world catch of fish, molluscs, crustaceans and other seafood accounted for 5 million tonnes per year. Today, the global catch is almost 20 times higher: 92.3 million tonnes were caught in 1999 out of a maximum theoretical yield of 100 million tonnes per year. This apparent progression hides the real facts: from an annual catch of 18 million tonnes at the beginning of the 1950s, the tonnages increased by 6% each year until 1969 but then by only 2% a year throughout the 1970s and 1980s. They then stabilized at a level that has scarcely varied since that time. However, fishing has not decreased, it has increased, with traditional methods coming up against fierce competition from factory ships, which locate fish using an array of detection devices. It is clear, therefore, that the stagnation is not a result of a decrease in fishing but of the overexploitation of fish stocks.

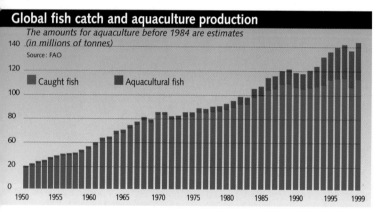

Global fish catch and aquaculture production

The amounts for aquaculture before 1984 are estimates (in millions of tonnes)

Source: FAO

■ Caught fish   ■ Aquacultural fish

China in the lead

China is the world's leading fishing nation, accounting for 20% of the global catch in 1998. After it come Japan, the USA, the Russian Federation, Peru, Indonesia, Chile, India, Thailand and Norway. In 1998, fish catches totalled only 86.3 million tonnes, a drop of 8% compared with the previous year. This decrease reveals the significance of the 1997–8 El Niño phenomenon: since they were poorer in nutrient-rich salts, the coastal waters of Peru contained fewer fish, and the volume of catches fell from 17 million tonnes to 8 million between 1996 and 1998. It also shows how dependent each fishing area is on one or two species: the Peruvian

In the north-east Atlantic, stocks are dwindling. Proof of this is that the size of catches has remained constant since the 1970s.

anchovy and the Chilean jack mackerel in the South Pacific, the Alaska pollock and the Japanese anchovy in the north-west Pacific, the skipjack tuna and the yellowfin tuna in the central-west Pacific, and so on.

A boom in catches in tropical waters

For a long time, the temperate and cold waters of the northern hemisphere provided most of the global catch. They still provide a significant amount – with 36 million tonnes, the north-west Pacific and north-east Atlantic supplied almost 40% of total global production in 1998. However, in recent years the size of the catches in these zones has been stagnating and sometimes even decreasing.

Production in the north-east Atlantic has remained at 11 million tonnes since the 1970s. Catches of Alaska pollock dropped from 6 million tonnes in the 1980s to 4 million in 1998. In contrast, the amount of fish taken from warm tropical waters is constantly rising. An increase has been detected in the central-west Pacific (9.3 million tonnes in 1998): this is due not only to shoals of tuna but also to other fish (sardinella, various species of mullet and bonitos), molluscs (carpet clams, venus clams, cuttlefish) and crustaceans (prawns).

Creating reserves

The future of fishing seems to lie in the central-west Pacific and the eastern Indian Ocean, fishing grounds that produced record catches in 1998. This situation is also the result of an overexploitation of resources, especially in the Southern Ocean and the south-east and north-west Atlantic. Of the 441 fishing stocks that have been assessed by the FAO, 9% were exhausted, 15–18% overexploited and 47–50% already fully exploited. Three-quarters of the world's fishing areas therefore need to be subjected to restrictions in order to ensure their recovery. It is very unlikely that new fishing grounds will be found; in fact, 87% of the total biomass of fish and other edible marine animals are found in coastal waters or in upwelling zones, where cold, nutrient-rich water rises to the surface from the depths. These areas represent a mere 2% of the water in the world's oceans. Fishing grounds have already been regulated, quotas established, the number of boats restricted and the mesh size of nets prescribed. This is obviously not enough. Consequently, scientists have recommended the creation of reserves within which certain species will be protected. However, in order to allow shoals to recover, traditional quotas must also be applied outside the reserves. This is obviously not popular with fishermen and the problem has not been solved. At present, only around one hundred reserves have been created, most of which cover no more than 12km² – less than 0.01% of the surface area of the world's oceans.

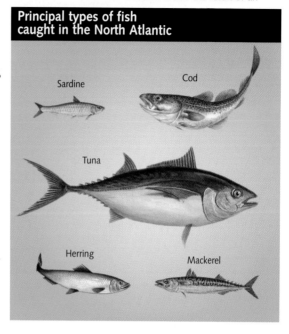

Principal types of fish caught in the North Atlantic

Sardine

Cod

Tuna

Herring

Mackerel

Fishing monitored by zones

The overwhelming majority of fish are caught in the continental shelf area. Fish like albacore, bigeye and skipjack tuna, however, are caught in the open ocean. In order to monitor world fish stocks, the FAO does not divide the global ocean into continental shelf and open ocean areas; instead, it splits the global ocean into 16 zones, defined by their latitudes and longitudes. There are six zones in the Atlantic, six in the Pacific, two in the Indian Ocean, one in the Mediterranean and the Black Sea, and one in the Southern Ocean.

Various methods of fishing

Fishermen all over the world use nets, lines, dragnets and pots. Nets can be conical and dragged by one or two boats along the ocean floor or through mid-water: half the global

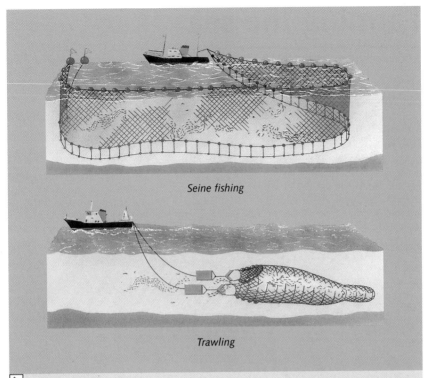

Seine fishing

Trawling

Fishing techniques vary depending on the type of fish being caught: seine fishing is used to find fish that school close to the surface, and trawling to catch those found near the bottom.

catch is produced by trawlers. The nets can also be made up of several layers of mesh suspended vertically, either fixed or drifting: these are called 'gill nets'. Sometimes, they are dragged in such a way that they encircle shoals of fish swimming near the surface: these so-called 'seine nets' are used to catch anchovies and sardines in particular. Lines can be of variable length (up to 150km) and equipped with hooks (as many as several thousand) that are directly attached to the line or connected by secondary lines called 'paternoster lines'. This system is used to catch mackerel and tuna. Fishermen also use metallic dragnets to collect shellfish from the ocean floor, pots to catch large crustaceans, and various other types of trap.

Freshwater fish

The global fish catch, as defined by the FAO, includes fish caught in both salt and fresh water. The amount caught in fresh water is quite large: in 1999 it was 8.2 million tonnes, or almost 9% of the total catch. This figure was an increase from only 6.7 million tonnes in 1994. China is also the world's leading nation in freshwater fishing, being responsible for 30% of the catch.

Farming the sea

Aquaculture, increasingly industrialized, is enjoying a boom.
It provides mussels, oysters, seaweed and fish – one-third
of the world's seafood products.

An ancient practice

The farming of aquatic environments is a practice which has been carried out for centuries in Asia, and was known to the ancient Greeks and Romans. Noticing that young fish, molluscs and crustaceans come into coastal lagoons and ponds to grow before returning to the sea, people had the idea of trapping them. Techniques were developed, such as the tambaks (brackish-water fish ponds) in Asia and the valli (brackish lagoons used for fish farming) in the Po Delta. Today, traditional methods are gradually giving way to industrial techniques, which can yield around 33 tonnes of aquatic organisms a year.

Oyster farming (the extensive breeding of oysters in beds) is an aquacultural activity which is very widespread in western Europe and in many countries in Asia (as here in Japan).

Cultivating young larvae

Larvae are taken from the sea or obtained from hatcheries and nurseries, and then kept in controlled areas and fed. This so-called 'extensive' aquaculture is used for rearing carp in eastern Europe and China, milkfish in Asia, mullets, gilthead bream and sea bass in the Italian valli, and prawns throughout the Indo-Pacific region. Mussels, oysters and clams are cultivated in the same way all over the world, in France, Spain, Japan and the USA. Nevertheless, intensive – rather than extensive – aquaculture is becoming the predominant farming method.

Salmon alevins bred in pools find protection among artificial algae.

The fish-farming industry

The 'intensive' aquaculture system is used for fish, in particular salmon. These are fed on cheap granulated fish flour in artificial pools with a strong current of fresh water (18°C maximum) flowing through them. Norway has become the leader in this sector: in 1996 it produced over half of the 618,000 tonnes of salmon farmed that year. Rainbow trouts, eels, yellowtail, gilthead bream and sea bass will soon be farmed in the same way. However, mass farming is still problematic, since breeding is not well controlled and feeding is expensive.

The leading producers

Already the world's leading fishing nation, China is also the leader in aquaculture. In 1998 it produced almost 27 million tonnes of seafood products, well ahead of India (2 million), Japan (1.3 million), the Philippines (955,000 tonnes), Indonesia (814,000), the Republic of Korea (797,000), Bangladesh (584,000), Thailand (570,000) and Vietnam (538,000). The market value of the seafood products farmed by all the other nations combined (US$12.5 billion) was only half of that achieved by China (US$25 billion).

The predominance of seaweed

Today, around 60% of aquaculture is carried on in fresh water. The brackish water so beloved of Japanese prawns is used in only 6% of aquaculture. Salt water is mainly used to produce seaweed and, to a lesser degree, molluscs.

Traditionally used in Asian cooking, seaweed is also used for feeding animals, as well as in agriculture, horticulture, the pharmaceutical industry and as a raw material for food production. It is cultivated on a large scale by 'seeding' floating nets several kilometres long with spores. Many species of seaweed have been studied with a view to their aquacultural exploitation. The cultivation of seaweed is of less concern to environmentalists than the rearing of fish, which can cause pollution.

Hunting for treasure

The ocean floor and its waters contain many valuable commodities other than fish. Some of the most highly prized marine resources are salt, bromine, magnesium, gas and oil.

Salt pans

Man has been extracting salt from the environment ever since the Neolithic period. In the

In salt pans (seen here in France), evaporation of the seawater is promoted by circulating it through a series of pools.

Mediterranean, salt could simply be collected from the shores of numerous saltwater lakes, where it had accumulated as a result of the action of the sun and wind. Elsewhere, people in the Middle Ages had the idea of getting seawater to evaporate by circulating the water through a series of pools called 'salt pans' in order to harvest the salt. Over the years, the technique has been refined: the hydraulic circulation has been adjusted and the large pools divided into smaller units. This method is very effective in hot, dry regions such as the shores of the Black Sea, the Mediterranean, the Gulf of California, the Sea of Oman, and the inland seas in eastern and south-eastern Asia. One-third of the world's salt production is derived from the sea. Bromine is also extracted (90% coming from the water in salt pans), as is magnesium (60% of which comes from seawater).

Offshore oil rigs

Since 1947, oil has been pumped from the sediments on the bottom of the ocean. This is known as offshore drilling and involves the use of gigantic oil rigs. More recently, continental shelves have been drilled down to maximum depths of 500m. Today, oil platforms resting on the ocean floor have largely been replaced by floating rigs. These can be used to prospect for oil up to 2,000m below the surface, often in the deltas of large rivers. In total, almost 3 billion tonnes of oil were extracted from the sea in 1999. A third of this came from underwater oil deposits situated mainly off the coasts of Middle Eastern countries; the remaining two-thirds came from the waters around Africa, Venezuela, Indonesia, Alaska and western Canada, and from the Gulf of Mexico and the North Sea. As for natural gas, a tenth of it is extracted from the depths of the sea.

A freshwater reservoir

At a time when fresh water is extremely scarce in many areas of the planet, the desalinization of seawater seems to be the perfect solution.

Several techniques, based either on evaporation or the use of filtering systems, have been developed. A number of desalinization plants have been set up in the USA, Kuwait, Russia, Japan and Australia.

Fixed oil rigs, which pump oil from deposits in the ocean sediments, are now being replaced by floating structures.

Mineral deposits and sources of energy

Coal and iron ore deposits extend into the sea, but they are less frequently exploited there than on land. The seas and oceans also contain sulphur deposits (the sulphur field off the coast of Louisiana provides 90% of global production) and rocks from which phosphate can be extracted in up-welling zones. Muds and nodules rich in metals are beginning to be exploited in deep ocean waters, and some people are already dreaming of recovering minerals from the hydrothermal springs on oceanic ridges. The muds yield iron, zinc, lead, copper, gold and silver; the polymetallic nodules are sources of manganese, iron, nickel, copper and cobalt.

Finally, in addition to tidal energy, there are plans to harness the ocean's energy in other ways.

These polymetallic nodules are found at a depth of over 5,000m.

Wave energy, the energy in strong currents, and the thermal differential between warm surface water and the considerably cooler deep ocean water could all be used to generate electricity.

GLOSSARY

[Offshore drilling] A technique that involves extracting fossil fuel from beneath the sea bed.
[Nodules] Spherical concretions containing metal oxides, most commonly found at depths of over 3,550m.

Sovereignty rights

Competition for the oceans' resources sometimes creates conflict between states and those working in the maritime sector.

One conference after another

The first United Nations Conference on the Law of the Sea took place in 1958 in Montego Bay (Jamaica). Four conventions were adopted to define the status and limits of territorial waters, the continental shelf, the high seas and fishing. Controversy ensued, leading to a second Conference in 1960 – and a second failure. Some states found, on achieving independence, that their sovereignty over the sea covered a mere 3 nautical miles (1.852km), while others had sovereignty over an area extending as far as 200 nautical miles from the coast. After much bitter argument, the Convention on the Law of the Sea was finally adopted in 1982. However, several major nations (including the USA, the United Kingdom, Japan and Spain) still refuse to ratify it.

> **GLOSSARY**
>
> **[Sovereignty]**
> The so-called sovereign states lay down their conditions for access to natural resources without holding the ordinary legal rights of possession.

Defining a territory

The Convention set the limit of territorial waters at 12 nautical miles (around 22km) from the coast. Responsible for ensuring safe navigation and obliged to let ships pass freely, the state in question is in some respects the 'owner' of the zone: it can assert its rights there regarding fishing, research and the exploitation of natural resources.

Exclusive Economic Zones (EEZs) extend the exploitation rights of coastal nations to 200 nautical miles (370km) from the shore. However, the freedom for third parties to navigate in, fly over or lay underwater cables or pipelines in an EEZ cannot be challenged by the coastal state. In accordance with international agreements, a state can authorize land-locked countries to exploit the natural resources in its EEZ.

In the event of an oil slick, the owners of the ship responsible for the disaster are liable for any damage caused – but only if their country has signed the Convention.

Up to 200 nautical miles (370km) from the shore, coastal states are liable for the safety of any ships passing through the area. Moreover, these states can authorize fishing and marine research in their EEZ.

The freedom of the high seas

In accordance with the Convention signed in Montego Bay, the high seas remain outside the territorial waters of the EEZs. All states, land-locked or coastal, are free to sail in this area, fly over it, lay cables and pipelines and carry out scientific research and fishing. Ships on the high seas are subject to the jurisdiction corresponding to their flag, and only vessels licensed with a flag from the same state can police them, except in cases of piracy, drug traffic or pollution.

The deep bed of the high seas and its resources are considered to be the common assets of mankind, and all permits to exploit or study it are issued by the International Seabed Authority (ISA). In the future, this authority may redistribute part of the profits obtained from exploitation to developing countries. However, some would prefer the ISA to simply be a co-ordinator between countries wishing to exploit the high seas and the seabed.

Marine pollution

Sovereign states and the International Seabed Authority are obliged to preserve the marine environment. This protection is carried out through treaties, which oblige ship owners or those wishing to exploit natural resources to take the necessary steps to deal with any damage caused by pollution, in line with the Barcelona Convention for the Protection of the Mediterranean Sea Against Pollution, signed in 1976. Since each ship is the responsibility of the country in which it is registered, it has to respect only those conventions signed by that country: this is one of the reasons why ships with flags of convenience come in for such a lot of criticism.

E xcept for the Arctic and the Southern Oceans, where the entire surface area is limited to polar waters, the oceans generally stretch from one hemisphere to the other, separating continents. The Pacific Ocean is the largest, the deepest and the oldest of the world's five oceans, covering 180 million km². However, the Atlantic Ocean (106 million km²) is the only one to connect the two poles. The Indian Ocean is bounded in the north by the Arabian Peninsula, Iran and India and is affected by the monsoon system with its changing winds.

The uniformity of the oceans is only superficial: each one has unique characteristics that set it apart from the others.

The vast oceans

The Pacific Ocean

*The Pacific, a paradise of coral reefs and mangrove swamps,
is also liable to volcanic eruptions and deadly earthquakes.
Its sea currents and atmospheric currents affect the climate of
a large proportion of the planet.*

The ocean that holds all the records

The Pacific Ocean is the largest ocean and the world's largest body of water. It covers almost one-third of the Earth's surface, or around 180 million km². This figure includes all its secondary seas, as well as its part of the Southern Ocean. If the Southern Ocean is excluded, the Pacific measures around 147 million km². The Pacific Ocean holds half of all the water on the planet. Its average oceanic depth (4,200m) is the greatest in the world, and the lowest point on the Earth's surface – the 11,022m-deep Marianas Trench – lies within this ocean. The highest mountain in the world is not Everest, but a Pacific volcano, Mauna Loa (Hawaii), which rises to a height of 9,200m above the seabed (4,171m above sea level). The Pacific is also the oldest of the oceans (200 million years old).

A multitude of coral reefs

Moving like a conveyor belt at an exceptional speed (8–18cm a year as opposed to 2–5cm a year in the Atlantic) and away from the axis of the underwater volcanic mountain chains or

Created by underwater volcanoes, some Pacific islands have turned into beautiful coral atolls.

Depth of the Pacific Ocean (in metres)

0–1,000	5,000–6,000
1,000–4,000	6,000–8,000
4,000–5,000	

Circulation of currents

⟶

0   2,000km

scale at the equator

'ridges' where the ocean crust is formed, the Pacific Ocean's basalt floor passes over 'hot spots'. Here the underlying molten rock gives rise to volcanoes whose summits can rear up in the form of volcanic islands, as in the case of the Hawaii Archipelago, the Society Islands and the Caroline Islands. Coral reefs form on the perimeters of these island chains; in time they will turn the islands into atolls. Other reefs adjoin the many other Pacific islands. Over 2,400km long, the Australian 'Great Barrier Reef' is the largest coral formation on Earth.

This fire in Indonesia started as a result of a drought caused by El Niño.

Underwater riches

The extraordinarily rich coral reefs are home to thousands of species, while the low-salinity warm waters that surround them appear to be oceanic deserts. Thanks to the diversity of its coasts and climates, the Pacific Ocean contains a wide variety of living organisms. In northern Australia and southern China, mangrove swamps are home to many different types of shellfish, crustaceans, fish and reptiles. Meanwhile, the currents of cold water along the American coast promote the development of a forest of seaweed (kelp) inhabited by small invertebrates, sea bass, sea otters and sea lions. The coasts of Peru are famous for their shoals of anchovies, the abundance of which depends on the El Niño phenomenon.

GLOSSARY

[Hot spot]
An area on the Earth's upper mantle from which a plume of hot liquid rock (magma) rises up, breaking through the crust that covers it and creating a volcano. This volcano becomes extinct when the continental plate moves.

▌Ring of Fire

In the west, the Pacific Plate collides with and slides underneath the Indo-Australian and Philippine Plates. This results in a series of trenches (the Tonga Trench, the Marianas Trench, the Japan Trench, the Kuril Trench) and island chains with very active volcanoes (Japan, the Tonga Islands, the Mariana Islands) as well as the development of marginal seas which – depending on whether they are open or enclosed – are associated with large earthquakes. These elements all combine to form the Pacific 'Ring of Fire', which contains, within a perimeter of over 70,000km, more than half of the world's 1,000 or so active volcanoes.

El Niño's birthplace

Given its name (meaning 'the Christ Child' in Spanish) because it generally begins at around Christmas, El Niño is an event typical of the Pacific Ocean and reveals the inseparable link between atmosphere and ocean. It occurs when the normal east-to-west trade winds weaken: as a result, the warm surface waters in the east Pacific are driven to the west less efficiently, or they flow back towards the South American coast, which increases the effect of the phenomenon.

The El Niño phenomenon causes torrential rains to fall in central and south-eastern America. This photograph was taken in Ecuador.

The result is serious droughts in Indonesia and Australia and torrential rains in Peru. The cold upwellings also weaken, bringing fewer nutrients and cold waters to the surface, if any at all. Fish abandon their usual habitats, and fishing is seriously disrupted. Nevertheless, the presence of deep-sea tuna means that the Pacific Ocean is still a very profitable fishing ground, and aquaculture, which has been carried out for many years in Asia, has recently become extremely popular.

A 'lazy' ocean

Subjected to torrential rains in its tropical belt, the Pacific also receives quantities of low-salinity water from the Southern Ocean. The amount of evaporation that occurs in the Pacific is not sufficient to compensate for the input of water, which is why the average salinity of this ocean is low. As a result, water density remains low, even in the north-west Pacific, where winter temperatures are extremely cold. The Pacific Ocean does not form cold, deep water itself, but receives it instead from its neighbours.

The Indian Ocean

The Indian Ocean is the second smallest and the most complex of the five oceans. Its surface currents reverse twice a year under the influence of the monsoon winds.

Closed off in the north

Completely closed off in the north by the coasts of the Arabian Peninsula, Iran and India, the Indian Ocean is the second smallest of the Earth's five oceans after the Arctic Ocean. It

covers an area of 'only' 49 million km^2 if one includes the adjacent seas (this nevertheless represents a surface area equivalent to Europe, Africa and the USA combined) and a maximum of 75 million km^2 if one also includes its part of the waters in the Southern Ocean. The average depth is 3,800m, less than that of the Pacific but greater than that of the Atlantic. This is due to the poor development of the continental shelves and the presence of several trenches on the ocean's eastern edge: the Ob Trench and Diamantina Fracture Zone, which

Some of the Indian Ocean islands are very popular with tourists, including the Seychelles (above).

extend westward from the south-west coast of Australia; the Java Trench, the deepest at 7,450m; and the Sunda Trench on the southern edge of the Indonesian Archipelago.

Characteristic topography

The underwater relief of the Indian Ocean is unique. The ridge is not peripheral like the Pacific Ocean's famous 'Ring of Fire', but axial as in the Atlantic, with three branches: one is the continuation of the African Rift Valley and the other two join up with the Atlantic and Pacific Oceans respectively. In addition, ridges rise up all over the ocean floor and divide the Indian Ocean up into a multitude of basins: the Arabian Basin, the Somali Basin, the Madagascar Basin, the Mid-Indian Ocean Basin, the South Australian Basin, and others.

Different salinity levels

Heavy rains in the area around Java cause a drastic lowering in the salinity level of the ocean: it is never greater than 34‰ on the surface, and can drop to 30‰ during the rainy season. Conversely, the desert climate encountered off the coast of Australia and to the south of the Arabian Peninsula leads to high levels of evaporation and thus high salinity levels: they can reach levels of over 40‰ in the Red Sea and the Persian Gulf.

The monsoon regime, which is due to a reversal of the prevailing winds, brings torrential rains and flooding in summer.

Persian Gulf

ASIA

Red Sea

Sea of Oman

Gulf of Aden

Laccadive
Islands

Bay of
Bengal

Andaman
Sea

AFRICA

Carlsberg Ridge

Somali Basin

Maldives

East Indian Ridge

Sumatra

Equator

Seychelles

Chagos
Archipelago

Mid-Indian
Basin

Java

Mauritius
Réunion

Mid-Indian Ridge

West
Australian
Basin

North
Australian
Basin

Madagascar

Indian
Ocean

Ninety East Ridge

Madagascar
Basin

South-west Indian Ridge

Amsterdam &
St Paul Islands

Crozet
Basin

Natal Basin

South
Australian
Basin

Kerguelen
Islands

Crozet
Islands

South-east Indian Ridge

Agulhas
Basin

South Indian
Basin

Indian-Atlantic
Basin

ANTARCTICA

Depth of the Indian Ocean (in metres)

0–200	2,000–3,000	5,000–6,000
200–1,000	3,000–4,000	6,000–7,000
1,000–2,000	4,000–5,000	7,000–8,000

over 8,000

Circulation of the currents

0   1,500km

scale at the equator

Influenced by monsoons

On the whole, the climate of the Indian Ocean is tropical and affected by monsoons.

To the north of Madagascar, the air temperature over the ocean always ranges between 23°C and 27°C. On the other hand, precipitation varies widely from one part of the ocean to another. During the summer monsoon, rainfall is plentiful in the Bay of Bengal and along the coasts of South-East Asia – up to three metres a year off the coast of Sumatra. At the same time, however, the waters off the coasts of Australia and the Arabian Peninsula experience a desert climate. Moreover, the north of the Indian Ocean is subject in winter to moderate, cold, dry winds, which generate a great deal of evaporation, while regions below a latitude of 10° S are ravaged by cyclones. All of the above naturally affects the circulation of the water, its plankton content, and its plant and animal life.

An abundance of reefs

Like the Pacific and the tropical waters of the Atlantic, the Indian Ocean has many coral reefs. They are found along the coasts of the Red Sea and eastern Africa, as well as around numerous islands, such as the Comoros, Mauritius, the Mascarene Islands, the Seychelles and the Maldives.

GLOSSARY

[Monsoon]
Seasonal winds in tropical regions which change direction according to the season. In the Indian Ocean, the dry winter monsoon is characterized by winds blowing from the land to the sea, while the wet summer monsoon blows from the ocean towards land, bringing torrential rains.

A regime of variable currents

In the northern part of the Indian Ocean, currents change direction with the seasons. Owing to to this complex regime of changing currents, upwellings of nutrient-rich substances occur along the eastern coast of Africa in summer, while in winter they take place off the coast of India and in other parts of the Indian Ocean. As a result, nutrient-rich minerals do not rise up in the same places throughout the year. This leads to significant temporal and spatial fluctuations in the oceanic distribution of phytoplankton.

Highly sought-after fish stocks

Because the currents are very strong, phytoplankton are carried several hundreds of kilometres away from their place of origin. This promotes the development of zooplankton, which will in turn lead to the appearance of carnivores. Thus, in the end, the places with the highest concentrations of fish are located well away from the upwelling zones. In those zones with high fish populations, one can find tuna, mackerels and sardines, as well as sharks, sea turtles and humpback whales. In most parts of the Indian Ocean, but especially in the rich waters of the north, fishing is still carried out using traditional methods. The plentiful stocks of fish are highly sought after.

The coelacanth, native to the deep waters of the Comoros Islands, was thought to be extinct until a live specimen was discovered in 1938.

The Atlantic Ocean

The second largest ocean in terms of surface area, the Atlantic Ocean is the only one that links the waters of both polar regions. In this regard, it plays an important role in regulating our planet's hydrologic balance.

Linking the poles

Bordering the Arctic Ocean in the north and the Southern Ocean in the south, the Atlantic is the only ocean that links up the cold waters of both polar regions. Half the size of the Pacific, it covers an area of 88 million km² including the adjacent seas (106 million km² if one includes its part of the Southern Ocean waters).

The Atlantic is bordered by vast continental shelves (notably in the north) which account for almost 14% of the surface area of its floor, in other words twice as much as in the Pacific or Indian Ocean. The floor of the Atlantic Ocean is dominated by a large S-shaped

Many adjacent seas

In addition to its prominent and numerous continental shelves, the Atlantic is bordered by a large number of epicontinental seas: including the English Channel, the Baltic Sea, the North Sea and the Irish Sea. There are also deeper bordering seas, such as the Mediterranean, the Sargasso Sea and the Caribbean, as well as many gulfs (the Gulf of Mexico, the Gulf of Guinea, etc).

mid-ocean ridge (extending up to 2,000km in width from the centre of the ridge in places). It is made up of a vast chain of underwater reliefs, which emerge here and there in the form of volcanic islands (the Azores, Iceland, etc). For the above reasons, the average depth of the Atlantic (3,300m) is less than that of the Pacific and Indian Oceans. Some abyssal trenches, however, are very deep (8,400m for the Puerto Rico Trench).

The volcanic archipelago of the Azores.

Hudson Bay

Labrador Sea

Iceland

North Sea

NORTH AMERICA

West Europe Basin

EUROPE

Mediterranean Sea

Azores

Bermuda Islands

Mid-Atlantic Ridge

North Atlantic Ocean

Madeira

Canary Islands

North American Basin

Gulf of Mexico

Sargasso Sea

Canary Basin

AFRICA

Cuba

Haiti

Cape Verde Islands

Caribbean Sea

Cape Verde Basin

Equator

SOUTH AMERICA

Brazil Basin

Atlantic Ridge

Angola Basin

St Helena

Rio Grande Rise

South Atlantic Ocean

Cape Basin

Mid-

Argentine Basin

Falkland Islands

Atlantic-Indian Ridge

Scotia Sea

Scotia Rise

Atlantic-Indian Basin

ANTARCTICA

Depth of the Atlantic Ocean (in metres)

Circulation of the currents

0–200
200–1,000
1,000–2,000

2,000–3,000
3,000–4,000
4,000–5,000

5,000–6,000
6,000–7,000
7,000–8,000

over 8,000

0   1,000km

scale at the equator

A series of basins

A notable feature of the Atlantic Ocean is its wide range of salinity levels. In some places, particularly the Mediterranean, the Atlantic is subject to intense evaporation. It contains half of the planet's fresh water, being fed by many large rivers such as the Saint Laurent, the Orinoco, the Amazon, the Congo and the Niger. Furthermore, the Mid-Atlantic Ridge is punctuated by fractures and transversal rises, which divide the ocean floor up into around a dozen basins. As a result of this, the deep water can only circulate by crossing a number of sills. On passing over these sills, the water loses some of its density and thus often also some of its salinity.

⌐ The influence of the Gulf Stream

The variations in the flow of the waters of the Gulf Stream have been linked to enormous climate changes in the northern hemisphere. Around 100,000 years ago, the waters of the North Atlantic Ocean flowed three to five times more slowly than they do today. The North Atlantic Drift – a continuation of the Gulf Stream – was then situated at a latitude of around 40° N. Thus, at that time, the coasts of Europe did not benefit from the Gulf Stream's warm currents.

This phenomenon is also at work in the adjacent seas. In the Mediterranean, for example, the deep water has a salinity of 39.10‰ in the south-east of the sea, but only 38‰ when it leaves the Strait of Gibraltar.

A wide range of climates

As a result of its geographical location, its shape and the variety of climates to which it is subjected, the Atlantic is the most active of the oceans, transporting large quantities of surface water (the Gulf Stream has a flow of 130 million m³ per second). It is also a place where

The coasts bordering the Atlantic Ocean, which opens onto polar waters to the north and south, have a wide variety of climates.

For a long time the North Atlantic was a fisherman's paradise, but those days have gone.

deep water is formed (particularly in the Norwegian Sea). In turn, this activity plays a vital role in the regulation of climates. Thus, water vapour transported by the Gulf Stream heats the western coasts of Europe, to the extent that a city like Lisbon in Portugal has winter temperatures on average 10°C warmer than those in New York, a city situated at practically the same latitude. As a result, plants and animals are very different on the two sides of the Atlantic. They also vary considerably depending on the latitude and the nature of the coast – sandy beaches are inhabited by shellfish and sea worms, rocky coasts are covered in algae, with fjords, mangrove swamps, coral reefs, and so on all providing niche habitats.

Exhausted fish stocks

Large-scale fishing first developed in the North Atlantic region, because of the greater extent of its continental shelves and the predominance of industrialized countries. Today it has become stagnant, because fish stocks (Atlantic herring, mackerels, sardines, Atlantic cod, tuna) have been overexploited. However, the fishing industry is booming in the south-west Atlantic, particularly in the waters near Argentina. As for aquaculture, there is extensive oyster farming (Portugal and France) and mussel farming (Holland, Spain and France), and seaweed is collected for use in agriculture or in the cosmetics industry. More importantly, intensive fish farming is also practised (for example, salmon farming in Norway). In addition, the Atlantic Ocean contains all kinds of natural resources that have been exploited over many years: salt, sand, gravel and, more recently, diamonds (Namibia) and oil (the North Sea, the western coasts of Africa, the Gulf of Mexico).

The vast oceans

The polar oceans

The Arctic and Southern Oceans play an essential role in regulating the circulation of the Earth's water masses. Deep, cold, nutrient-rich water is created in these oceans.

'False' oceans

The Arctic Ocean is the northern part of the Atlantic Ocean. The Southern or Antarctic Ocean links the southern tips of all the other oceans (apart from the Arctic). Thus, neither of them should really be called an 'ocean'.

Nevertheless, the designation is justified because of their influence on the global circulation of deep water. With a surface area of 14 million km², the Arctic Ocean is the smallest of the oceans. The Southern Ocean is much larger: 77 million km², halfway between the size of the Atlantic and the Indian Oceans. Of the two, the Arctic Ocean is the more hospitable. Linked to the Southern Ocean by a 500m-deep sill stretching from eastern Greenland to northern Norway, the Arctic Ocean receives salt water (almost 35‰) from it that is quite warm (2–9°C) considering the air temperatures typical of these high latitudes (as cold as

In winter, only a small part of the Arctic Ocean remains ice-free. Hence the need for icebreakers.

−60°C at the North Pole during winter). These temperatures explain why it contains a permanent, huge sheet of pack ice, which is on average three metres thick. In winter the Arctic Ocean is surrounded by an ice floe which stretches out as far as the coasts, only leaving a tiny section of the ocean, the Barents Sea, free of ice. Polar bears can move around over the frozen ocean as they would do on land.

Richness of the Arctic waters

On the coasts around the Arctic Ocean, temperatures can reach 10°C in summer. With this rise in temperature, thousands of icebergs break off from the continental glaciers, making navigation dangerous. However, fishermen still go out, as the waters are full of fish. The con-

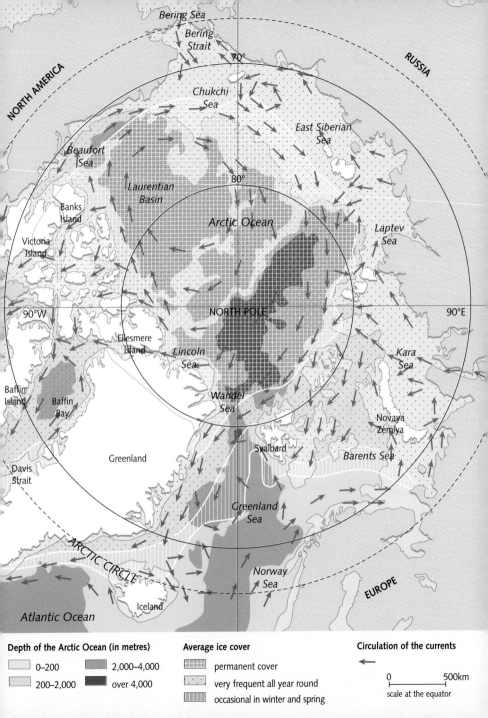

Bering Sea			
Bering Strait			RUSSIA
NORTH AMERICA	70°	Chukchi Sea	East Siberian Sea
Beaufort Sea	80°		
Banks Island	Laurentian Basin	Arctic Ocean	Laptev Sea
Victoria Island			
90°W		NORTH POLE	90°E
Ellesmere Island	Lincoln Sea		Kara Sea
Baffin Island		Wandel Sea	Novaya Zemlya
Baffin Bay		Svalbard	Barents Sea
Davis Strait	Greenland		
		Greenland Sea	
ARCTIC CIRCLE		Norway Sea	EUROPE
Atlantic Ocean	Iceland		

Depth of the Arctic Ocean (in metres)

- 0–200
- 200–2,000
- 2,000–4,000
- over 4,000

Average ice cover

- permanent cover
- very frequent all year round
- occasional in winter and spring

Circulation of the currents

⟵

0   500km

scale at the equator

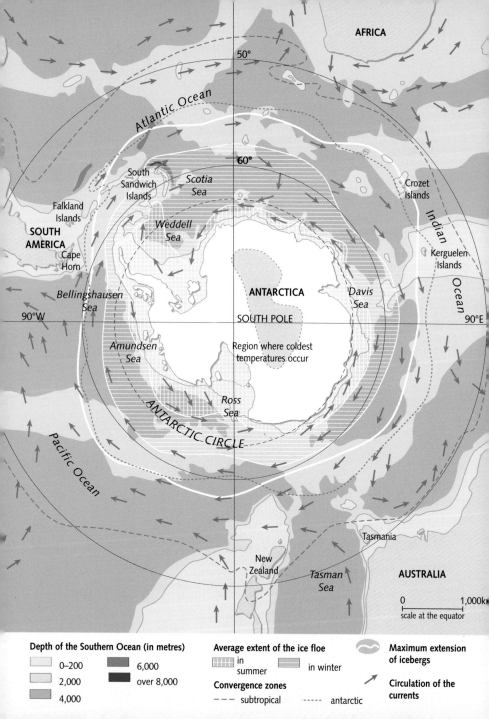

AFRICA

50°

Atlantic Ocean

60°

South
Sandwich
Islands

*Scotia
Sea*

Crozet
Islands

Falkland
Islands

*Weddell
Sea*

Indian

SOUTH
AMERICA

Kerguelen
Islands

Cape
Horn

*Bellingshausen
Sea*

ANTARCTICA

SOUTH POLE

*Davis
Sea*

90°W

90°E

Ocean

*Amundsen
Sea*

Region where coldest
temperatures occur

*Ross
Sea*

ANTARCTIC CIRCLE

Pacific Ocean

Tasmania

New
Zealand

*Tasman
Sea*

AUSTRALIA

0   1,000km
scale at the equator

Depth of the Southern Ocean (in metres)

0–200	6,000
2,000	over 8,000
4,000	

Average extent of the ice floe

in
summer   in winter

Convergence zones

- - - subtropical   .... antarctic

**Maximum extension
of icebergs**

**Circulation of the
currents**

tinental shelf covers 37% of the ocean bottom: from Alaska to Svalbard, the depth is on average only 50m up to a distance of 600–700km from the coasts. Plankton develops on this shelf and attracts molluscs, crustaceans and other organisms, which in turn serve as food for many fish that are economically important, such as Atlantic cod, smelt, plaice, halibut and sturgeon.

Cold, salty water

The Antarctic waters are feared by navigators, who speak of 'the roaring forties', 'the furious fifties' and 'the screaming sixties' in reference to the extreme violence of the winds in these latitudes (180–360kph near the coasts). In winter, the temperature of the surface water ranges between 0°C and 2°C, while it drops as low as –60°C on land. The salinity level of the waters drops in summer when the ice melts, but rises again in winter, reaching 34.5‰. The waters then become denser and sink along the coasts. This so-called 'Antarctic bottom water' feeds the circulation of deep water all over the world by spreading northwards from Antarctica under other water masses.

In summer, on the other hand, upwellings of extremely nutrient-rich water occur near the coasts. This water encourages the development of phytoplankton, which is at the origin of a vast food chain. Fish, penguins and particularly whales devour krill, which is made up of huge swarms of tiny crustaceans. However, because of the cold, a number of species stay in these waters only in the summer in order to feed.

Unequal shelves

While the Arctic Ocean is characterized by its broad, shallow continental shelf, in the Southern Ocean around the continent of Antarctica the shelf is narrow and very deep (500m on average). Indeed, the great weight of the ice tends to make the shelf sink. Beyond the shelf, the ocean rapidly reaches depths of 4,000m.

GLOSSARY

[Pack ice]
A large area of free-floating sea ice, consisting of pieces that have been driven together by wind and currents to form a solid mass.

Penguins, habitual residents of Antarctica, feed on krill (tiny crustaceans), which is plentiful in the coastal waters in summer.

In full bloom

Dr David S Reay, University of Edinburgh

Massive amounts of agricultural fertilizer and human sewage are ending up in our streams, rivers, and eventually our estuaries and coastal waters. This enrichment of the waters around our coasts, called eutrophication, *promotes huge algal blooms which, as well as looking bad and often smelling even worse, can be dangerous to both animal and human health.*

Take a trip down to the beach this weekend, and you might well see a notice warning that 'shellfish in this area should not be eaten, as they contain a naturally occurring toxin'. Such notices can be found just about anywhere along our coastline, and if you see one you would be wise to heed its warning. The toxins in question are produced by microscopic algae called phytoplankton, on which shellfish feed. Dense growths or 'blooms' of these algae can be so intense that they literally make the sea change colour; the most widely known are the red algae, whose blooms produce 'red tides'. As shellfish consume these algae, they become increasingly loaded with algal toxins. Eating these shellfish can therefore pose a real danger to human health.

The threat of shellfish poisoning due to these toxin-producing algae can exist even without any obvious algal bloom, because the toxins can become concentrated in the tissues of shellfish over time. Types of shellfish poisoning include paralytic, diarrhetic, neurotoxic, and amnesic poisoning. In the UK, diarrhetic shellfish poisoning (DSP) and paralytic shellfish poisoning (PSP) toxins have been particularly problematic. DSP, which can cause stomach-aches and diarrhoea, was blamed for the poisoning of 49 people in London in 1998. PSP can be much more serious. It starts to take effect within about half an hour of eating the poisoned shellfish and, as its name suggests, begins to paralyse the body, making the limbs go numb and the face tingle. If a large amount of poisoned shellfish has been eaten, the toxin can kill a person within just two hours. The chief culprit for PSP around the UK is an alga called *Alexandrium tamarense*. In 1968, mussels containing the PSP toxins made by this alga caused 78 people to become sick.

Taking extra care over the shellfish you eat does not guarantee your safety from toxic algal blooms, as just swimming through such a bloom can leave you with a very bad stomach upset, if not worse. It is also not only humans that are in danger; many fish and bird species rely on shellfish for food, and so can run a real risk of fatal poisoning. Indeed, there are some algal toxins that, while not dangerous to humans, can be very damaging to wild birds and fish.

Shellfish poisoning is not the only problem caused by algal blooms. Though most algae do not produce the dangerous toxins of the 'red-tide' species, some, like the spiny *Chaetoceros* algae, can clog the gills of fish. Where a dense bloom of these spiny algae coincides with fish that are unable to swim out of the way (such as those in fish farms), large-scale suffocation of the fish can result. Some other species of algae, such as *Phaeocystis*, produce great amounts of gelatinous mucilage which, when churned up by the wind and waves, forms an unsightly scum on the surface of the sea and on the seashore. As well as looking unpleasant, some of these algal blooms smell very bad. An intense coastal bloom in summer can transform a beautiful day at the beach into a smelly trip to a scum-covered shore.

The 'naturally occurring' tag for algae and the toxins they produce disguises the fact that algal blooms can be prompted by the over-enrichment of our coastal waters with agricultural fertilizers and sewage. This process, called eutrophication, is anything but 'natural', with millions of tonnes of extra nutrients entering the seas around Europe each year as a result of human activity.

Concern over eutrophication in our rivers and seas has increased greatly in the last few decades as its impact has become more widely understood. Much progress has already been made, both by farmers and by local authorities, in reducing the amounts of fertilizer lost from the land and in cutting the volume of sewage flowing into our coastal waters. As the European Union moves more and more towards environmentally aware land and water management,

GLOSSARY

[Eutrophication]
The over-enrichment of a body of water, either naturally or as a result of artificial pollution.

we will hopefully start to see less and less eutrophication in our rivers, estuaries and seas.

Though the number of algal blooms around our coastlines currently seems to be on the increase, this perception is due at least in part to our increased awareness of the problem. Today, a greater understanding of the threat posed by toxic algal blooms, combined with a sophisticated system of satellite monitoring, water testing and local observation, means that people are quickly alerted to any danger of toxic shellfish, and severe poisoning like that seen in 1968 is thankfully rare.

Toxic algal blooms will always be a concern, even when we have managed to shut off their extra fertilizer-based food supply. Algal blooms can occur naturally, so close monitoring of our waters will always be needed in order to give early warning of any potential poisoning risk. Indeed, even big reductions in fertilizer and sewage pollution may not go far enough in dealing with the problem. The predicted warming of our seas due to climate change may end up making things worse before they get better. Higher water temperatures could lead to an increase in the severity of algal blooms around our coast, increased human contact and, potentially, more poisoning incidents.

Cold retreat

Dr David S Reay, University of Edinburgh

Climate change is already having a big impact on life in the waters around Britain. In the North Sea, a combination of over-fishing and warming waters has drastically reduced the cod population. In the English Channel, exotic species are beginning to replace some of the cold-water-loving species. By the year 2050, we could be swimming with loggerhead turtles and eating locally caught barracuda.

It is nine o'clock on a warm summer morning and the local market is alive with shoppers, eager to get the weekend's food bought and home before the day gets too hot. Among the multicoloured stalls is an eye-catching fishmonger's with a beautiful display of the morning's catch – huge spider crabs, shiny slipper lobsters and even some rather unnerving barracuda staring back blankly with their toothy grins. Such a scene is repeated every week in dozens of towns in the south of Europe. However, this is not southern Europe, nor is it anywhere else where such warm-water species are usually caught. In fact, it is Britain in the year 2050, with its much warmer seas playing host to new and exotic marine wildlife.

It might not feel like it when you next take a teeth-clenching dip at the seaside, but the sea around Britain is warming up at an alarming rate. Global warming may well increase our seawater temperatures by several degrees during this century. Such warming will have a big impact, both on marine life in British waters and on the people who depend on the sea for their livelihood.

The temperature of waters around Britain is already at record levels, and with just a 1°C rise we could see some of our marine wildlife pushed entirely out of British waters, their ranges retreating northwards to cooler seas. At the same time, warmer British waters will allow new species from the south to extend their ranges, with more and more frequent visits from exotic species like those being sold on our market stall in 2050. Such shifts in the ranges of marine species may be very rapid, particularly where a species is already at or near its southernmost extreme – or where fishing and pollution pressures have drastically reduced the existing population, as in the case of cod.

Nowhere is the threat to British livelihoods from climate change starker than in its predicted impact on commercial fish species, such as cod, haddock and plaice. As regards cod, a combination of over-fishing, government quotas and warming waters has already forced many fishermen out of business. However, even with the fishing pressure easing, the future for cod in British waters looks bleak. If history is anything to go by, stocks may never return to their previous highs. The population of herring in the English Channel during the 1950s crashed as a result of a short-lived upward shift in temperature and intense fishing pressure. The herring were replaced in many areas by horse mackerel and, though temperatures in the Channel eventually dipped again, the herring were never able to re-establish themselves fully.

Some of the warm-water species making their new homes in British waters, such as red mullet and Japanese oysters, may provide an alternative for commercial fishing, though we as consumers would have to get used to eating this more 'exotic' fare. Overall, warming of our seas spells bad news for our fishermen and the many people dependent on the fishing industry.

As well as commercial fish species, other marine species are also under threat. The ranges of some seabirds, such as guillemots and fulmars, may be forced further north as temperatures rise, while the already threatened seagrass beds and salt-marsh habitats around the coast of Britain are extremely vulnerable to any rises in sea level. Even the seal population in British waters may be at risk from global warming, with higher water temperatures threatening the stability of their food supply and promoting the spread of disease. As mentioned on pages 116–17, warmer seas around Britain may also worsen the problem of toxic al-

gal blooms or 'red tides', increasing the risk of poisoning for fish, birds and humans alike.

So, climate change is likely to mean warmer waters around Britain, with the consequent disappearance of some of our existing marine species and the arrival of some new ones. However, there is a possibility that the current warming trend will not continue. Recent evidence suggests that the Gulf Stream – the current that brings warm water to our west coast and so maintains our temperate maritime climate – is slowing down. If we were to lose the Gulf Stream we could be plunged into much colder, continental-style weather, with longer and more extreme winter conditions like those seen at similar latitudes in Canada and Scandinavia. The reason for the apparent slowing of the Gulf Stream seems to lie once again with climate change. As temperatures in Greenland rise, more and more of its massive ice sheet begins to disintegrate. With the melting of the Greenland ice sheet comes a growing flood of fresh water into the northern Atlantic Ocean and, as this giant wedge of fresh water builds up, it could cause more and more disruption to the flow of the Gulf Stream.

Scientific understanding of the precise impacts that climate change will have on Britain's seas remains poor. Much effort is being put into predicting exactly what might happen, and how such impacts might best be mitigated. The 'warming seas' scenario, rather than the 'frozen Britain' scenario, still looks the most likely, but one thing is for certain: our seas are changing.

Glossary

[Abyss]
The abyss, or abyssal benthic zone, is the floor of the deep ocean and is situated at depths of over 2,000m.

[Antarctic convergence zone]
The name given to a transition region in the Southern Ocean where cold and dense surface water from Antarctica meets warmer water from the oceans of lower latitudes and sinks beneath it.

[Benthos]
A collective term for organisms living on or near the bottom of a body of water.

[Bioluminescence]
Light produced by living organisms by means of a chemical reaction. It is primarily a marine phenomenon.

[Biomass]
Biomass is the term used to describe the total living organisms in a specific ecosystem, population or other unit area at a given moment.

[Chop]
A series of wind-driven waves that do not form a regular train.

[Continental ice sheet]
A vast continental glacier found in high latitudes (Antarctica, Greenland), which masks the underlying relief.

[Continental shelf]
The zone bordering continents that lies under the sea and which extends from the shoreline to the start of the continental slope. The continental shelves were formed

when land was flooded by the rise of seawater during the Quaternary era.

[Diatom]
Diatoms are microscopic, single-celled algae with shells made of silica. They are particularly common in cold waters.

[El Niño]
El Niño is a climatic phenomenon that occurs off the coast of Peru when the normal east-to-west trade winds weaken: as a result, the warm surface waters in the east Pacific are driven to the west less efficiently or they flow back towards the South American coast. This has a dramatic effect on weather patterns all over the planet.

[Ensign]
The flag flown by a vessel at its stern to denote its nationality.

[Epicontinental sea]
A shallow sea covering the continental shelf or part of a continent.

[Epifauna]
Animals that live on the surface of the substrate or sediment and that move by crawling, walking or swimming.

[Extensive aquaculture]
In extensive aquaculture, aquatic animals and plants are reared in a natural environment, requiring large quantities of water. This leads to low productivity per unit volume.

[Fetch]
The fetch is the distance over

which wind blows without changing direction.

[Fjord]
A deep and narrow inlet, where the sea has flooded a valley carved by a glacier. Fjords are common in Norway, New Zealand and western parts of Scotland.

[Foraminifer]
Foraminifera are single-celled, microscopic organisms related to amoebae. These protozoa have a calcareous shell and are very abundant near the ocean floor.

[GPS]
The Global Positioning System (GPS) is a navigation system using the American network of satellites known as NAVSTAR.

[Gyre]
Gyres are large wind-driven swirls of oceanic surface water. They are anticyclonic in the subtropical regions and cyclonic close to the poles.

[Gyrocompass]
An electrical device with a spinning disc as in a gyroscope, used to indicate true north. The gyrocompass is linked to a ship's automatic pilot.

[Holoplankton]
Organisms that live their entire life cycle as plankton.

[Hot spot]
An area on the Earth's upper mantle from which a plume of hot liquid rock (magma) rises up, breaking through the crust that covers it and creating a volcano. This volcano becomes extinct when

the continental plate moves.

[Iceberg]
Icebergs are blocks of ice which break off from the seaward front of glaciers in a process known as 'calving'.

[Ice floe]
An ice floe is a sheet of floating ice at least 2–3m thick and with a variable surface area. It is formed by the freezing of seawater.

[Infauna]
Animals that live in the sediment or substrate and that move by boring holes or burrowing.

[Infrared radiation]
Electromagnetic radiation whose wavelength is between the red end of the visible spectrum and microwaves.

[Intensive aquaculture]
In intensive aquaculture, aquatic animals and plants are reared in artificial pools of limited dimensions, a process that requires the addition of nutrients from outside. High productivity is achieved with intensive aquaculture.

[Latent heat]
Heat energy that is stored and then released by a substance undergoing a change of state, such as the condensation of water vapour.

[Mangrove swamp]
A mangrove swamp is a forest community made up of mangrove trees, which can grow partially submerged in water. Mangrove swamps are found in salt marshes and on mudflats along tropical seacoasts on both sides of the equator.

[Meroplankton]
Temporary zooplankton: any of the various animal organisms that spend part of their life cycle (larval or adult stages) as plankton.

[Monsoon]
Seasonal winds in tropical regions which change direction according to the season. In the Indian Ocean, the dry winter monsoon is characterized by winds blowing from the land to the sea, while the wet summer monsoon blows from the ocean towards land, bringing torrential rains.

[Nautical mile]
A unit of length used in marine navigation, equivalent to 1,852 metres.

[Nekton]
Microscopic aquatic organisms which can swim actively against water currents.

[Nodules]
Spherical concretions containing metal oxides, most commonly found at depths of over 3,550m.

[Oceanic ridge]
An extensive underwater chain of volcanoes formed where two adjacent plates diverge and new ocean crust is generated by the process of sea-floor spreading and volcanic eruptions.

[Oceanic trench]
A deep (usually over 5,000m), steep-sided depression in the ocean floor.

[Offshore drilling]
A technique that involves extracting fossil fuel from beneath the sea bed.

[Pack ice]
A large area of free-floating sea ice, consisting of pieces that have been driven together by wind and currents to form a solid mass.

[Pelagic]
Relating to the deep open sea (as in pelagic sediment, pelagic fauna, etc).

[Photic zone]
The photic zone of the ocean is the sunlit upper zone where there is sufficient light for algae and other living organisms to photosynthesize.

[Plankton]
Minute plant organisms (phytoplankton) and animal organisms (zooplankton) which are found in aquatic ecosystems. They float passively, being unable to swim against water currents.

[Plate tectonics]
Theory formulated in the 1960s to explain the movements of the plates of which the Earth's crust is composed. Types of plate movement include divergence, convergence, subduction, shearing and lateral slipping.

[Polyp]
Polyps are tiny rudimentary organisms, related to jellyfish. They form colonies of billions of individuals and live attached to rocky substrate or on top of other animals. Polyps secrete an external skeleton: calcareous in the

case of coral polyps and chitinous or calcareous in the case of bryozoan polyps.

[Potential temperature]
Water temperature corrected to take into account the effects of pressure. This value is used to compare different masses of deep water.

[Sea lily]
Sea lilies are marine organisms related to sea urchins and starfish. They live attached to the ocean floor by means of a stalk.

[Spreading rate]
The rate at which the sea floor spreads. Spreading rates are usually calculated for only one side of a ridge, and are often called 'half-spreading' rates to avoid confusion. In the Atlantic and Indian Oceans, this half-spreading rate has been 0.8–2.5cm per year for the last 5 million years. In the Pacific Ocean, it can be as much as 16–20cm per year.

[Storm surge]
An abnormal rise in the coastal water level caused by a drop in atmospheric pressure and strong winds blowing onshore. A storm surge generally makes the sea level rise by 30cm, but in exceptional circumstances it can even increase by 1m.

[Sverdrup]
A unit used to measure the volume of ocean currents. Sverdrup is often abbreviated as Sv and is equivalent to 1 million cubic metres per second (m³/s).

[Swell]
Undulating movement of the surface of the open ocean. Unlike a tide, a swell does not move the water horizontally and thus does not create any currents.

[Thermocline]
The layer of water in the ocean where temperature decreases most rapidly with depth. The thermocline is usually situated at depths of between 100m and 1,000m and tends to disappear in winter.

[Thermohaline circulation]
The density-driven circulation system of the world's oceans. Deep, very slow-moving currents move cold water from one ocean to another. This movement is generated by the differences in temperature, salinity, and therefore density, between masses of oceanic water.

[Thermohaline convection]
Thermohaline convection is a vertical energy transfer between the ocean surface waters and the bottom waters, caused by the instability of the layers of water. It causes cold, dense water to descend into the water column below the warm water and the less dense, warmer water to rise up.

[Tidal coefficient]
A figure between 20 and 120 indicating the amplitude of the tide. The higher the number, the higher the tide.

[Tidal range or amplitude]
The tidal range, or tidal amplitude, is the difference in height between consecutive high and low tides in a given place.

[Trade winds]
The trade winds are north-easterly and south-easterly winds of the Atlantic and the Pacific, which are found between the latitudes 30° N and 30° S and blow towards the equator all year round.

[Transpiration]
Plants constantly lose some of their water in the form of water vapour through the tiny pores in their tissues. The loss of water through evaporation from the soil and transpiration from plants is known as 'evapotranspiration'.

[Trawl net]
A trawl net is a long conical fishing net with many short lines and hooks attached to it. It is dragged through deep water or along the ocean bottom behind a trawling vessel.

[Undercurrent]
A current which transports water only beneath the surface.

[Upwelling]
Upwelling of deep water most commonly occurs in lower latitudes on the western coastlines of the continents. It takes place when winds blow the lighter surface water away from the coast and denser, cooler water rises to replace it.

Useful addresses and websites

Aquaria (UK and Ireland)

Blue Planet Aquarium
Cheshire Oaks, Ellesmere Port, Cheshire, CH65 9LF
http://www.blueplanetaquarium.com/

Blue Reef Aquarium
Three locations:
Towan Promenade, Newquay, Cornwall, TR7 1DU
Grand Parade, Tynemouth, Tyne & Wear, NE30 4JS
Clarence Esplanade, Southsea, Portsmouth, PO5 3PB
http://www.bluereefaquarium.co.uk/

Dingle Oceanworld
The Wood, Dingle, Co. Kerry, Ireland
http://www.dingle-oceanworld.ie/

The London Aquarium
County Hall, Westminster Bridge Road, London, SE1 7PB
http://www.londonaquarium.co.uk/

The National Marine Aquarium
Rope Walk, Coxside, Plymouth, PL4 0LF
http://www.national-aquarium.co.uk/

Sea Life Centres
There are 17 Sea Life Centres all over Europe. Full details can be found on their website.
http://www.sealifeeurope.com/uk/uk.htm

The St Andrews Aquarium
The Scores, St Andrews, Fife KY16 9AS
http://www.standrewsaquarium.co.uk/

Science and Research Information (UK)

British Antarctic Survey
http://www.antarctica.ac.uk/

The Centre for Environment, Fisheries and Aquaculture Science
http://www.cefas.co.uk/homepage.htm

The Marine Biological Association
http://www.mba.ac.uk/

National Marine Biological Library
http://www.mba.ac.uk/nmbl/

Port Erin Marine Laboratory
http://www.liv.ac.uk/peml/

Proudman Oceanographic Laboratory
http://www.nbi.ac.uk/

Scott Polar Research Institute
http://www.spri.cam.ac.uk/

Suggestions for further reading

Byatt, A et al, *The Blue Planet: A Natural History of the Oceans*, BBC Worldwide, London, 2001.

Herring, P, *The Biology of the Deep Ocean*, Biology of Habitats Series, Oxford University Press, Oxford, 2002.

Jennings, S, Kaiser, M J and Reynolds, J D, *Marine Fisheries Ecology*, Blackwell Science, Oxford, 2001.

Kunzig, R, *Mapping the Deep: The Extraordinary Story of Ocean Science*, Sort of Books, London, 2000.

Little, C and Kitching, J A, *The Biology of Rocky Shores*, Biology of Habitats Series, Oxford University Press, Oxford, 1996.

Norton, T, *Reflections on a Summer Sea*, Arrow, London, 2002.

Open University Oceanography Course Team, *The Ocean Basins: Their Structure and Evolution*, Butterworth-Heinemann, Oxford, 1998.

Pauly, D and Maclean, J L, *In a Perfect Ocean: The State of Fisheries and Ecosystems in the North Atlantic Ocean*, Island Press, Washington, DC, 2002.

Index

Illustration credits

Photographs

Drawings and computer graphics

For the English-language edition:

Translator
Sheila Hardie

Consultant
Dr Audrey Brown

Editor
Camilla Rockwood

Prepress
Kirsteen Wright

Prepress manager
Sharon McTeir

Publishing manager
Patrick White

Originally published by Larousse as *Petit atlas des espèces menacées*
by Yves Sciama

© Larousse/VUEF, 2003

English-language edition
© Chambers Harrap Publishers Ltd 2004

ISBN 0550 10160 8

Typeset by Chambers Harrap Publishers Ltd, Edinburgh
Printed in France by IME, Beaume-les-Dames

Yves Sciama

Endangered Species

CHAMBERS
World Library

Contents

Foreword

Today, the study of the diversity of living organisms and their worldwide evolution is still in its infancy. Although around 1,700,000 species have been described, the total number of species on Earth is estimated at between 5 million and 100 million.

This is an extraordinary degree of uncertainty: in fact, we have a far better idea of the number of stars in our galaxy than the number of living species on our planet. Other figures given in this book – the number of species in any given natural environment, the number of extinct species, the number of endangered species, the number of species that used to inhabit our planet, and so on – are just as imprecise.

There are two basic reasons for this lack of knowledge regarding living organisms. The first reason is that the identification and classification of individual species is complex, and the criteria are in a state of constant flux.

The second reason is that the study of living organisms has not been seen as a scientific priority. For over a century now, it has been in decline and has not been given sufficient funding, doubtless because it is not a profit-making activity.

As a result, figures indicating biodiversity are often uncertain and controversial. In this book, we have tried to present these figures as honestly as possible and have therefore given the most realistic estimates. The figures may be debatable but there is a consensus as regards the general effect of man's actions: we are rapidly destroying the Earth's biodiversity. Because it is so widespread, this destruction is likely to be the most important environmental issue for many years to come.

⌐ **Coral reefs** are the tropical forests of the sea. Today these amazing examples of biological diversity are at great risk. At the present rate, half of the world's reefs will have vanished in the next 20 years, taking with them thousands of species of plants and animals.

Species are like individual organisms: they are born, they develop and grow, and then they die. This process is part of everyday life. Nevertheless, all the signs are that the pace at which species are becoming extinct has increased dramatically over the last few centuries, and especially in the last few decades. Our planet is now entering a phase of mass extinctions, often known as the 'sixth extinction', which will drastically reduce the number and diversity of the Earth's living organisms. The consequences for future generations are hard to assess at present, but will inevitably be very serious.

The unique animal life of the Galapagos Islands, including these marine iguanas, is threatened by pollution and the development of tourism.

The birth and death of species

The birth of species

New species are constantly appearing. They evolve from old species by becoming ever more closely adapted to their environment. But this process – called speciation – is often very slow.

One mutation after another

Ever since life first appeared on Earth over 3.5 billion years ago, the number of living species has increased steadily. This rise has been punctuated by several waves of extinction, which have had the effect of drastically reducing the diversity of the biosphere.

The peppered moth (*Biston betularia*) is a European moth whose light colouring provides a perfect camouflage against predators. When trees became darker during the Industrial Revolution, dark-winged mutants, until then very rare, became widespread.

Nevertheless, this global and seemingly inevitable tendency towards an increase in the number of species has not been reversed. Today, there is a greater variety of living organisms on Earth than ever before.

How do new species come about? The development of a new species is based on a series of infrequent mutations which occur randomly in the genes of individuals. Mutations are accidental changes in the hereditary information present in genes. Most turn out to be harmful or neutral, but some are beneficial. Animals or plants with beneficial mutations find it easier to survive: they can run faster, they have a more toxic venom, they have keener senses than other members of their species, and so on. Thus, they have more descendants, their mutations are inherited and are spread throughout the whole population. If the process is repeated for a sufficient number of mutations, a new species appears, clearly differentiated from its predecessor.

10

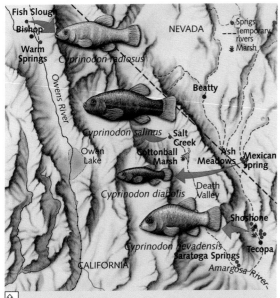

Fish Slough
Bishop
Warm
Springs
NEVADA
Cyprinodon radiosus

Owens River

Beatty

Sprigs
Temporary
rivers
Marsh

Cyprinodon salinus Salt
Creek
Owen
Lake   Cottonball
Marsh Ash
Meadows Mexican
Spring

Cyprinodon diabolis Death
Valley

Shoshone

Cyprinodon nevadensis
Saratoga Springs Tecopa
CALIFORNIA
Amargosa River

🔍 **Fish species in the Mojave Desert** (United States) have been separated from one another for 10,000 years. The vast network of rivers and lakes that covered the region during the Quaternary period was gradually replaced by desert. This led to an extreme fragmentation of the fish habitat. Remarkably, the devil's hole pupfish (*Cyprinodon diabolis*) occupies a single pool just a few square metres in size, its population consisting of only 150 to 400 individuals.

New species develop

A new species can develop if one section of a given population becomes geographically isolated from the rest. This is known as allopatric speciation. Let us take the example of a large lake in which the water level has dropped. Small peripheral lakes may form in the hollows around the main body of water.

Generally, fish that become trapped in this kind of environment begin to develop particular adaptations linked to the specific requirements of the new habitat (warmer or shallower water, water with a special chemical composition, and so on).

If – several hundreds of thousands of years later – the lake's water level rises again, the new species might come into contact with its 'mother species'. Nevertheless, it will have become sufficiently different to prevent hybridization, which would deprive it of its identifying characteristics.

Another process, called 'sympatric speciation', can also be observed. Let us take the example of a population of insects that feed on one specific type of plant. If different plants grow nearby, some insects might stray into them and develop adaptations to their digestive secretions, biological rhythms, camouflage techniques, and so forth. This could then lead to them becoming radically different from the mother population, even in the absence of any geographical barrier, so forming a new species.

GLOSSARY

[Allopatric speciation]
The creation of new species from populations separated geographically by natural obstacles (river, mountain range, creek, etc), with the result that interbreeding between the resulting populations is prevented.

[Sympatric speciation]
This occurs when two populations physically in contact with one another become genetically isolated, for example when their reproductive cycles no longer coincide.

Map *(following pages)*

✴ *Since 1600, at least 296 known species of vertebrates and 313 known species of invertebrates have become extinct. These figures are undoubtedly very conservative, especially in the case of invertebrates. This phenomenon – largely caused by man and pre-dating European colonization – has affected islands in particular. In Europe, the main extinctions occured much earlier, in Neolithic times (about 5,000 years ago).*

Species extinct since 1600

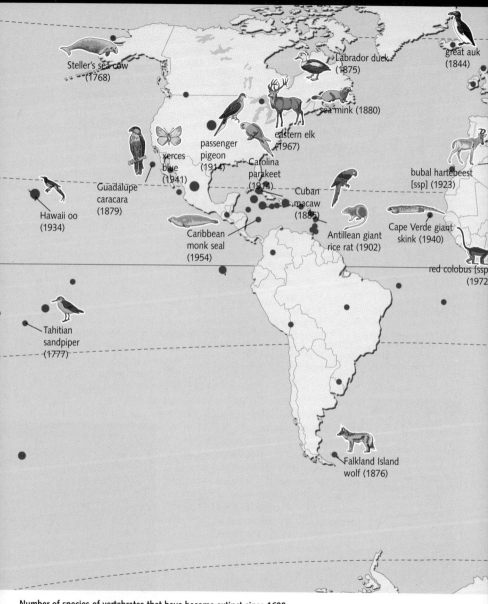

Steller's sea cow (1768)

Labrador duck (1875)

great auk (1844)

sea mink (1880)

eastern elk (1967)

passenger pigeon (1914)

xerces blue (1941)

Carolina parakeet (1914)

Cuban macaw (1885)

bubal hartebeest [ssp] (1923)

Guadalupe caracara (1879)

Hawaii oo (1934)

Caribbean monk seal (1954)

Antillean giant rice rat (1902)

Cape Verde giant skink (1940)

red colobus [ssp] (1972)

Tahitian sandpiper (1777)

Falkland Island wolf (1876)

Number of species of vertebrates that have become extinct since 1600

- from 1 to 3
- from 4 to 11
- from 12 to 41
- from 42 to 102

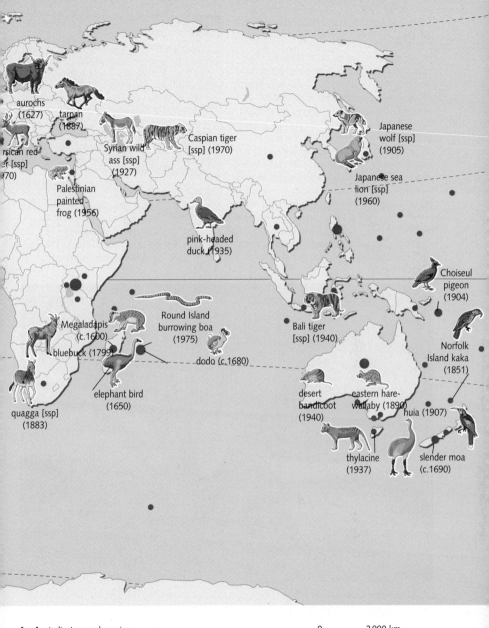

aurochs (1627)

tarpan (1887)

rsican red er [ssp] 970)

Syrian wild ass [ssp] (1927)

Caspian tiger [ssp] (1970)

Japanese wolf [ssp] (1905)

Palestinian painted frog (1956)

Japanese sea lion [ssp] (1960)

pink-headed duck (1935)

Choiseul pigeon (1904)

Megaladapis (c.1600)

Round Island burrowing boa (1975)

bluebuck (1799)

dodo (c.1680)

Bali tiger [ssp] (1940)

Norfolk Island kaka (1851)

elephant bird (1650)

desert bandicoot (1940)

eastern hare-wallaby (1890)

huia (1907)

quagga [ssp] (1883)

thylacine (1937)

slender moa (c.1690)

[ssp] : indicates a subspecies

(1650) : date when the species became extinct

0   2 000 km
scale at the equator

The astounding inventiveness of life

It is impossible not to be amazed by the extraordinary capacity that living things have for innovation. Admittedly, these 'inventions' are of varying significance. Some really revolutionary inventions have been adopted by millions of species: for example, the many types of leaves and flowers in the plant kingdom have radically changed the appearance of the biosphere. Similarly, insect wings and the appearance of the placenta in mammals were 'landmark' innovations in the animal kingdom. The majority of evolutionary innovations have been far more modest. However, whether it be a digestive enzyme for breaking down a particularly difficult molecule, a change in embryonic development improving the use of a joint, or even a mutation that increases a seed's resistance to the cold, each evolutionary improvement represents, on its own scale, an achievement on behalf of living things.

Shared territory

The appearance of a new species does not necessarily lead to the disappearance of the preceding one. The latter might be expelled from one particular habitat to which its 'daughter species' may be better adapted, but nevertheless retain the rest of its range, or even the whole of its environment, should the newcomer settle in another one. Likewise, two species can live in the same habitat, either by coexisting or by dividing up the territory. Of course, the new species does sometimes cause the old one to disappear because it is better adapted.

The feathery antennae of a moth, which are covered in chemical scent sensors, are the reason for this insect's extraordinary sense of smell.

Organs are not created overnight

Life's tremendous creativity needs very many years to come to fruition, despite some instances of rapid evolution. It took almost a billion years for bacteria to surround their nuclei with a membrane and another billion years for these single cells to form rudimentary organisms. Plants acquired conductive tissues only after several hundred million years. The efficiency of certain organs created by evolution is simply astonishing – for example, the chemical sensors that male butterflies have on their antennae allow them to detect a female up to 8km away. However, the evolution of organs such as these – particularly in the case of complex self-regulated systems such as mammals' immune systems – was an extremely long process, with each step forward being based on the one before.

The ginkgo or maidenhair tree, also known as the Tree of Forty Gold Crowns (*Ginkgo biloba*), has survived almost unchanged since the Permian period (the last period of the Palaeozoic era, around 250 million years ago) – a truly exceptional life span.

Usually occurring within just a few decades, the disappearance of a species due to human intervention thus represents the destruction of an extraordinary accumulation of innovations which are impossible to replace.

The genome – running out of ideas?

The creation of new species has been continuous, ever since the appearance of life on Earth. However, all the current phyla and divisions of the animal and plant kingdoms were already present in the Cambrian period, over 500 million years ago. It would therefore appear that, since that time, there has been a series of variations on the same theme, without any major innovations as regards the basic structure of living organisms. According to some scientists, this is due to a progressive loss in the 'plasticity' of the genome throughout the history of life on Earth. Whatever the reason, it only makes the disappearance of entire groups of organisms as a result of man's actions all the more serious.

GLOSSARY

[Phylum, Division]
Groups of species with the same structure (molluscs, arthropods, vertebrates, vascular plants, etc) are said to belong to the same phylum (animals) or division (plants).

Extinction: an irreversible phenomenon

When a species becomes extinct, its genetic capital is lost forever. Despite rapid advances in biological science, we are still unable to recreate species that have died out.

Gone forever

The fact that extinction is irreversible makes it a particularly serious phenomenon. Natural ecosystems can often recover from ecological disasters fairly quickly, at least on a historical or geological timescale. Even the largest oil slick disappears completely after a few decades. This is not the case with extinctions; when a species dies out it can never be reproduced, neither by nature — which took several hundred thousand years to create it — nor by man. All the same, there have been several attempts (some serious, some less so) to resurrect extinct species by using selective breeding to retrieve the genes of the extinct animals and eventually produce individuals as similar as possible to those that have disappeared. In Europe, scientists have tried to 're-breed' the aurochs (*Bos primigenius*), a large wild ox which died out several centuries ago and is thought to be the ancestor of our domestic cattle. In order to do this, various breeds of cattle, each displaying certain characteristics of the aurochs (size of animal, length and shape of horns, coat colour, the male's aggressive and territorial behaviour, etc), were successively crossbred. The resulting animals certainly look fairly convincing. But appearance is only one of an animal's characteristics and, in reality, a large number of the aurochs' genes have been lost forever.

Genes are unique

The problem with extinction is a genetic one. Species develop original genes that programme the synthesis of molecules or groups of molecules which allow them to adapt to the constraints of their environment. These molecules can improve the digestive system, the animal's structure, its resistance to disease, and so on. Similarly, certain groups of genes are responsible for complex behaviour, and those animals that possess them have a better chance of survival. Genes are original, sophisticated inventions of living things.

The last aurochs is reported to have died in Poland in 1627. Efforts to resurrect the species through selective breeding will never be able to totally recreate its genetic heritage.

The disappearance of one (or a particular combination) of these genes is an irreparable loss. Scientists are still unable to identify extinct genes, far less recreate them. This point is worth stressing because recent advances in genetics (such as cloning or genetically modified plants and animals) have sometimes given the impression that scientists are able to create beings from scratch, or that they will be able to do so in the near future. However, transferring a few genes from one plant to another is not the same as recreating a living organism. Not only do organisms contain several tens of millions of genes, these genes are also in a state of constant interaction.

Jurassic Park – science fiction, not science fact

Scenarios such as that in the film *Jurassic Park*, where the discovery of the DNA of a fossilized dinosaur enables the extinct animal to be recreated, are totally implausible, and there is little likelihood that this will change in the near future. Indeed, even in the event of perfectly complete and functional DNA from an extinct species being found (which is highly unlikely bearing in mind how fragile these molecules are), we would have to know which living cell to insert the DNA into in order to rebuild a complete living organism. Moreover, the successful insertion of the entire DNA from one species into the egg of another is an operation that for the moment remains beyond the reach of science.

The fossilization of dinosaur DNA, hypothesized in the film *Jurassic Park*, is in itself highly unlikely. The DNA molecule deteriorates very quickly when it comes into contact with water or air. The rest of the scientific scenario in the film is equally unrealistic.

Extinction goes hand in hand with evolution

The evolution of living organisms has always been accompanied by a steady succession of extinctions. Indeed, the list of extinct species is longer than the list of living species.

Programmed destinies

Although the extinction rate is now alarmingly high, in reality extinction is the natural fate that faces all species. Like all living organisms, species are born, develop and then disappear, only to be replaced by others. The average life span of a species ranges from one million to four million years (although figures for microbes are rather uncertain). Our own species (*Homo sapiens*) – which can be described as young since it is probably no more than 200,000 years old – will inevitably die out one day too.

Not one of the forest-dwelling plant species of the Carboniferous period – such as this giant horsetail (*Calamites* sp) – has survived. The life expectancy of a species is generally too short for this to be possible.

Ninety-nine per cent of all species have died out

Scientists estimate that our planet has been home to at least 30 billion different living species over the course of its existence. Despite the uncertainty surrounding both this figure and the number of species currently found on Earth, it is reasonable to suppose that since life appeared more than 99% of species have become extinct. As the palaeontologist Richard Leakey once jokingly remarked, a rough estimate might suggest that *all* species have become extinct.

Extinctions are inseparable from evolution – or, in other words, from life, which is characterized by change above all else. When a major change in the environment occurs (temperature, sea level, atmospheric conditions, etc) this always leads to an upheaval within living communities. Some species die out, others proliferate and others are created through adaptation.

Constantly changing living conditions

Even in the absence of global changes in the environment, the 'ordinary' living conditions of a species are sufficiently changeable to cause constant renewal. This is known as the 'Red Queen effect'.

The constant need to improve, even if only in order to find food – as in the case of this cheetah trying to catch a gnu – is the driving force behind the innovation of living things and explains the amazing feats of which some species are capable.

For example, there is a real 'arms race' between predators and prey. The former are constantly improving their sensory equipment, their speed, their strategies, and even their poisons. The latter respond to this by refining their camouflage, their escape techniques, and their ability to detect danger and produce antidotes.

The appearance of a new species of predator in an ecosystem can also radically change the whole community's living conditions. If a new predator is more efficient than the existing one, it can force the latter to resort to hunting herbivores it had previously ignored (for example, because they were too small). The increased scarcity of these herbivores might favour certain plant species, which will in turn have a knock-on effect on certain insects, and so on. All the members of a community are thus ultimately affected by the newcomer and this is how species can disappear. Extinctions are not abnormal – quite the reverse. When a species becomes extinct it frees up an ecological niche, which can then be filled by new species. The mass extinctions of the past were always followed by active phases of speciation. Proof of this is the extraordinary rise in the number of mammal species during the Tertiary period that followed the disappearance of the large reptiles of the Mesozoic.

The birth and death of species

Extinctions that are difficult to quantify

Although there is consensus on the general trends underlying extinction, it is difficult to estimate the phenomena at work with any precision.

Controversial estimates

The concept of extinct species is not a new biological idea. Baron Georges Cuvier was the first to put forward the hypothesis of extinction at the end of the 18th century after studying mammoth bones. He found that the bones did not match those of any species on Earth and so deduced that the species concerned was extinct. However, although the concept of extinction is extremely old, scientists have great difficulty in providing accurate, acceptable estimates – both for recent events and for those that have occurred over a geological timescale. Estimates of current and past extinction rates are at odds with one another (a fossil species is far more difficult to define than a living one), and this leads to doubts about how grave the current situation really is.

Few fossils are as complete as this bat from the Eocene (52 million years ago). Often, shapeless fragments are all scientists have to help them identify extinct species.

Fossilization: a rare and selective process

There are several reasons for these doubts. The first is the incomplete character of the geological 'record'. In order for a living organism to be preserved for millions of years, even in fragmentary form, a set of exceptional circumstances is required. The normal fate of a corpse in nature is decomposition by invertebrates and later by microbes. It is only on a few rare occasions (for example, if the animal is caught in mud or resin) that this does not happen. Moreover, fossilization occurs far more readily in an aquatic environment than on land, which can result in misleading data. Lastly, animals without a skeleton or shell (of which there are a large number) are very rarely preserved. Palaeontologists are thus forced to make all kinds of extrapolations, which can lead to inaccurate and questionable results.

Previously classified as extinct, the ivory-billed woodpecker (*Campephilus principalis*) was reclassified as critically endangered after unconfirmed sightings in 1999. Despite intensive searches, there have been no confirmed sightings of this bird since the 1940s.

Recent and even current extinctions are not much easier to quantify. Indeed, the time from when the progressive decline in a population begins to the moment when the last member of the species is lost can be decades or even centuries, even in what may be classified as a rapid extinction. Furthermore, many species live in very specific habitats, which are difficult to reach and are untouched or rarely visited by humans. The evaluation of the conservation status of fish populations, for example, requires periodic fishing and counting, and all the skills, material and labour that this entails. These operations often fail and we have to make do with estimates.

Where's the proof?

The palaeoanthropologist Louis Leakey was right when he said that absence of proof is not proof of absence. However, it is often negative proof (the lack of observations over a long period of time) that justifies the conclusion that a species has become extinct. It is extremely rare for a scientific publication to confirm the extinction of a species, as there is always the chance that another individual will be discovered. The Madeiran land snail (*Discus guerinianus*) was listed as extinct by the IUCN (World Conservation Union) in 1996 because it had not been recorded for 130 years. However, it was discovered in 1999 on a part of the island not previously surveyed because it was not known to be part of the snail's historic range. Such incidents allow some people to point to an absence of scientific proof and thus to deliberately understate the extent of environmental damage caused by humans.

Underestimated figures

Scientists like to proceed cautiously and, in the absence of formal proof, they consider a species to be extinct only if no specimens have been observed for around 50 years. During a four-year campaign carried out recently on the Malaysian peninsula, scientists observed only 122 of the 266 species of freshwater fish that had previously been recorded there. Not all of the remaining 144 are considered to be extinct, but some of them will no doubt have died out.

The 'sixth mass extinction'

The history of living organisms has been punctuated by large extinctions. The current mass extinction event stands out due to the fact that it has been caused by a single species – our own.

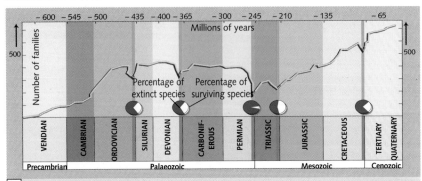

The history of life on Earth has been punctuated by several mass extinctions, whose causes are not very well known. In spite of this, the number of living species on our planet has continued to rise.

Five major biological catastrophes

Palaeontology and dating techniques reveal that extinctions are not at all regular or continuous. Whilst it is true that the process does not stop, it is nevertheless subject to cyclical patterns of acceleration during which species die out in large numbers. The history of life on Earth has been marked by five large extinctions, during which over 60% of all living species have disappeared in just a few million years. Whilst the best-known extinction is that of the dinosaurs at the end of the Cretaceous period (65 million years ago), the most remarkable was at the end of the Permian (245 million years ago), which resulted in the elimination of 90% of all known marine species. Around a dozen smaller extinction events have also been recorded. During these, 15–40% of existing species died out, which is a huge number.

Causes of controversy

The hypotheses that would help explain these planetary catastrophes are controversial and diverse. The relative periodicity in the sequence of these events (one crisis approximately every 26 million years) would seem to suggest the existence of cyclical phenomena.

GLOSSARY

[Marine regression]
The retreat of the sea and a drop in the sea level, causing shallow seas situated on the edges of continents to disappear, and with them the numerous species that lived there. Regressions result from changes in the size of ocean basins.

The impact of one or several meteorites may explain certain extinction events, in particular the one that occurred at the end of the Cretaceous period. However, this explanation does not fit the data available for other disasters, although it could explain the periodicity – if the Earth regularly passed through a cloud of meteorites or comets, for example. Some scientists have put forward the hypothesis of an intermittent recurrence of volcanic activity with large-scale emissions of dust and carbon dioxide. Certain biologists have remarked that major marine regressions are often associated with extinctions, though they are not necessarily the cause, especially in view of the fact that some large regressions have had no effect at all on the diversity of living organisms. A global climate change could explain certain mass extinctions: for example, periods of cooling, which encourage a build-up of water in the form of ice, help to create marine regressions. Finally, some scientists favour a scenario based on the simultaneous occurence of several independent phenomena.

The K/T (Cretaceous/Tertiary) extinction

The most famous and most analysed mass extinction is also the most recent. It took place at the end of the Cretaceous and the beginning of the Tertiary periods (hence the abbreviation 'K/T', with the 'K' standing for Kreide – 'chalk' in German – which describes the chalky sediment layer from the Cretaceous period, and the 'T' standing for Tertiary). The K/T event sounded the death knell for the large reptiles of the Mesozoic era, the dinosaurs in particular, paving the way for the development of mammals and our own species. It was caused by an asteroid around 10km in diameter crashing into our planet. The impact sent enough dust and debris into the atmosphere to plunge the planet into darkness for several months. The impact crater, today covered by thick layers of sediment, was discovered in the Chicxulub region at the tip of the Yucatán Peninsula in Mexico.

Violent volcanic eruptions may explain mass extinctions. Indeed, the gas and dust produced by volcanoes – if sufficiently abundant – would be capable of dramatically changing the Earth's climate.

The birth and death of species

The extinction of the thylacine (*Thylacinus cynocephalus*) in 1937 was entirely due to man. This carnivorous marsupial from Tasmania, also known as the Tasmanian wolf or Tasmanian tiger, was regarded as a threat to livestock and was hunted, trapped and poisoned.

Rapid, widespread and global extinctions

Whatever the real causes were, these mass extinctions are all characterized by species being wiped out extremely rapidly. These extinctions have involved all living organisms (even if some groups have been more affected than others) all over the world. Moreover, their duration has become shorter and shorter on a geological timescale as more evidence has come to light. These features apply perfectly to the process currently underway: this is why many scientists speak of the 'sixth extinction' to describe the times in which we live.

The current era is indeed characterized by an extinction rate 1,000–10,000 times higher than the 'normal' rate observed in nature. Taken over all geological periods, this 'normal' rate is estimated at one species becoming extinct every four years. At present, one species is being lost every day. According to the biologist David Raup, if habitat destruction continues at the current rate, by the end of the 21st century 17,000–100,000 species will become extinct each year. If we are optimistic and just take a low figure of 30,000 species, the speed at which they will disappear will be 120,000 times greater than the geological average. A mass extinction event certainly does appear to be in progress.

Only one species to blame: *Homo sapiens*

What is unique about this 'sixth extinction' is its cause. Although several processes are involved, it has been brought about by a single species: our own, *Homo sapiens*. Throughout history, there have in fact been many examples of global impact resulting from the appearance of a

The dodo from Mauritius was hunted for its meat and its eggs. Its extinction in the 17th century illustrates the vulnerability of island animal life.

particular living organism. The most important was that of the first single-celled photosynthetic organisms over 3.5 billion years ago. Through photosynthesis they started releasing oxygen and thus brought about an enormous upheaval in the biosphere: they gradually increased the amount of oxygen in the atmosphere twentyfold, causing the death of countless existing organisms and creating conditions where others could evolve. This revolutionary development also made life as we know it today possible. From being a very harmful poison, oxygen became a precious and essential commodity for all those organisms that had been able to adapt. However, this transformation was spread over several million years and involved a huge number of organisms; this is very different from the current case of a single species exerting an effect for only a few thousand years.

The degradation of natural habitats, such as the decline of the tropical montane cloud forests in Costa Rica, is the main cause of the 'sixth mass extinction'.

Living organisms will recover ... but will man?

The mass extinctions of the past always ended with an upturn in biodiversity and a higher speciation rate. In the end, they did not stop living forms from continuing to diversify. Nevertheless, it would be a serious mistake to underestimate the gravity of the current situation. It should be remembered that the whole history of human civilization only spans a few thousand years, whereas the regeneration of the biosphere after an extinction generally takes five to ten million years, far longer than the life expectancy of our species. For future generations, the colossal reduction in the number of species currently observed is an irreplaceable loss.

Extinctions and biodiversity

The number of extinct species and the speed at which the extinctions occur only tell part of the story of the decline in global biodiversity.

The difficulty of measuring biodiversity

The number of extinctions is often used as an indication of the decline in biodiversity. For example, if 10% of the species disappear from a given habitat, it is usual to consider that one tenth of the biodiversity has been lost. It is a simplistic method and not always meaningful. In fact, biodiversity can be viewed on three levels: a genetic level, a species level and an ecosystem level. A species may well not be extinct and may even be in a satisfactory state of preservation, even though it has lost an important part of its genetic wealth. The American bison is a case in point: at the beginning of the 18th century, around 60 million bison inhabited the North American plains. The massacres that took place during the 19th century reduced the population to a few hundred individuals by the beginning of the 20th century. Numbers have risen to around 200,000 today. However, when the population of a species drops to several hundred animals, a large number of the genes (carrying the genetic information necessary for resistance to disease, for overcoming other environmental difficulties, and so on) disappear. Even if numbers later rise, the lost genes are not recreated. Thus, there is a decline in this living organism due to the loss of genetic variation. This is why small populations are very fragile. It is often thought that when the population drops below 500 individuals a species can disappear at any moment.

Even though the numbers of American bison (*Bison bison*) have risen greatly since the massacre of this species during the 19th century, it is still genetically fragile.

Distinctions are subjective

The boundaries between species are a constant source of disagreement. According to some scientists a species is not a category with any sort of biological reality but something created by the human mind. Nature itself only recognizes populations, so it is difficult to decide exactly when two isolated populations displaying large genetic differences should be considered separate species. For example, the Pyrenean brown bear (*Ursus arctos pyrenaicus*), which only lives in France and Spain, is a subspecies of the brown bear (*Ursus arctos*). There are only a few dozen individuals of the former left and, despite all attempts to save them, they appear doomed to

A tiny brown bear population still survives in the French Pyrenees. Various groups have invested a lot of time and effort in attempting to preserve this emblematic animal.

extinction in the near future. Statistically speaking, the disappearance of this population, deplorable though it is, will have no effect on the global situation of the species *Ursus arctos*, which is itself far from becoming extinct, especially in Siberia and in North America.

Extinction modifies the ecological system

In the end, the disappearance of species is only partially responsible for the disappearance of ecosystems. In theory, it is possible to create countless different ecosystems using the same species, by simply varying predatory relations, habitat occupation, relative densities, behaviour, and so on. While it is true that the biodiversity of a country or a territory is defined by the number of species it contains, it is also defined by the diversity of its ecosystems. A territory containing a variety of ecosystems is obviously more diverse than another more uniform area. And recreating an ecosystem that has disappeared is no more possible than bringing back to life an extinct species.

In the case of this strawberry poison dart frog (*Dendrobates pumilio*) from Central America, some populations are bright red and others dark blue. Can we really talk of a single species?

The birth and death of species **27**

Polar environments, tropical forests, deserts, steppes and vast ocean floors all contain endangered species. No ecosystem is spared. However, the threat is more acute in tropical environments and poor countries. Central and South America (Brazil, Colombia, Ecuador, Mexico, etc), East Africa (Tanzania), South-East Asia (China, India, Indonesia and Malaysia) and the island of Madagascar are all seriously affected. Scientists have identified 25 biodiversity 'hotspots', where the threat is believed to be greatest.

Large numbers of wetlands, particularly rich in species but judged to be 'unproductive', have been destroyed all over the world.

Where are the endangered species?

Distribution of biodiversity

In certain parts of the world, life consists of a handful of organisms, whereas in other areas there is an extraordinary diversity of species. It all depends on the topography and the climate.

Uneven distribution

The number of species varies greatly depending on the geographical location. In the British Isles, for example, 80 species of birds nest in around 10,000km² of coastline, compared to 270 in similar-sized areas in Indonesia and 350 in Costa Rica. The environments with the greatest biodiversity are the tropical rainforests; it is estimated that they contain 60–75% of the world's biodiversity although they account for only 7% of the Earth's landmass and 2% of the planet's total surface area. The Amazonian rainforest alone is home to 81 species of primates; in other words, almost half of all primate species worldwide. A famous study carried out in 1980 in the Panamanian forest recorded 1,200 species of beetles on only 19 trees; remarkably, 80% of these species were unknown to science.

The heat, humidity and stability of the tropical rainforest make it the ecosystem with the highest biodiversity on Earth.

The importance of climatic conditions

Why are there such large variations? Firstly because of the climate: heat and humidity are favourable to life. Heat speeds up metabolic reactions and provides organisms with energy, whilst humidity stops them drying out. Moreover, seasons create problems for living things. In temperate climates, plants have to adapt to long periods of cold. These various adaptations (dormancy in cereals, storage of reserves in the roots of plants, and so on) often use up a lot of energy and are sometimes inhibited by the vagaries of the weather. Animals, meanwhile, have to migrate or live at a slower pace for many months, or

European and African lakes

Lake Geneva in Europe contains 14 endemic fish species and 11 more that have been introduced by man. This is a paltry number compared to the 300 endemic species in Lake Tanganyika or the 500 in Lake Malawi. However, 20,000 years ago, Lake Geneva was covered in ice whilst the African lakes have been covered in water for several million years.

Very few species manage to survive in the Arctic tundra. In addition to the ice, which makes liquid water unavailable for most of the year, the cold and violent winds limit the number of living organisms.

find enough food to survive on in the absence, or virtual absence, of all plant activity. This is why fewer species are recorded in temperate zones than in the tropics.

Historical and geographical explanations

The history of different environments also helps to explain their biodiversity. North America, for example, is far richer in freshwater fish species than Europe. During the ice ages, the fish that inhabited the basin of the largest North American river, the Mississippi, managed to migrate south and take temporary refuge in warmer areas. In Europe, only the lower reaches of the Danube, south of the Alpine zone, played a similar role. Thus the successive advances and retreats of the ice during the last 500,000 years forced species to abandon their habitats and to return when conditions were more favourable. Those that were unable to do so became extinct. In the tropics, the glaciations did not have much influence and organisms were able to evolve for a long time in a stable environment, which therefore favoured species formation. The shape of continents is also a factor. The continuity of the landmass between North America and the tropics allows many birds to move between the two zones. On the other hand, the Sahara and the Mediterranean separate Europe from Africa, thus making migration more difficult.

> **Map** *(following pages)*
>
> *The threat facing global biodiversity is concentrated in 25 'hotspots'. These zones, which are the focus of biodiversity conservation, are the richest and most endangered reservoirs of plant and animal life on Earth (tropical rainforests, Mediterranean regions, etc) and/or they contain a large number of endemic species (Pacific islands, Madagascar, etc). Furthermore, 200 'ecoregions' have also been designated in order to preserve not only the 'hotspots' but also a representative sample of ecologically exceptional terrestrial, marine and freshwater environments.*

Where are the endangered species? **31**

Centres of biodiversity

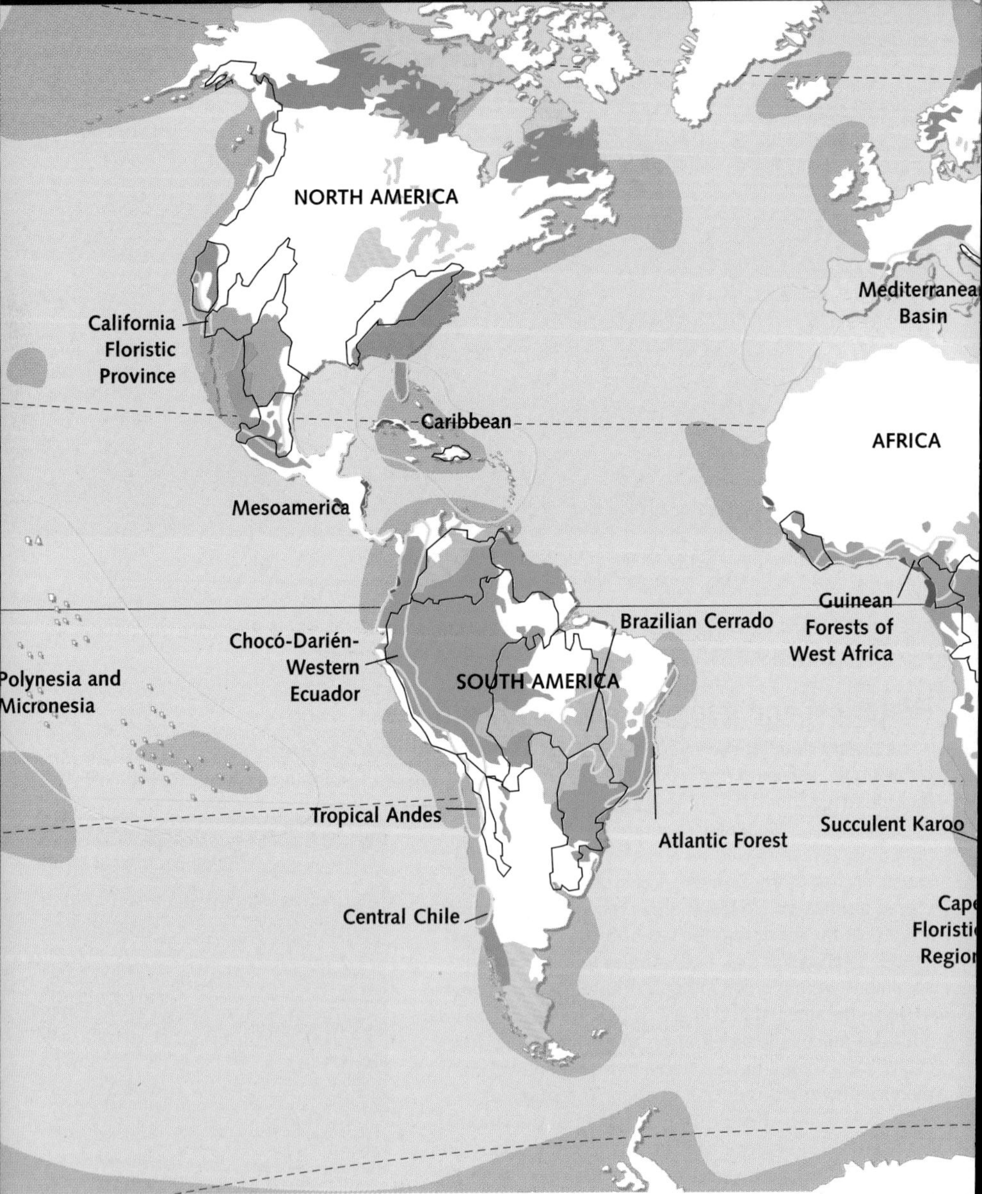

NORTH AMERICA

California
Floristic
Province

Caribbean

Mesoamerica

Mediterranean
Basin

AFRICA

Chocó-Darién-
Western
Ecuador

Brazilian Cerrado

Guinean
Forests of
West Africa

Polynesia and
Micronesia

SOUTH AMERICA

Tropical Andes

Atlantic Forest

Succulent Karoo

Central Chile

Cape
Floristic
Region

Global distribution of the 200 ecoregions

- tropical forests
- temperate forests
- boreal forests/taiga

- tropical grasslands and savannas
- temperate grasslands/pampa
- montane grasslands and shrublands
- Mediterranean forests, woodlands and scrub

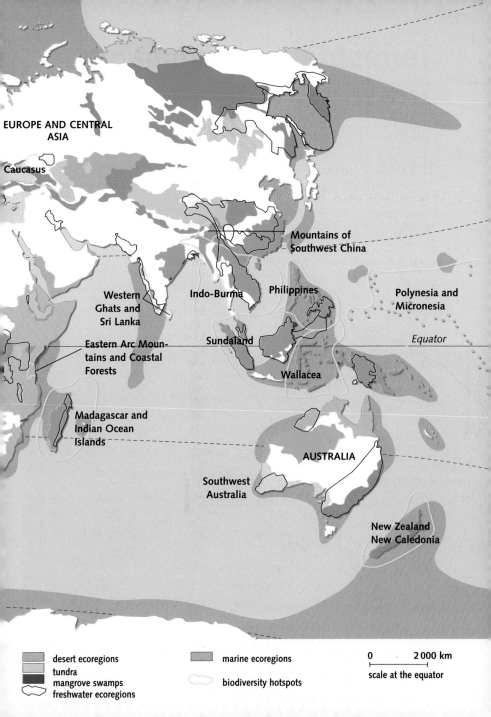

EUROPE AND CENTRAL
ASIA

Caucasus

Mountains of
Southwest China

Western
Ghats and
Sri Lanka

Indo-Burma

Philippines

Polynesia and
Micronesia

Eastern Arc Moun-
tains and Coastal
Forests

Sundaland

Equator

Wallacea

Madagascar and
Indian Ocean
Islands

AUSTRALIA

Southwest
Australia

New Zealand
New Caledonia

desert ecoregions
tundra
mangrove swamps
freshwater ecoregions

marine ecoregions

biodiversity hotspots

0   2 000 km

scale at the equator

Terrestrial environments

Although not enough is yet known about ocean environments, scientists believe that the diversification of species is greatest on land, with tropical forests containing most.

The lush tropical forests

Without any doubt, the prize for greatest biodiversity goes to the tropical forests (which contain around 20 million species), whether they be lowland, montane or monsoon forests. These forests display a vertical stratification: several layers are superimposed between the soil, where it is dark and damp, and the canopy, which is brightly lit and dry. There is a great diversity of plant life in these forests: for example, in the coastal tropical rainforest of Brazil, known as the Mata Atlântica, there are as many as 300 species of trees per hectare, in addition to all the ferns, mosses, lianas and epiphytes such as orchids. Borneo's tropical forest is home to 11,000 plant species, 40% of which are endemic. All these plants are home to millions of species of invertebrates – mainly insects – the majority of which are dependent on them. Finally, a large number of vertebrate species, in particular amphibians and almost 90% of all primate species, live in

In the tropical rainforests the humidity is so high that many amphibians, such as this toad from Thailand, are able to live far from rivers and lakes and make their home high up in the trees.

tropical forests. The other types of forest are generally less rich in biodiversity. Nevertheless, in temperate zones broad-leaved forests are home to many species, especially at ground level. As for the vast boreal forests, they are dominated by only a few species of trees, in contrast to the wide variety of lichens and mosses to be found there. Moreover, the long periods of cold weather mean that the number of invertebrates capable of survival is limited. The biodiversity is thus reduced, all the more so since the boundaries of the forests are shared by other, not dissimilar types of environment. On the other hand, the continental masses in the southern hemisphere and their environments are divided up into areas of land surrounded by numerous islands, and this isolation favours endemisms (a high percentage of species indigenous to one specific territory).

The large herds of herbivores on the African steppes (here in the Serengeti in Tanzania) can give the impression that these are rich ecosystems. In reality, the aridity and poor quality of the soil limit the number of species.

The Mediterranean grassland ecosystem

Mediterranean environments have a high level of plant and animal biodiversity. These areas – located not only around the Mediterranean Sea but also in California, Chile, South Africa and Australia – are home to a large number of species, despite accounting for only 1–2% of the planet's surface area. The Cape Floristic Region, for example, contains 8,200 different vascular plants on only 0.04% of the planet's dry land.

Grassland ecosystems, well-known because in Africa they are home to populations of large, familiar mammals (giraffe, elephant, buffalo, zebra, rhinoceros and gnu), have very poor quality soil and are not very productive, in particular because water is often scarce. This means that mammals are found in relatively low densities, despite their vast herds. Being gregarious animals, their vulnerability is thus increased.

Man and his influence

'Traditional agriculture' sometimes generates a high level of biodiversity, even greater than in pre-existing environments. Thus, hay meadows and hedged farm land house many species, especially insects (grasshoppers, bees, stag beetles, ladybirds, etc). Conversely, urban environments, environments adjacent to cities, areas shaped by intensive agriculture and zones cleared by burning tropical forests or mangrove swamps are often like biological deserts.

Where are the endangered species? **35**

Aquatic environments

Freshwater environments appear to contain a greater biodiversity than the oceans. However, research into oceanic environments may well bring new discoveries.

In the oceans, life is concentrated in the surface waters where light is abundant. Many endangered species such as seahorses can be found there.

The mysteries of the deep

Although coastal environments have been relatively well studied, the biodiversity of the pelagic zone (the open sea) is not well known. Recent research has revealed that this area is of greater importance than oceanographers previously suspected. The open sea, which receives light down to depths of 200m, has a high biological stratification and contains complex food chains, which are based on plankton. At the top of these chains are mammals (in particular cetaceans: dolphins, whales, etc) and birds. The great depths of the sea, where the biomass is very low, also appear to be home to quite a large number of species.

Coral reefs

The richest marine ecosystems are without doubt the coastal environments, especially coral reefs, which are considered to be the oceanic equivalent of tropical rainforests in terms of biodiversity. These tropical ecosystems cover 627,000km^2, the most spectacular being the Great Barrier Reef, which extends for over 2,000km off the north-east coast of Australia. Coral reefs benefit from strong sunlight, which passes almost unfiltered through the crystal-clear water. Corals are simple animals that live in symbiosis with zooxanthellae – algae with powerful photosynthetic activity. Corals provide food and protection to a whole host of marine animals, crustaceans, molluscs, worms, and so on, and to almost 4,000 species of fish.

The Amazon Basin

The Amazon Watershed and Ucayali Subbasin in the tropical part of South America constitute the richest reservoir of freshwater species in the world. Around 2,300 species of fish (ten times more than in all European rivers combined) live in the waters of this river or in the flooded forest environment (*várzea*). There are at least 500 species of catfish and 40 species of electric eel. However, the building of dams has upset this unique ecosystem, creating zones devoid of oxygen, trapping toxic sediments and destroying a high percentage of the species that once lived there.

Coral reefs contain an impressive biological diversity: fish, crustaceans, sea urchins, molluscs and sea worms abound among colonies of madrepores.

The total biodiversity of the reefs is estimated at a minimum of 450,000 species, of which only 10% have been described. Mangrove swamps are another type of well-known coastal environment. Although their biodiversity is quite low, they play an important ecological role because they are used as breeding grounds by many marine species.

Very fresh water

Watercourses and lakes represent only around 0.01% of the total volume of water on Earth. This figure scarcely changes when we add the contents of all the wetlands (peat bogs, marshes, mud flats, etc). Nevertheless, this tiny fraction of the biosphere is home to an amazing variety of species. Indeed, 40% of the 10,000 recorded species of fish live in fresh water. This diversity can probably be explained by the heterogeneity of the freshwater environment. A simple river contains many different habitats between its source and its mouth: cold, clear waters around the source, warmer, slower-running water in the middle course and then a marshy estuary. Moreover, freshwater habitats are generally quite compartmentalized, the genetic mixing is poor and the conditions are thus far more favourable for speciation than in the sea.

> **GLOSSARY**
>
> **[Biomass]**
> Biomass is the total mass of living organisms in a specific ecosystem, population or other unit area at a given moment.

The ecosystems most at risk

Not all environments are exposed to the same dangers. Some, such as coral reefs and tropical forests, have been severely disrupted and even destroyed by man, whilst others have suffered only slight disturbance.

Habitats at risk

There is no natural environment that remains entirely untouched by man's activities. Some ecosystems are particularly at risk because they are highly desirable for some reason or because they find it hard to recover from disruption. A high level of biodiversity does not necessarily mean a place is of economic interest. However, it is unfortunately often the places richest in biodiversity that suffer the greatest damage. This is particularly true of the tropical forests: exploited for precious wood – which is exported – and cleared by local farmers, they are unable to regenerate spontaneously after they have been destroyed.

Endangered corals and freshwater organisms

Coral reefs are damaged by fishing techniques which use cyanide and dynamite, and are seriously affected by environmental changes such as pollution and a rise in temperature due to global warming. These stresses cause the death of the zooxanthellae algae which give the corals their colour, resulting in the 'bleaching' and death of the coral. Sixty per cent of Caribbean reefs have already been affected. Freshwater organisms also suffer from human activity. Various kinds of toxic waste are simply poured into rivers and streams. Rainwater carries residual substances from modern agricultural techniques (pesticides, fertilizers, organic waste, etc) into watercourses, and rivers and lakes have only a limited capacity for diluting this waste matter. Wetland ecosystems are also at risk: forming borders between terrestrial and aquatic environments (peat bogs, marshes, mangrove swamps, etc),

Mangrove swamps are forest communities which can grow partially submerged in water in coastal areas. They play a vital role as nurseries for young fish, crustaceans and molluscs.

The polar bear, like all large carnivores at the top of the food pyramid, ingests large concentrations of pollutants which are a result of human activity (dioxins, mercury, pesticides, etc).

they are often considered sterile and a threat to human health. In reality, however, they contain many species and play an essential ecological role in regulating the flow of water. Humans often turn them into 'productive zones', draining them or filling them in to create agricultural or industrial land. Recent floods in Europe are perhaps linked to this harmful activity.

Polar zones – far from safe

The biodiversity of species in the polar zones is particularly low; nevertheless, these regions contain large mammals (polar bear, seal, walrus, whale, etc) and aquatic invertebrates, as well as many species of birds and fish. However, industrial fishing and atmospheric pollution generated by industrial activity elsewhere (dioxins, mercury, etc) have caused serious damage. Global warming has already had serious repercussions: the size of emperor penguin populations in the Antarctic has declined by over 50% in the last 25 years due to the rise in temperature of the Southern Ocean.

Forest and plantations

There are over one million square kilometres of forestry plantations on Earth. These generally consist of rows of fast-growing trees belonging to the same species (mainly eucalyptus, pines and poplars). Admittedly, these plantations do fulfil some ecological roles (regulating water, stabilizing the soil, storing carbon, etc), as well as providing wood for industrial purposes and relieving the economic pressure on ancient forests. However, their biodiversity is far lower than that of the forests they replace.

The 'hotspots'

> Biologists have identified 25 zones in which they consider species to be at risk. It is essential to protect these areas, which have been adversely affected by human activity.

Defining priorities

Faced with the apparently inexorable decline in the number of species on Earth, scientists have tried to identify those areas of the planet in greatest need of protection. The aim of this procedure is clear: to identify conservation priorities in order to make the best use of the limited funds available and to focus cost-effective efforts on those priorities. In February 2000, the British biologist Norman Myers from the University of Oxford published the results of this work in the journal *Nature*. He identified 25 'hotspots', whose future is crucial for the future of global biodiversity. This list is now a vital point of reference for the scientific community.

Madagascar has been designated one of 25 global biodiversity hotspots due to the variety of threats facing this island environment, which contains many endemic species such as Grandidier's baobab tree.

The criteria

Two criteria were used to select the hotspots. The first was the number and diversity of plant and animal species. In order to assess this, the authors focused on flowering plants. These were used as 'qualifiers' because they are relatively well known to researchers (unlike invertebrates, for example) and, moreover, they are at the bottom of the food chain. Thus, when making an initial evaluation, scientists can assume that an area containing an exceptional variety of plants will also have a great diversity of other living organisms. Up to the present, around 300,000 flowering plants have been described worldwide. In order to be designated a hotspot, a given area has to support at least 1,500 endemic plant species, or 0.5% of the global total. The second criterion is that the area must be at significant risk. This is assessed by calculating the proportion of the original primary vegetation that has disappeared. In order to qualify as a hotspot, the region must have lost at least 70% of its original habitat.

Costa Rica, despite its modest surface area (51,000 km²), is known to have twice as many bird species (for example, this Amazon parrot) as the whole of Europe.

Disturbing results

The 25 hotspots described by Myers and his colleagues cover 2.1 million km2, in other words 1.4% of the Earth's total land surface. They contain 133,149 higher plant species (44% of the world's total) and 35% of all terrestrial vertebrate species. On average, the hotspots have already lost 88% of their original primary vegetation; in three cases over 95% has been lost. In some of the regions the situation has become critical. These hotspots are situated in Madagascar, the Philippines, Indonesia, the Brazilian Atlantic Forest, the Caribbean and the Mediterranean Basin.

Around 38% of the hotspots are protected areas, but often this protection exists only on paper. According to the authors of the report, to protect all these zones would cost 500 million dollars a year and at present only one twelfth of this is being spent. The amount needed is a relatively derisory sum on a global scale, as is borne out by the fact that the annual military budget of the USA alone is 600 times higher than the amount needed to protect the hotspots.

What about the oceans?

Similar work began recently to identify ten critical sites among the coral reefs. Because less is known about the marine environment than the terrestrial one, there is more room for uncertainty. However, scientists estimate that the zones they have selected, although only covering 0.012% of the oceans, are home to 34% of endemic species. Eight of these sites are adjacent to terrestrial hotspots. The Philippines and the Gulf of Guinea are the joint leaders of this depressing list.

A large number of species are at risk from human activities which destroy their habitats: 91% of all endangered plants, 89% of all endangered birds and 83% of all endangered mammals, according to the IUCN (International Union for the Conservation of Nature). There are no precise figures for the other categories of living organisms, which are less well known, but the percentages are probably similar. A number of particularly rich habitats are currently suffering irreversible damage: these include forests, arid and subarid regions, wetlands and coral reefs.

In Borneo, vast wooded areas are cleared to make way for oil palm plantations (seen here in the background).

Man, destroyer of habitats

Deforestation: a by-product of poverty

In the tropics, hundreds of millions of poor, generally illiterate farmers have to clear forests to feed their families. They use the felled timber for firewood and reclaim the land for crops.

Deforestation at an alarming rate

Between the years 900 and 1900, the forest cover in Europe was drastically reduced, dropping from 90% to 20%, in order to create farmland. Today, European forests are gaining ground, especially in France (up 3% over the last 20 years) and in Poland (up 35% since 1950). On the other hand, forests are declining dramatically in tropical regions. The statistics for deforestation are difficult to establish because they are often provided by the countries concerned, and these base their figures on those provided (willingly or otherwise) by the forestry companies. Many people exploit the forests illegally and even the authorized companies occasionally conceal some of their activities (according to the Brazilian government, the illegal timber trade is four times bigger than the legal trade). Eventually, satellite photos will help solve this problem. Another difficulty is that it is hard to say at what stage of degradation a forest can no longer be called a forest. The FAO (Food and Agriculture Organization of the United Nations) estimates that at least 200 million hectares of primary forest (in other words, 10% of the world's tropical forests) – greater than the total surface area of Mexico – were lost between 1980 and 1995. And an additional 14 million hectares (over three times the size of Switzerland) are destroyed each year.

From an agricultural point of view, the deforestation of the slopes of Borneo constitutes an ecological disaster with serious repercussions for the soil, which the slightest amount of rain washes away forever from the slopes, down into the valleys.

<figure>
⊞ **The search for wood** for heating and cooking is a daily priority for these children from the high plateaux of Madagascar. If deforestation continues at the current rate, in thirty years this tropical island will be turned into a desert.
</figure>

Radical change in residual forests

In addition to this rapid deforestation, there is another problem, that of the qualitative degradation of the remaining forests, which are often split up into a large number of separate plots. If one compares similar-sized areas, a group of several forest islands contains much less biodiversity than a single large unit. Large animals need extensive territories to find food, and many small animals depend on the presence of larger ones. In the Amazon, for example, several species of frogs living in 100-hectare plots have disappeared rapidly because the surface area of their habitat is too small for peccaries, which dig out the ruts in which the frogs shelter. Moreover, isolated populations result in genetic decline: a population of 50 individuals cut off from the rest of their species will become far more vulnerable to disease or natural disasters. Finally, biologists have long known of the existence of the so-called 'edge effect': the forest habitat only functions properly·800m from its edge, because this is where the undisturbed area begins. This edge effect obviously affects a fragmented forest more than a larger one.

A forest can also be degraded by the selective harvesting of trees that are of commercial value: the movement of machinery, the tracks that are cut, the work itself – all cause serious damage to the local plant and animal life. Likewise, forests near urban centres are very often exploited for firewood. The larger trees survive, but the others are chopped down. Although such activities do not appear in the deforestation statistics, they have a profound and lasting detrimental effect on the ecology of forest habitats.

Map (following pages)

✷ Habitat degradation (deforestation, drying out of wetlands, coastal developments, etc) is the main threat facing animals and plants worldwide. The mass deforestation accompanying the development of human societies over the last 2,000 years first affected European forests. For the last 30 years, this destruction has been increasing rapidly in tropical zones.

Degradation of coasts and forests

NORTH AMERICA

AFRICA

SOUTH AMERICA

Forest cover throughout the world

- temperate and boreal forests
- tropical dry or moist forests
- forest cover 2,000 years ago

Coastal development

- high
- moderate
- low

Slash-and-burn agriculture on a small scale does not have too dramatic an impact on tropical environments. However, its generalized use does threaten a number of forest species, such as this curious Malagasy leaf-tailed gecko (Uroplatus sp).

A socioeconomic problem

Many different factors cause forest degradation, and they vary from place to place. One of the main causes is the presence of around 500 million poor people (one human in twelve), who have no means of subsistence and live on the edges of the large primary forests. In order to survive, they practise slash-and-burn agriculture, which consists of clearing plots of land by burning the existing vegetation and then planting crops which will provide just enough to live on. This means of cultivation exhausts the soil within two or three years, after which time the farmer and his family have no choice but to leave their plot of land, go deeper into the forest in search of more fertile ground and start the process all over again. Two-thirds of the forest cover lost each year disappears as a result of this practice. Deforestation is thus a very complex problem – a problem that is not only ecological, but also socioeconomic and human.

Planned destruction

Generally speaking, it is clear that the world's forests will not be saved without halting the increase of worldwide social inequality and eradicating the mass poverty that is blighting our planet. It is undeniable that the governments of many tropical countries have often made the situation worse by using primary forests as 'safety valves' in order to avoid dealing with problems of unemployment, anarchic urbanization, crime and agricultural reform (in Brazil, 1% of the population owns 46% of the farm land). Moreover, 'colonization' policies have sometimes been adopted, which actively encourage slash-and burn agriculture in the primary forests. Some countries have also encouraged their populations to clear and occupy forest zones in order to affirm their sovereignty (for example, on the borders of Peru, Ecuador and Colombia).

The responsibility of the rich countries

However, the ultimate responsibility lies with the richer, more industrialized countries of the northern hemisphere. Not content with plundering natural resources such as precious tropical woods, which they import in massive quantities, they crush the countries in the southern hemisphere beneath the weight of huge debt and thus prevent them from developing. When a debt becomes too large, it ends up consuming a country's entire revenue and the country then has no means of educating its population. According to the World Bank, in the ten countries where deforestation is principally carried out, the debt burden as a percentage of GNP rose from 26% to 60% between 1976 and 1996.

The firewood problem

In developing countries, firewood accounts for 80% of wood consumption. Worldwide, 3 billion individuals use wood as their main source of energy and it is unlikely that substitute fuels will be available for these people in the near future. In rural areas, wood is used as it is, whilst the inhabitants of urban areas most often use wood charcoal, which burns with a hotter flame. This use of wood puts considerable pressure on the surrounding forests, which, if they are not irreparably damaged, are nevertheless seriously degraded. Madagascar, for example, will lose all its forests in 30 years if nothing is done.

Agriculture and the timber trade

The tropical timber trade is flourishing, whilst traditional agriculture is dying out in the face of its industrial equivalent. Natural environments are being degraded and forests are rapidly disappearing.

From subsistence agriculture to industrial agriculture

The increasing industrialization of agriculture is largely responsible for the decline in natural habitats. In Europe and the United States, natural grasslands have been replaced by vast monocultures of rape, maize or wheat. The expansion of artificial ecosystems, saturated with pesticides and herbicides, has been accompanied by extreme degradation of the existing

Part of the Monteverde Cloud Forest (Costa Rica) has already been sacrificed on the altar of the North American 'hamburger chain': the cattle are raised on hills cleared of trees.

plant and animal life. In tropical regions, the creation of modern agricultural units, generally geared towards export, often leads to the uprooting of the farmers who previously cultivated these areas. Thus, in Honduras in the 1970s, thousands of poor farmers had to leave their land to make way for oil palm plantations in the valleys of the northern coasts. Almost inevitably, these farmers ended up carrying out slash-and-burn agriculture, either with the active support of the authorities, who may even have organized their relocation, or quite simply because it was the only type of agricultural practice they knew. Where there is no existing agricultural land available, forests are cleared to make way for new areas of cultivation. Thus, the primary forest has often simply been replaced by plantations of oil palms, rubber trees, coffee trees, cacao trees, and so on.

These hardwood logs from the tropical forest of Borneo will be exported to Japan, which is by far the largest consumer of valuable wood in the world.

Cattle replace the forest

Extensive cattle-ranching also takes a heavy toll on tropical forests, particularly in Latin America. Livestock farms were traditionally established on relatively dry lands on the western side of the continent, but the opening up of the North American markets has led to an expansion in cattle-ranching and it has now spread east into the moist tropical forest areas. Many breeders have used poor farmers to clear new grazing lands by means of chainsaws and burning. The FAO estimates that between 1955 and 1995 the total area of grazing land in Central America grew from 3.9 million to 13.4 million hectares, almost entirely to the detriment of the forest. In addition, this increase in grazing land leads to rapid erosion, which is estimated at 200 tonnes of soil per hectare per year, whereas in a dense forest there is scarcely any erosion at all.

Valuable wood

The extraction of valuable wood (teak, mahogany, rosewood, etc), usually intended for export, accounts for around 15% of deforestation. In certain parts of Asia where there are a large number of particularly desirable tree species, this figure reaches 50%. In Malaysia, for example, the volume of timber felled quadrupled between 1976 and 1992. The valuable wood is generally extracted selectively, leaving the surrounding trees standing. However, the intrusion of huge machines, the creation of permanent camps (sometimes housing hundreds of workers), roads and tracks used by a constant stream of lorries cause irreparable damage. Governments generally grant short-term concessions to the forestry companies and these, having no motivation to manage their land properly, adopt a predatory attitude. The percentage of tropical forest that is well managed from the long-term point of view has been estimated at a mere 1%.

Man, destroyer of habitats **51**

Desertification

Dense grasslands give way to poor grazing land. With few plant roots to bind the soil together, the wind erodes the top layers and rain begins to wash the soil away, and the desert advances.

A downward spiral

The degradation of the land in arid and semi-arid zones, linked to climatic variations and human activity, is a serious problem for the Earth's ecosystems. The FAO estimates that 70% of the planet's arid lands (around 3.6 billion hectares) have already been degraded. Desertification generally produces a reduction in plant cover, accompanied by an inexorable decline in the local animal life. If the vegetation disappears completely, the soil, no longer held in place by the roots of plants, tends to become loose. It is then eroded through the action of the wind and rain, making it more difficult for new

GLOSSARY

[Overgrazing]
Overgrazing occurs when land is overexploited to such an extent that the vegetation and soil are significantly degraded.
[Salinization]
Salinization is a process in which soluble salts build up in soil, making it unsuitable for cultivation.

Sahelian Africa loses a little more of its plant cover each year and the Sahara Desert is advancing southwards, as illustrated in this photograph taken in Mali.

Desertification, the climate and man

Global warming undoubtedly contributes towards desertification. However, there were already signs of a climate change before the industrial era, and thus before the mass emissions of carbon dioxide: the last ice age occurred around 20,000 years ago and the Earth has been warming up since then. Nevertheless, even if there is a 'natural' warming process at work, man worsens it considerably through the overuse of fossil fuel. Thus, man's intervention is at least partially responsible for the degradation of arid lands.

plants to take root, and the remaining soil becomes even more fragile. Normally, the underground network of plant roots efficiently traps water and maintains a moist layer in the subsoil. A desert, even after rain, dries out again very quickly and it is therefore more difficult for plants to become re-established. Desertification in a moderate form is a reversible process and to a certain extent natural. Climatic variations cause the vegetation boundary around the Sahara to move each year, and this border can vary by up to 200km. However, once plant destruction and soil erosion pass a certain threshold, spontaneous regeneration is no longer possible: human intervention and considerable financial resources are required and these are rarely available in tropical countries.

Unsuitable agricultural practices

Of all human activities, poor agricultural practice is the main cause of desertification. Overgrazing, in particular, prevents grassland from regenerating properly and also leads to the land being trampled, thus hindering the natural regrowth of plants. Overintensive farming and inappropriate working of the soil (for example ploughing too deeply, insufficient fertilization or unsuitable crops) soon destroy land that is too dry. Irrigation, which can of course enrich the earth when it is carried out properly, sometimes affects the functioning of the water table and leads to the salinization of the soil. The gathering of firewood is equally catastrophic if carried out too intensively. It should, however, be pointed out that the presence of humans does not always lead to a decline in the quality of land. On the contrary, good agricultural practices can improve it. In Yemen, a vast system of irrigated terraces for crops was developed from a desert area. Sadly, the farmers were tempted away by the money they could make in the oil industry, and the land became desert again.

Tropical rains wash away deforested soils, sweeping the arable land into the oceans. An example of this irreversible loss can be seen in this photograph of the confluence of two rivers in Central America.

Industry, mining and urbanization

Polluting mines consume wood on the one hand, and create sprawl-ing, fast-growing cities on the other – natural environments are being eaten away from the inside and the outside simultaneously.

Rapid urbanization

The destruction of natural environments also occurs, admittedly on a more local level, as a result of a certain number of urban developments. Urbanization is a rapid phenomenon that occurs on a global scale, devouring increasingly large areas of our planet. The number of cities with over one million inhabitants rose from 10 to 500 between 1900 and 2000. Mediterranean environments (the area surrounding the Mediterranean Sea, California and coastal regions of South Africa) are particularly associated with desirable climatic conditions, in other words lots of sunshine, pleasant temperatures and rain that only falls during a few months of the year. These environments, which contain a large number of endemic species, are thus subjected to much property speculation and a steady rise in population levels. However, the growth of built-up areas occurs in all climates. Major communication networks also have a great impact on the environment, especially forests. The opening up of the famous Transamazon Highway provided slash-and-burn farmers and Brazilian cattle-ranchers with access to millions of square kilometres of forest. On a more modest level, simply opening up roads for motor vehicles in forests has led to an increase in the number of cars, walkers, hunters, and so on, and this can make the environment uninhabitable for fragile species that are sensitive to disturbance.

Both land and sea in coastal zones are often of great biological value. Unfortunately, as in the case of Cancún in Mexico (shown above), these areas are also highly sought after by property developers.

All sorts of mines, some gigantic

Mining, prospecting and oil extraction are also important factors that lead to the

54

Driven by 'gold fever', poor populations end up deforesting vast regions in order to dig the earth with their bare hands. This picture was taken at the border between Burkina Faso and Mali.

destruction of natural environments. Opencast mines in particular can destroy extremely large areas of land. This is particularly true when they are located in tropical forests: for example, the huge gold mines in Brazil, the Indonesian coal mines or the copper mines in Zambia. These mine workings naturally lead to the destruction of that part of the forest situated above the mineral deposits. However, the main problem is caused by the large concentration of workers that the industry brings into the middle of the forest. They need to be fed and this leads to the intense trade in 'bush meat' – in other words, mammals and birds (mainly) that are hunted in the surrounding area. The fact that many of these species (in particular the primates) are protected is ignored by the hunters, and there is no real control over their activities. In addition, the development of large roads creates access routes into the forest, which are soon used by slash-and-burn farmers.

Energy taken from the forest

The energy requirements for these installations are generally met by burning wood taken from the area around the sites. The energy consumption of a 'village' of several hundred workers, even if they are very poor, is quite considerable. There are also often industrial processes, which consume far more fuel. And many of these activities involve the dumping of toxic waste in the ecosystem. This is the case, for example, in gold mining, in which large quantities of mercury are used. This metal, which has serious neurotoxic effects, is now present in several watercourses within the Amazon Basin.

The development of water-courses

Rivers and wetlands often contain a large number of endemic species and a high level of biodiversity. The construction of dams on rivers, and large ports on coasts and in estuaries, can cause irreparable damage.

The Three Gorges Dam, on China's Yangtze River, will open in 2009. This colossal construction will radically change the course of the river and have a huge negative impact on the biodiversity of the area.

The problem with dams

Symbols of development and modernity, dams began to increase rapidly in number at the beginning of the 20th century in countries in the northern hemisphere and then later in the southern hemisphere. Dam schemes are intended to bring cheap energy and protection against floods, as well as making navigation easier and providing water for irrigation. However, the way in which dams have fulfilled their potential, especially in tropical regions, is often controversial. Their detractors accuse them of having increased their country's burden of debt, made parasitic diseases more widespread and disrupted the water cycle. Whatever people think of the economic outcome, it is obvious that from the point of view of the natural environment the effect of dams has almost always been disastrous. In general, the zones that were flooded were previously wetlands of biological importance, containing a wide diversity of animals and plants.

They have been replaced by homogeneous, but ecologically poor stretches of water. Moreover, dams trap sediment, which is often full of pollutants produced upstream. The Aswan High Dam, for example, built on the upper reaches of the River Nile, prevents the river from flooding and has thereby eliminated the fertilizing effect these waters once had. The amount of fertilizer used by farmers has thus rocketed, causing serious pollution problems. Dams are also generally linked to other installations (dykes, gates, locks, etc) which are all designed to stop the river flooding and to facilitate navigation by guaranteeing a regular flow and stable depth of water. However, rivers are naturally variable environments, inhabited by species which are adapted to this variability.

The construction of huge port areas in large estuaries has sounded the death knell for the original biodiversity of these aquatic environments situated on the boundary between land, fresh water and sea water.

The 'domestication' of these watercourses always leads to a great decline in their biodiversity. Dams are also obstacles for migratory fish, such as salmon and eels, and generally reduce the diversity of living organisms.

The problem with estuaries

The development of estuaries has also frequently had deadly consequences for natural environments. Estuaries of large rivers often form shifting deltas, which support a profusion of living organisms: aquatic invertebrates, birds and fish. However, estuaries also generally contain busy ports with extensive installations, which need maintenance (by dredging, for example) in order to cater for increasingly large ships, and these activities have a detrimental effect on the natural environment.

In general, wetlands and marshes have long been considered sterile areas, making them prime targets for development. They have been drained, filled in, dried out, planted with poplars, rice or maize, and so on – all kinds of different operations have turned them into biological deserts.

The Three Gorges Dam

The era of gigantic construction projects is not yet over. The most famous of these projects is currently under way in China on the Yangtze River: the huge Three Gorges Dam, which will be 185m high and over 2km long when completed. It will create a 1,000km² reservoir and interrupt the flow of the giant Yangtze River (over 6,000km long), whose basin is home to over 200 million Chinese. The supporters of the project, however, estimate that it will save China 50 million tonnes of coal each year. A considerable saving indeed, but only in the short term.

Man, destroyer of habitats

Although habitat destruction is the main cause of extinctions, another problem is that many chemicals dumped in the environment can be deadly to vulnerable species. The introduction of alien species, far from enriching the environment, also causes a large number of species to die out. Moreover, direct removal – by hunting, fishing and collecting – has an extremely detrimental effect on natural habitats. And what are the reasons for this species removal? It is done to provide meat, medicine, decorations for people's houses and gardens, or unusual pets to impress one's neighbours.

Monkeys, like the young gorilla (left) and the greater white-nosed monkey (right), carried in this photograph by a poacher, are often killed as bush meat.

Hunted or displaced species

Invaders that drive out other species

'Biological pollution' – as the introduction of non-indigenous species is sometimes called – impoverishes the biosphere. This is the second major cause of extinction after habitat destruction.

Ancestral traditions

For thousands of years, man has been transporting living species from one place to another, even if only for agricultural purposes. Wheat, cultivated for the first time almost 7,000 years ago in Mesopotamia, thus gradually conquered the world. Maize, potatoes and tomatoes spread all over the globe within a few centuries of America being discovered by Europeans. But man not only transports crops and animals for breeding, he also takes with him a certain number of other species: pets such as dogs and cats; parasites such as fleas, mosquitoes and bacteria; and mice and rats. Rats are without doubt one of the most destructive and prolific colonizing species on Earth. More-over, 'introductions' of plants and animals were very fashionable from the 17th to the 19th centuries.

People travelled all over the world to find new and interesting species with which to enrich the plant and

Islands – first in the line of fire

Island ecosystems are particularly sensitive to introduced species. The percentage of exotic species introduced into continents may be anything up to 20%. This figure can be as high as 50% for islands (47% for Hawaii), which is even more remarkable if one considers that it was reached in only a few decades. Moreover, the invading species are generally far more deadly to local species in island environments because there is a finite amount of habitat for local species to colonize if displaced. Thus, a small parasitic fly (*Philornis downsi*), accidentally imported to the Galapagos Islands in 1997, now infests 97% of the endemic finches' nests on the archipelago, threatening all finch species there with extinction.

Maize, which is now found all over the world, is the cultivated form of teosinte, a plant that originated in Mexico. It is one of many thousands of species that man has introduced into countries outside of their continent of origin as a source of food or for decoration, hunting or fishing.

The cane toad (*Bufo marinus*) is a giant Brazilian toad that was introduced into Australia in 1935 in the hope of eliminating two pests that attacked sugar cane (the grey-backed cane beetle and the frenchie beetle). This introduction has in fact caused a far greater ecological imbalance.

animal life of their homelands. The introduction of new species into an ecosystem is a paradoxical matter, however: although in theory it should create greater diversity, it often results in a reduction in the number of species.

Troublesome invaders

Introduced species tend to proliferate. Basically, this is because these species are generally evolutionary 'success stories' – adaptable, fertile, resistant, and so forth. More importantly, however, they succeed because their new environment is generally free of pathogens and predators which are adapted to them, and this gives them a considerable advantage over indigenous organisms. Furthermore, human action favours these invasions by making the 'host' ecosystems more fragile, because a disturbed ecosystem (due to pollution, species removal, etc) is more vulnerable to invaders than a healthy one. A species that proliferates rapidly is bound to have a great impact on its new habitat.

GLOSSARY

[Pathogenic]
This adjective is used to describe any microorganism that can cause disease in a living organism. Such microorganisms include viruses, bacteria, parasites and fungi.

Map *(following pages)*

The future of around 30,000 species is threatened by overfishing and the international wildlife trade. Fish stocks in the North Pacific and the North Atlantic have almost run out. At the same time, over 350 million wild plants and animals are being removed from their habitats annually. The bush meat trade in tropical Africa also accounts for a million tonnes of animal meat a year.

The wildlife trade

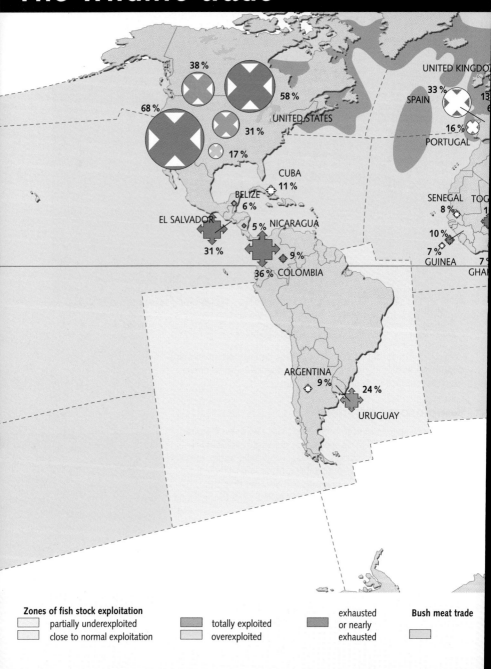

38 %

58 %

68 %

31 %

17 %

UNITED STATES

UNITED KINGDO

33 %

SPAIN

13

6

16 %

PORTUGAL

CUBA
11 %

BELIZE
6 %

SENEGAL   TOG

8 %

1

EL SALVADOR

5 % NICARAGUA

10 %

31 %

9 %

7 %

GUINEA   7

36 % COLOMBIA

GHA

ARGENTINA
9 %

24 %

URUGUAY

Zones of fish stock exploitation

- partially underexploited
- close to normal exploitation

- totally exploited
- overexploited

- exhausted
  or nearly
  exhausted

Bush meat trade

RUSSIA 8 %

BELARUS
ANCE 5 %
40 %

CHINA 18 % JAPAN 40 %

5 % 14 %

29 % 5 %
33 % 5 %
38 %

THAILAND SOUTH
KOREA 38 %

60 % 16 %
PHILIPPINES

Equator

TANZANIA
13 %

ZAMBIA 22 %
5 % MOZAMBIQUE INDONESIA
22 % 9 % 30 %

SOUTH AFRICA

22 %

0   2 000 km

scale at the equator

Main countries that import and export wild plants and animals

| import | primates | snakes | lizards | tortoises and turtles | parrots | orchids |
| export | primates | snakes | lizards | tortoises and turtles | parrots | orchids |

The rat: a great bird-killer

The black rat (*Rattus rattus*) is a prolific rodent and exceptionally adaptable. Originally from Asia Minor, this species is thought to have first reached western Europe in the holds of ships during the 4th century. Over the last five centuries, it has succeeded in colonizing even the tiniest islands inhabited by humans. It has almost always adapted well to its new environment, often massacring bird populations by plundering nests on the ground or in trees (the black rat is an excellent climber). The introduction of cats has had a similar result. Most of the dozens of bird species that have become extinct since 1800, in particular on islands in the Indian and Pacific Oceans, have disappeared because of the introduction of alien species. Today, it is estimated that one third of all birds currently considered to be endangered are victims of such 'invaders'.

There are often knock-on effects: the disappearance of hummingbirds, for example, can lead to the disappearance of the plants they pollinate. Similarly, the extinction of other insectivorous species can increase the populations of invertebrates.

Plants are killers too

In 1858, the common brushtail possum (*Trichosurus vulpecula*), a small Australian marsupial, was introduced into New Zealand for its fur. Now, around 150 years later, 70 million possums are destroying the forests of New Zealand, plundering birds' nests, eating eggs and killing chicks.

The Nile perch (*Lates niloticus*), introduced into Lake Victoria in Africa in 1954 in order to develop freshwater fishing, has wreaked havoc on what was previously one of the most diversified lake systems in the world. Due to its voracious appetite, this species alone is responsible for wiping out 200 of the 400 endemic species previously found there. And the plant kingdom is not to be outdone: the water hyacinth (*Eichornia crassipes*), an ornamental plant originally from South America, has proliferated on ponds and lakes in tropical zones all over the world. Today, it completely chokes

Admired for its pale mauve flowers, the water hyacinth, originally from South America, was introduced into Asia and Africa. Its proliferation has caused havoc to aquatic ecosystems.

Red-eared sliders (*Trachemys scripta*), which are popular as pets when small, rapidly outgrow their aquariums. When released into the wild by their thoughtless owners, they can cause indigenous turtles to die out.

these habitats, stopping light filtering beneath the surface of the water and depriving any life below of oxygen. This has terrible economic and ecological consequences.

Widespread invasion

Today, increasingly large numbers of species are being transported from one place to another. Plants are moved for agricultural purposes and also to exploit their ornamental qualities. This also occurs with animals (birds, fish, etc). However, there are other reasons for moving animals: for hunting, fishing and for the pet market. Moreover, ship's ballast (heavy material such as water, used to keep the boat steady when it has little or no cargo)

One imported species in 100 proliferates

For every 100 species introduced by man into a new environment, around a dozen adapt to the new surroundings and one proliferates. Their spread is generally brought to an end by a pathogen or a predator; however, this will not bring back the species that have disappeared as a result of the invader, and the environment will have been irreparably degraded.

has proved to be an effective means of spreading living organisms. In one American port, as many as 357 different species were found in the ballast water released by 159 Japanese cargo ships. Many larvae and other planktonic species are spread in this way. A number of molluscs and other animals also move around by clinging to the hulls of ships and boats, especially in fresh water. The network of navigable canals in Europe has allowed the zebra mussel (*Dreissena polymorpha*) from the Danube Basin to invade western waters. Fruit cargoes transported from one continent to another can also contain large numbers of invertebrates. Lastly, the creation of new communication routes (the Panama and Suez Canals, for example) has brought together animals that had previously been separated for millions of years. In one century, around 300 species have moved from the Red Sea and the Indian Ocean into the Mediterranean via the Suez Canal.

'Bush meat'

> In Africa in particular, meat from illegally killed wild animals is traded on a professional, organized basis. This bush meat trade has a disastrous effect on indigenous animals.

Pressure from local populations

The term 'bush meat' is used to describe all the animal products in a natural environment

that are used for food, whether they come from tropical forests or other more open habitats (as in the case of elephants, for example). The problem of bush meat is particularly serious in Africa, but it also has a negative impact on the animal life of Asia and South America. Local populations in tropical zones have always hunted without causing any lasting damage to the environment because the hunting was carried out by a small number of poorly equipped people. However, the situation has been changing rapidly over the last few decades. Human populations living close to wild areas – especially forests – have grown considerably, due to the rural exodus and the appalling living conditions in the shanty towns. In Africa, 90% of the rural population consumes less than half of the minimum daily protein allowance recommended by the FAO for survival, and the situation is not much better on other continents. Meat from wild animals is thus vital for these populations, both as a source of food and – more recently – a source

This poacher 'proudly' displays an arm cut from an adult gorilla, which is destined for the local bush meat market; unless – the height of bad taste – the hand ends up being turned into an ashtray and sold to trophy hunters looking for something original for their mantelpiece.

of money. However, the consumption of bush meat can lead to viruses such as Ebola and probably also AIDS being transmitted to humans.

The poaching business

Over the last 20 years, a veritable bush meat trade has been established. As a Congolese civil servant wrote in a recent report: 'Those behind this illegal trade are often highly placed people with a certain reputation, holding positions of responsibility in the civil service or politics. These people provide arms, ammunition and other material to their local representatives who, in turn, recruit gangs of poachers.

Popular bush meat species in Africa

Antelopes are the most highly sought-after species, but many other animals are also traded: primates (small monkeys, but also chimpanzees and gorillas), rhinoceroses, African elephants, hippopotamuses, African buffaloes, bush pigs, etc. Growing poverty in some regions has led to taboos about certain species (rodents, snakes and even insects) being ignored. As a result, even more havoc has been wreaked on the ecosystems.

They are real businesses (…) and their activity is so profitable that many people now specialize in this trade'. Nowadays, poachers are equipped with army rifles, sophisticated rope traps, modern means of communication, lorries, and so on.

Inadequate protection

Local consumption is gradually taking a back seat, as thousands of tonnes of meat are smoked or salted before being sent off to the cities or to other countries, and sometimes even to other continents (Europe, USA). This catastrophic situation is not improved by the lamentable state of the local nature protection organizations. At present, the creation of a new nature reserve in Africa almost automatically leads to the arrival of poachers – some of whom have travelled a long way – because they are sure of finding a high density of animals there. Moreover, these reserves are poorly protected. In the Lobeke National Park in Cameroon, a mere ten guards have to look after 200,000 hectares. To make matters worse, the guards earn less than the poachers, are not as well armed and are demoralized due to the lack of resources at their disposal.

Protected by a guard, this black rhinoceros may have a better chance than others of surviving the poachers' bullets. However, due to the lack of adequate funds to pay for its protection, the future of this species looks extremely bleak.

The impact of 'natural' medicines

Much hunting and gathering of endangered species is carried out because of the therapeutic properties attributed to them (rightly or wrongly) by various schools of traditional medicine.

The impact of traditional medicine

Around 80% of the Earth's inhabitants use only traditional medicine and have no access to modern medical facilities. In Mozambique, for example, there is one traditional healer for every 200 inhabitants, and one modern doctor for every 50,000. Moreover, even in countries with a well-established medical system, alternative medicines or those based on natural products are becoming more popular. The best-known of these systems is Chinese traditional medicine, which has hundreds of millions of devotees throughout Asia. Over 1,000 living species (80% of which are plants) are included in its pharmacopoeia. Similar systems are practised throughout the world. To describe all of these as charlatan practices which should be abolished would be both unfair and simplistic. Chinese law severely punishes any trade in substances deriving from tigers or rhinoceroses, and those who break this law risk the death penalty. Nevertheless, the trade continues on a large scale. Obviously, there is a need for dialogue between nature conservation organizations and communities relying on traditional medicine in order to try and find common solutions to these problems.

Rhino horn (pictured is a white rhinoceros) is a reputed aphrodisiac and has an extremely high market value in Yemen and Asia.

Products derived directly from the natural environment

This is a serious problem. The great majority of the 'natural' products that make up the traditional pharmacopoeias are not derived from cultivated plants or farmed animals but are

simply collected in the wild. Many of them come from endangered species, often at risk precisely because of such pharmaceutical practices.

In addition to the tiger and the rhinoceros (whose blood is highly prized as well as its horn), a very large number of animal species are exploited for medicinal purposes. These include several species of sea lions, many felines (panthers, leopards, etc), birds (vultures etc), turtles and snakes. Around 20 million sea horses (sold for US$1,000 per kilo on the black market) also die because of this trade each year.

The Chinese pharmacopoeia contains many substances derived from endangered species, such as these dried sea horses and tiger derivatives, available over the counter in this Hong Kong shop.

Medicinal plants under threat

The problem of collecting medicinal plants appears to be just as serious as that of the removal of animals. One study carried out in Europe has revealed that manufacturers of plant-based preparations import over 120,000 tonnes of plants a year from over 120 countries. Around 150 species of European plants are currently at risk as a result of this practice. For example, each year around 6,000 tonnes of yellow gentian are collected each year – 2,500 tonnes in France alone. In Spain, 75 million thyme plants are removed each year (90% are exported). Admittedly, the populations of the above plants in these two countries appear to be thriving, but it is hard to predict whether these species can stand this sort of removal for much longer. Little information is available for tropical countries, but everything appears to indicate that intensive plant collecting is also carried out there. Exports of medicinal plants from Brazil to the United States alone amount to over US$50 million. Scientists believe there is an urgent need to record all the species in question and to estimate how many are being removed.

The yellow gentian is one of the European species suffering most from plant collecting. Would it not be preferable if such species were cultivated instead?

The damage caused by fishing

Rapid advances in fishing techniques have not been accompanied by a significant growth in selectivity. More birds, mammals, turtles and young fish than ever are being decimated by new fishing practices.

Efficient but destructive techniques

Thanks to very efficient means of detection (radar, sonar, etc), industrial fishing boats can find their bearings and position themselves above shoals of fish with great accuracy.

Modern fishing vessels such as the one above, photographed off the coast of South Africa, can store thousands of tonnes of fish.

The world fishing fleet now includes many factory ships, where all stages of fish preparation, right up to freezing, are carried out. As a result, these ships can stay in the fishing areas for longer. Another problem is that some traditional fishing grounds have become very dangerous: coral reefs are often 'exploited' using dynamite and cyanide (in the Philippines, 150 tonnes of cyanide are used for this purpose every year) and lobsters are flushed out by armies of divers using gas cylinders.

Overexploited fish stocks

The FAO estimates that 60% of the world's fishing grounds are badly managed or not managed at all, and that 35% of them are overexploited. Deep-sea fish, which have a very wide range, can sometimes compensate for the pressure of fishing by increasing their fertility; at least as long as there is enough plankton. On the other hand, large, slow-growing fish, which are not as fertile (swordfish, tuna, marlin and especially sharks), are very hard hit by this pressure. For example, there has been a 42% drop in the number of marlin in the North Atlantic over the last 40 years. Species that live in a restricted habitat (sturgeons, grouper that inhabit coral reefs, etc), or those that gather in dense shoals in limited breeding grounds, can rapidly become endangered.

The highly vulnerable Atlantic cod

The Atlantic cod (*Gadus morhua*) is currently classified as vulnerable by the IUCN. According to estimates, a stock of only 38,000 tonnes of sexually mature individuals now remains. A complete fishing ban lasting five to six years would be needed for the population to return to a viable level.

Disastrous 'collateral' damage

The greatest damage inflicted by commercial fishing comes from its side effects. Trawlers scrape the seabed and the hard wire on the leading edge of the nets destroys the invertebrate animals and larvae that live there. These nets are deadly devices; in effect they are vertical walls, up to 2.5km long, that scoop up everything too large to escape through the meshes. Fishing is the principal cause of death among seals (50%), porpoises (20% of them end their lives in a fishing net), marine turtles and immature fish. Around 25% of all fish caught are

Like this sea lion, strangled by a fishing net, many marine mammals are accidentally killed by fishing hooks or in nets.

discarded because they are too small. In total, the volume of accidentally caught fish (commonly known as 'by-catch') thrown back dead into the sea is almost the same as the

amount kept. Floating lines, bearing up to 3,000 baited hooks, are also a source of danger. As a result of these practices, all 16 known species of albatross are at risk, as are 29 species of petrels. Solutions do exist: trawling nets equipped with devices which allow large animals to escape, a ban on fishing in areas where there is a very large by-catch, and so forth. But the fishing industry is quite hostile to these proposals, since they entail extra costs.

Marine turtles not only suffer collateral damage from industrial fishing (a large number die in nets) and pollution, many of them are also poached.

The extent of world trade

Around 350 million endangered plants and animals enter the international wildlife trade circuit each year. This trade is hard to control and sometimes has tragic consequences for the survival of the species.

The trade in endangered species, dead or alive, is often carried out through a network of small businesses, like this modest shop selling stuffed and mounted animals in Bangkok (Thailand).

What do a mahogany armchair, a shark's tooth pendant and a Mexican redknee tarantula have in common? Trade in all of them falls within the provisions of a convention signed by over 150 countries: the Convention on the International Trade of Endangered Species of Wild Fauna and Flora, or CITES, which came into force in 1975. CITES regulates the buying and selling of endangered species and their derivatives, such as furs, leather, bones, timber and goods made from these materials. The aim of this convention is to prevent plant and animal species from becoming extinct as a result of international trade.

Species are classified by CITES in three appendices, according to the level or type of protection they are granted. Appendix I lists the most endangered species, threatened with extinction.

CITES generally prohibits all international trade in these species. International trade in species in Appendix II may be authorized if the relevant authorities grant export certificates and permits. This will only be done if certain conditions are met. Appendix III lists species for which there are local restrictions, but that can be traded on the presentation of the appropriate permits or certificates, which are granted by member states. The trade in endangered plants and animals generates several billion dollars each year.

Millions of specimens each year

Existing statistics on the wildlife trade are not easy to evaluate because they are generally available (if at all) only on a species-by-species basis with the relevant signatory country providing information for each species within its territory. Nevertheless, according to CITES, in 1997 a total of 25,733 live primates were sold, as were 235,000 parrots, 948,000 lizards and 344,000 wild orchids. In addition, 1.6 million lizard skins, 1.5 million snake skins and around 800,000 crocodile skins were imported and exported. The USA is one of the main importers of reptiles in the world. In 1997, it imported over 1.7 million of these animals – mainly iguanas, ball pythons (*Python regius*) and boa constrictors.

A trade that is hard to stamp out

These startling figures are just the tip of the iceberg, since there are no real statistics for the illegal wildlife trade.

Illegal trade has certainly become extremely widespread and operates via a large number of decentralized networks, which the authorities have difficulty identifying and which re-form as soon as they are broken up. Those in charge of enforcing the law often receive little training, and the traffickers can easily trick them by passing off highly endangered species as other, non-endangered plants and animals.

It is indeed difficult for a non-specialist to distinguish at a glance the several dozen endangered orchid species from the 3,000 in existence. In addition, police and customs officers, who also have to control organized crime and drug trafficking, do not always appreciate the importance of trying to identify the species of a batch of parakeets or ornamental fish.

Parrots are stolen from the nest in order to meet both local demand and the demands of the international pet trade. Pictured is a young Amazon parrot captured in Central America.

Hunted or displaced species

C ompared with other major issues linked with human activity (finance, trade, health, climate, etc), the decline in biodiversity is of little interest to governments. Officially, 11,167 species are classified as threatened with extinction, but since there is still a huge proportion of the biosphere about which we know nothing, in reality this figure is likely to be in the hundreds of thousands. The following pages focus, necessarily somewhat selectively, on a few of the more significant groups of these threatened species. The size of these groups varies from a single species (the tiger) to 95% of all living organisms (invertebrates).

In order to take possession of this baby gorilla – a highly-valued prize for any trafficker in endangered species – the trafficker might also have to kill its mother and perhaps part of the clan into which it was born.

Which species are endangered?

How is an endangered species defined?

It is difficult to assess accurately whether a species is 'threatened', or indeed to what extent it is at risk. The IUCN has been working on this task for over 50 years.

The IUCN Red List

Although most of us have a good idea of what constitutes a 'threatened species', it is hard to

The concept of a threatened species is hard to define. For example, the capercaillie (*Tetrao urogallus*), whose population has declined in France, is flourishing in Scandinavia.

provide a scientific basis for the concept. The adjective 'threatened' conveys a certain notion of urgency, which is difficult to quantify, because there are many different situations in nature: abundant species that are declining; rare species whose populations are growing; species that appear stable but whose habitat is deteriorating rapidly, and so on. For over 50 years now, the IUCN (International Union for the Conservation of Nature, whose official name was changed to 'IUCN – The World Conservation Union' in 1990) has been assessing the preservation status of living organisms. It publishes the IUCN Red List of Threatened Species, which is constantly being updated. Thanks to its high level of scientific expertise (more than 10,000 scientists and experts from over 180 countries volunteer their

services to its six global commissions), together with its serious and objective approach, the IUCN has become a respected international source of reference. The threat categories defined by this institution provide an international benchmark to help with the programming of effective conservation efforts worldwide.

Categories defined by five criteria

The IUCN has defined criteria

Some IUCN categories

'Critically Endangered' This term describes a species (or taxon) facing an 'extremely high risk of extinction in the wild'.
'Endangered' A species is endangered when it is 'facing a very high risk of extinction in the wild'.
'Vulnerable' A species is vulnerable when it is 'facing a high risk of extinction in the wild'.
Other species which face lower risks and do not qualify as critically endangered, endangered or vulnerable are classified as being 'near threatened'. This is the case for species that are 'close to qualifying for or likely to qualify for a threatened category in the near future'.

The tuatara (*Sphenodon punctatus*) used to be found all over New Zealand. Its range is now limited to a few small islands.

which allow each country to assign a category to every species on its territory. These criteria take into account the main elements which define a species' state of health. They are: number of individuals; fluctuation of the population; size of the geographical range; fluctuation in the size of the range; and the extent to which populations and habitats have been fragmented.

A species only needs to fulfil one of the five criteria defining any given category for it to be included in that category. It does not matter if this species fails to meet the other criteria or if data relating to the other criteria is not available.

This system has one big advantage: species for which the number of individuals has not been counted, but whose range is restricted and in rapid decline, can thus be included in the list.

The striated caracara (*Phalcoboenus australis*), which inhabits Tierra del Fuego and the Falkland Islands, is classified by the IUCN as near threatened. There are now fewer than 500 pairs of this species left.

Although legitimate scientific estimates are allowed, fieldwork such as censuses and research into the species' distribution must still be carried out. However, the acquisition of this data is often costly and the number of species assessed still remains disappointingly low.

Map *(following pages)*

The IUCN has examined some 18,000 species and sub-species around the globe. Around 5,000 animal and 34,000 plant species are in danger of extinction in the medium to long term, whilst other species are on the very brink of extinction. However, many species that are still unknown (insects, for example) disappear without our even having been aware that they existed.

Which species are endangered?

Some endangered species

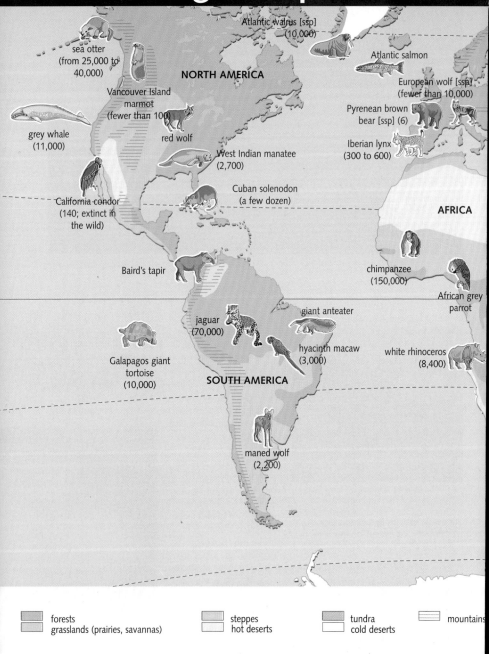

sea otter (from 25,000 to 40,000)

Atlantic walrus [ssp] (10,000)

NORTH AMERICA

Atlantic salmon

European wolf [ssp] (fewer than 10,000)

Vancouver Island marmot (fewer than 100)

Pyrenean brown bear [ssp] (6)

grey whale (11,000)

red wolf

Iberian lynx (300 to 600)

West Indian manatee (2,700)

Cuban solenodon (a few dozen)

AFRICA

California condor (140; extinct in the wild)

chimpanzee (150,000)

Baird's tapir

African grey parrot

jaguar (70,000)

giant anteater

Galapagos giant tortoise (10,000)

hyacinth macaw (3,000)

white rhinoceros (8,400)

SOUTH AMERICA

maned wolf (2,200)

forests
grasslands (prairies, savannas)

steppes
hot deserts

tundra
cold deserts

mountains

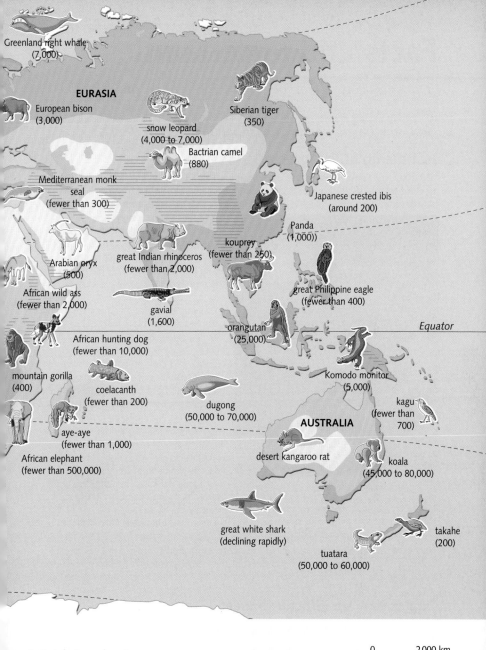

Greenland right whale
(7,000)

EURASIA

European bison
(3,000)

snow leopard
(4,000 to 7,000)

Siberian tiger
(350)

Bactrian camel
(880)

Mediterranean monk
seal
(fewer than 300)

Japanese crested ibis
(around 200)

Panda
(1,000))

Arabian oryx
(500)

great Indian rhinoceros
(fewer than 2,000)

kouprey
(fewer than 250)

African wild ass
(fewer than 2,000)

great Philippine eagle
(fewer than 400)

gavial
(1,600)

orangutan
(25,000)

Equator

African hunting dog
(fewer than 10,000)

mountain gorilla
(400)

coelacanth
(fewer than 200)

Komodo monitor
(5,000)

kagu
(fewer than
700)

dugong
(50,000 to 70,000)

AUSTRALIA

aye-aye
(fewer than 1,000)

desert kangaroo rat

koala
(45,000 to 80,000)

African elephant
(fewer than 500,000)

great white shark
(declining rapidly)

takahe
(200)

tuatara
(50,000 to 60,000)

[ssp] : indicates a subspecies

(8,400) : total population size of the species

0   2 000 km
├─────┼─────┤
scale at the equator

Facts and uncertainties

Our knowledge is still too sketchy for us to be able to define
precisely the threat levels for all categories of living organisms.
But one thing is certain: the situation is getting worse.

Just the tip of the iceberg

By 2002, the conservation status of only around 18,000 species and subspecies had been assessed by the IUCN, of which 11,167 were considered threatened to varying degrees. The only large groups to have been evaluated fully are the birds and mammals (with 4,763 and

9,946 species respectively) and 12% of the former and 24% of the latter are considered to be threatened. What can we deduce from these figures as regards the rest of the living world? Unfortunately, very little: knowing the status of 0.1% of all living species can only give a very vague idea of the fate of the remaining 99.9%; all the more so because birds and mammals are a special case. Firstly, they are generally well known and liked by humans (unlike snails, jellyfish or marine worms), and they are consequently given greater protection. International conservation programmes have been set up to save the tiger, the rhinoceros, the golden eagle, and the albatross. Secondly, birds and mammals are mainly terrestrial animals. Humans have little idea about what is going on in aquatic environments, which is one of the reasons why the condition of freshwater habitats all over the world has deteriorated so much. Thirdly, birds and mammals get special treatment because they are some of the giants of the biosphere. Animal life on this

The Iberian lynx (*Lynx pardinus*), whose population has dropped from 1,200 to under 600 in only 10 years, is very likely to be the first wild cat to become extinct for 2,000 years.

planet is mainly made up of invertebrates (and no doubt micro-organisms). If the fact that 12% of all known bird species and 24% of all known mammal species are threatened is worrying, then all the signs are that the rest of the animal kingdom is probably in an even worse state.

Targets that are difficult to meet

The IUCN's short-term goal (by 2005) is to finish assessing the status of all amphibians at the very least (around 6,000 species), reptiles (around 8,000 species) and freshwater fish (around

What is the conservation status of this little tree frog, endemic to south-east Madagascar? It is impossible to say without carrying out a comprehensive study. However, one thing is certain — the future of this species is currently threatened by deforestation.

10,000 species). In the years ahead, the organization also wants to complete the assessment of all sharks, rays and chimeras (only around 1,000 species, but they are ocean species, which are hard to assess) and freshwater molluscs (around 5,000 species). This will clearly require additional scientific resources and funds. Even after this work has been done, the IUCN will still need to determine the status of the invertebrates, plants and marine organisms. It is important to remember that not only does the list of threatened species get longer every year (partially due to improved documentation and new knowledge), but species (primates, albatrosses, petrels and penguins in particular) are being moved from the categories of least threat to those that indicate that there is an urgent need to protect them. The opposite also occurs, but the fact that this is much rarer indicates the general fragility of the status of threatened species today.

The freshwater habitats of North America

One association (TNC or The Nature Conservancy) has succeeded in assessing the conservation status of around 20,000 species in North America, including those found in freshwater habitats, which are generally poorly known. According to the TNC, 69% of the bivalves, 51% of the crayfish, 43% of the alderflies, 37% of the fish and 36% of the amphibians in North America are threatened. These figures are all the more startling if one considers that in North America the authorities and the law protect the environment, which is far from being the case in many other parts of the world.

alderfly

Threats facing invertebrates

The enormous numerical and ecological importance of invertebrates contrasts strongly with the low priority they are generally given and the great gaps in our knowledge about them.

A huge variety of species

We shall look at endangered invertebrates before we look at the better-known members of the animal kingdom in order to highlight the imbalance in our knowledge and the bias in our sympathies. Invertebrates form a mixed group which includes all animals that do not possess an internal backbone. It comprises a diverse assortment of sea urchins, jellyfish, earthworms, spiders, mussels, lobsters and butterflies, amongst others. Invertebrates have been very much neglected, bearing in mind that they represent 95% of all described species (over 75% are insects). When asked what he had learnt about the Creator after a lifetime of research, the biologist J B S Haldane (1892–1964) remarked that 'He must have had an inordinate fondness for beetles'. Indeed, one living species in four is an insect and the order *Coleoptera* (beetles) on its own contains ten times as many species as mammals, birds, reptiles, amphibians and fish put together. Future advances in science are likely to confirm the predominance of invertebrates. Biologists estimate that there are still 5,000 vertebrates waiting to be described. In contrast, there are between 5 million and 8 million undescribed

A victim of the use of pesticides in agriculture, the stag beetle (*Lucanus cervus*), one of the largest and most beautiful coleopterans in Europe, has disappeared from many regions.

species of insects and it is likely that the oceanic environments – still barely touched by science – will yield up an extraordinary wealth of other invertebrate species in the years to come.

Invertebrates at the heart of the biological cycle

Invertebrates are extremely important from an ecological point of view. Corals, made up of colonies of tiny invertebrates related to sea anemones, form the basis of one of the most diversified ecosystems on the planet. Invertebrates are also irreplaceable pollinators. A large number of plants, including agricultural species (sunflower, rape, fruit trees, etc), depend on a few species of insect – or even a single species in the case of many orchids – for their pollination.

82

Migratory locusts are a regular scourge of the African continent. However, the chemical methods used to combat them are harmful to the environment.

The disappearance of a large number of invertebrates would thus have huge repercussions on the plant world. Earthworms play a major role in fertilizing and aerating the soil. Coleopterans such as the dung beetle also help to fertilize the earth by decomposing animal dung, while ants 'clean up' most terrestrial ecosystems. On a more general level, bacteria can often not recycle matter efficiently unless it has been first broken down by invertebrates. It is also important to bear in mind that invertebrates play a key role in the large food chains, since many vertebrates are insectivores, especially birds. And in the oceans, plankton constitutes, either directly or indirectly, the basic food source for all fish.

Heavyweight invertebrates

In spite of their diminutive size, invertebrates are the planet's real heavyweights. The total biomass of all earthworms and terrestrial arthropods (spiders, insects, etc) in the United States is estimated at 1,000 kg/ha, whilst that of terrestrial vertebrates – including human beings – is in the region of 36 kg/ha, in other words 30 times less! In oceanic environments, the scales tip even further in favour of the invertebrates, due to the great mass of plankton found there.

A restricted and therefore vulnerable habitat

Wherever it has been studied, the conservation status of invertebrates has given cause for concern. Smaller and less mobile than birds and mammals, invertebrates are often more closely associated with one specific territory, and this increases their vulnerability. Thus, the Frigate Island giant tenebrionid beetle (*Polposipus herculeanus*) lives only on the dead trees of one small island (Frigate Island) in the Seychelles. As for the xerces blue (*Glaucopsyche xerces*), a butterfly endemic to the coastal sand dune systems of the San Francisco Bay area, it has the sad distinction – as a result of habitat loss due to urban development – of being the first insect species to have become officially extinct in the United States. However, the destruction of natural habitats is a global phenomenon, and growing numbers of other species, which often disappear without our even having been aware of their existence, are going the way of the xerces blue. The construction of watercourses also causes considerable damage. It is estimated that 20% of all North American insects are threatened by this kind of development. Many flying insects, in particular dragonflies, damselflies and mayflies, are in fact aquatic during the larval phase of their life.

Mayflies are particularly vulnerable: almost one in two species is threatened in the United States. In Europe, the semi-aquatic raft spider (*Dolomedes fimbriatus*) is declining alarmingly due to the drying out of wetland habitats. The construction of dams, often to control flooding, has caused many areas rich in invertebrate species to disappear.

Dragonflies are threatened by the decline in wetlands and the deterioration in the quality of the water in which they spend their larval phase.

Pesticides kill the harmless as well as the harmful

Phytophagous insects, which constitute the majority of insects, are frequently associated with a single plant species, and this makes them extremely vulnerable. Modern agriculture favours the more productive crops, which are not very resistant to insects, and so farmers use large quantities of insecticides. These products are generally tested to make sure they do not harm vertebrates, but they often wreak havoc amongst the so-called 'non-target' insect populations, which do no harm to the crops and are

Twenty-five times cheaper than a bird

American financial statistics highlight the lack of interest shown in invertebrates when it comes to the financing of conservation, even in nature conservation areas. In 1991, each species of protected bird received US$1.1 million towards its future conservation. This figure dropped to US$684,000 for mammals. As for protected invertebrates (of which there are very few), they were only allocated US$44,000 per species, 25 times less than birds!

[Phytophagous]
Used to describe animals, usually insects, which feed on plants (leaves, stalks, fruit, pollen, tree stumps, etc.)
[Coprophagous]
used to describe animals, such as dung beetles, which feed on animal dung and thus play an essential role in decomposing it.

simply unlucky enough to be in the wrong place at the wrong time. In an attempt to restrict the use of pesticides, biological control is sometimes used. This involves introducing a parasite or a predator of the unwanted species, which itself has often been introduced. However, the effects of this can be disastrous. The new parasite frequently attacks local species and sometimes prefers them to the intended target. On Hawaii, 83% of the parasites recorded on local butterfly species were originally introduced during biological control programmes. Similarly, some of the substances used to treat worm infections in cattle (ivermectin in particular) are toxic. These products decimate coprophagous invertebrates and the subsoil fauna, interrupting the cattle dung recycling process.

For decades, crops have been sprayed with pesticides or herbicides on an industrial scale (here in New Zealand). This practice pollutes many natural ecosystems and has a detrimental effect on invertebrate populations.

Which species are endangered?

Are the great apes doomed?

Great ape populations are declining dramatically. There is a great risk that soon the study of our closest relatives will only be possible in zoos.

A disaster waiting to happen

Amongst the primates, the great apes (gorilla, chimpanzee, bonobo and orangutan) are on

The great apes (from left to right and top to bottom: bonobo, orangutan and mountain gorilla) are, biologically speaking, man's closest relatives. They are well on the way to becoming extinct.

The other primates: not much better off

The status of all primates gives great cause for concern, as their numbers are declining rapidly. They have been badly affected by hunting, especially bush meat hunting (most affected are the greater white-nosed monkey, the chimpanzee and the African baboon). Other threats include deforestation (affecting orangutans, South American monkeys and Malagasy lemurs), the trade in young primates, animal experimentation and trophy hunting. Thus, over the last five years, the number of threatened species of primates has risen dramatically. After six years of research, scientists have concluded that the Miss Waldron's red colobus (*Procolobus badius waldroni*) has become extinct, the first primate to do so in the 20th century. This monkey, often hunted for its meat, has not been seen for 30 years.

the verge of extinction and some say it is inevitable that they will die out. These large animals are present in low numbers, and their reproductive cycle is particularly slow. In addition, most species of great apes inhabit forests, especially tropical forests, which are one of the natural environments that are disappearing most rapidly. The extinction of these apes would be a particularly serious disaster, as we still have a lot to learn from them about our own nature and origins – after all, humans share 99% of a chimpanzee's genes. Relationships within the great ape societies have only been studied for around 30 years. The social relations that researchers have discovered are truly amazing, being based on complex systems of alliance, loyalty and betrayal. Unique social strategies among the great apes have come to light and scientists have described the existence of subtle, differentiated personalities. This work has only just begun and there is a high risk that it will never be completed, due to a lack of subject matter.

Dwindling populations

It appears that the populations of orangutan, a species that mainly lives on Sumatra and Borneo, consist of only 14,000 to 110,000 individuals (the huge margin of error is instructive). The type of forest they inhabit is one of the most sought after and actively exploited on Earth, both for timber and for planting oil palms. Properly protected areas need to be created urgently. There are only 45,000 gorillas left, including a mere 300 mountain gorillas (*Gorilla beringei*) – the more endangered of the two gorilla species, which lives in the Democratic Republic of Congo, Rwanda and Uganda. The three subspecies of chimpanzee (*Pan troglodytes*) comprise around 200,000 individuals, but their numbers are declining very rapidly. The most endangered, *Pan troglodytes verus*, has been reduced to only 17,000 individuals. The number of bonobos (*Pan paniscus*) – cousins of the chimpanzee that exhibit truly astonishing behaviour and habits and particularly sophisticated social relations – has dropped to only 13,000. And the status of the family Hylobatidae – gibbons (*Hylobates* spp) and siamangs (*Symphalangus syndactylus*) – which live in South-East Asia, is equally critical.

The decline of the tiger

The tiger, a perfect symbol of nature in the wild, is disappearing in spite of the conservation measures apparently in place. This does not bode well for other species.

Constantly falling numbers

At the beginning of the 20th century, around 300,000 tigers inhabited a vast area stretching from the Caspian Sea to the Far East. Only 100,000 remained in 1945 and 15,000 in 1970. Current numbers are estimated at between 5,000 and 7,500. Of the eight subspecies of tigers that used to inhabit our planet, three have disappeared since 1945. Of the remaining five, the South China subspecies (*Panthera tigris amoyensis*) is the most critically endangered, and it is estimated that there are only around 30 left in the wild. Tigers are now found only in around a dozen countries, but it is India (with the famous Bengal tiger [*Panthera tigris tigris*]) that has the largest tiger population, probably over half the total species.

'Project Tiger' was launched in India in the early 1970s. A conflict between the rights of local village communities bordering the reserves and the conservation efforts resulted in the project being wrecked.

Not everyone is interested in conservation

The tiger's future has everything stacked against it. Its status as a large carnivore, and occasionally as a man-eater, is unlikely to win it any support from local populations. Its nutritional requirements are considerable, and hunting and human activity have reduced the amount of game available. It lives mainly in forests, an environment that is shrinking fast. Its exceptional fur is highly sought after. Most importantly, it has become a cult animal in Chinese traditional medicine, which has a billion followers throughout the world. Practically every part of the tiger's body (blood, brains, testicles, tail, stomach, etc) is supposed to play some therapeutic role, with the bones being the most highly prized. A freshly killed tiger is worth around US$6,000 in its country of origin; once properly marketed, its different body parts can bring in US$5 million. The average monthly income in the Asian countries where the tiger lives is rarely more than US$10. In an economic climate such as this, the tiger's commercial value encourages poaching, which has never been eliminated, especially since it is 'regulated' by the local authorities and these are often in the pockets of organized crime. Saving the tiger requires radical and costly policies in order to eradicate this illegal trade. These policies need to be supported by local populations, whom it is vital to interest in the protection of the species.

The cheetah (*Acinonyx jubatus*) is steadily declining.

Endangered big cats

The tiger is particularly threatened but many other big cats are also in a critical situation. They are at the top of the food chain and are thus particularly badly affected by the expansion of human activity. This is true of the ocelot population (9,000) in Latin America, the snow leopard (5,000) in Asia, the Iberian lynx (600) in Europe and the cheetah (25,000) in Africa. The lion, once found all over Africa and as far afield as Asia Minor, has disappeared from most of its historic range, and especially from the Moroccan Atlas Mountains (where it was last observed in 1922).

Cause for concern

The decline of the tiger is particularly worrying because it shows man's obvious inability to stop species disappearing. It is difficult to imagine a more famous and admired animal than the tiger: countless books and films have been devoted to the species, costly environmental campaigns have been carried out to protect it and its almost universal popularity should make it an easy cause to defend. How can subsoil invertebrates be saved if we cannot even save the tiger?

The ocelot (*Leopardus pardalis*), a small American nocturnal cat which is highly prized for its fur, is listed in Appendix I of CITES (in other words, all trade in the animal is banned).

Which species are endangered? **89**

Sharks: the hunter hunted

Sharks, large oceanic predators, are suffering the same fate as their terrestrial counterparts. Although they have few natural enemies, many species are showing a rapid decline in numbers due to human activity.

The **great white shark** (*Carcharodon carcharias*) has suffered greatly at the hands of trophy hunters, who like to have their photos taken beside a dead shark or to hang its huge jawbone in their living rooms.

Victims of collateral damage

The 400 or so species of sharks in our oceans have practically no predators apart from other sharks. Sharks have a long life (up to 70 years) and, like most large animals at the top of the food chain, reach sexual maturity quite late (often not until they are 20 years old) – when an animal has no predators, there is no evolutionary need for it to breed early or in large quantities. Unfortunately for sharks, which have inhabited our planet for 400 million years, one predator suddenly appeared several decades ago: *Homo sapiens*.

Most of the sharks that die as a result of human intervention are killed accidentally. Fishermen catch them in their nets or on their lines when they are looking for other species.

All the same, the sharks are dead when they are thrown back into the water. In 1995, 40,000 blue sharks were killed in this way by American fishermen in the North Atlantic and in the Gulf of Mexico. Very rarely declared, these so-called 'by-catches' have been estimated at a total of 700,000 tonnes for 1991 alone, an amount equal to the official catch.

These sharks' fins drying in the sun on Borneo will be sold to the Chinese market.

Growing commercial interest

In recent years, there have been major developments in commercial shark fishing. Sharks' fins are considered a delicacy in Asia, and their export figures have doubled over the last decade. The barbaric practice of obtaining the fins – cutting them off on board fishing boats while the animals are still alive and then throwing the mutilated sharks back into the water – is on the increase. The best that can be said for it is that it avoids storage problems. Shark liver oil, very rich in vitamin A, is also consumed, as is the animal's flesh; the spiny dogfish shark (marketed as 'rock shark' or 'rock salmon') is particularly popular in Great Britain. Sharks are also used in medicinal preparations. Shark liver provides the precious squalene, a fatty substance used in cosmetics and pharmaceuticals. In addition, shark cartilage is said to prevent or arrest cancer. Although it is doubtful that this cartilage is really effective, it certainly generates a great deal of money. One factory alone in Costa Rica reportedly turns 2.8 million sharks into cartilage pills each year. The dusky shark (*Carcharinus obscurus*) is one of the most endangered species in the world, and its North Atlantic populations have dropped by 80% in only a few decades. Thanks to the size of its liver (which accounts for up to 25% of the animal's body weight), the basking shark (*Cetorhinus maximus*), which is a giant plankton eater, is of great commercial importance. Finally, the great white shark (*Carcharodon carcharias*), the unwitting star of *Jaws*, has been a highly sought-after trophy ever since the film was released, despite the small size of its populations. The lower jaw of a great white shark sells for US$4,000 on the black market.

The blue shark (*Prionace glauca*) is a frequent 'collateral victim' of industrial fishing.

A strategic ecological role

It is estimated that 30 million to 100 million sharks of all species are killed each year. Inevitably, this has a great effect on the whole marine ecosystem, given the role the sharks play in it. In the animal kingdom, large predators keep the populations of their prey species healthy by selectively removing the diseased and handicapped individuals. These predators also help to create a balance between different species.

Which species are endangered?

Plants: the basis of life

The plant kingdom is currently undergoing a great upheaval, which will inevitably have repercussions on all other living organisms.

✎ **Plants** that were once common, such as the cornflower (*Centaurea cyanus*), are today at risk due to the increased use of herbicides in agriculture.

The basis for life on Earth

The biosphere (all living organisms and their environment) is supported by plants. They alone are able, through photosynthesis, to transform carbon dioxide, present in the atmosphere, into carbohydrates – sugars that are then used as 'fuel' and building blocks by all other living forms. Each year, plants produce a total of 120 billion tonnes of organic carbon (carbohydrates). Plants also carry out many other ecological tasks: they produce oxygen, prevent soil erosion, regulate water flow and even stabilize the climate at a local level. All of this makes the threat currently facing the plant kingdom particularly worrying.

Two thirds of all plants will be endangered by the end of the century

This statistic constitutes a threat that, although difficult to calculate accurately, is nonetheless real. According to the North American organization TNC (The Nature Conservancy), one third of all plant species on the American continent are at risk. In 2002, the IUCN recorded 5,714 threatened plant species on the planet. However, the number of plant species that have been assessed is very low (4% of the total), so this figure is very much an underestimate. Of greater significance is the status of the conifers, the only major plant group to have been comprehensively assessed on a global scale. It contains 140 threatened species, (16% of all conifers). In addition, the 16th International Botanical Congress of 1999, which was attended by over 5,000 botanists from all over the world, concluded that, unless something is done, two-thirds of all existing plant species will be at risk by the end of the 21st century.

✎ **On the slopes of Mount Kenya,** the original plants (here the giant lobelia) stabilize fragile soils, play an essential role in the water cycle and provide nectar for specialized birds (such as sunbirds).

In the tropical forest, thousands of organisms occupy different ecological niches, which are found on all levels, from stumps of trees to treetops.

Incalculable consequences

The extinction of certain plant species will be partially compensated for by the appearance of others, which will replace – though not necessarily exactly match – the functions of those that have disappeared. However, a rapid drop in plant diversity will still have a great impact on that of other living organisms. A large number of invertebrates are closely linked to one particular plant species, or perhaps a handful of species. This is also true of fungi: we are only beginning to discover the variety of their alliances with higher plants, and it appears that each higher plant species usually occurs in association with an average of around 50 species of fungi. In addition, most trees are considered to be carrier species, especially the large tropical trees. Indeed, each individual tree (the surface of which is often home to many parasitic and epiphytic plants) carries a whole ecosystem made up of several food chains. These chains include phytophagous invertebrates, which in turn form the prey of larger invertebrates, which are then eaten by insectivorous vertebrates (especially reptiles), and so on. If we consider that a single tropical tree can hold several hundred species of beetles, we get an idea of the diversity that would be lost if the carrier were to disappear.

Irreversible destruction

In many habitats, the disappearance of certain plants does not leave the way open for others to replace them. This is the case for arid environments, extinctions caused by overgrazing or where excessive species removal has hit precisely those plants capable of surviving there. All hopes of the ecosystem being regenerated then become hypothetical.

Which species are endangered? **93**

Lesser-known organisms

Certain categories of living organisms – significant ones at that – have been so poorly studied that it is impossible to estimate how their numbers are changing.

The invisible world beneath our feet

Certain groups of tiny living organisms are at present almost unknown to science. They are, however, extremely numerous: it is estimated that in an 'average' temperate deciduous forest over 7,000 invertebrates inhabit the soil that would be covered by a size 9 or 10 shoe. These animals belong to a wide variety of groups: worms, spiders, crustaceans, insects, etc. The nematodes (very small worms, generally invisible to the human eye) are a case in point: only 4,500 species have been described, whilst there are probably over one million on our planet. However, these tiny organisms, which

proliferate in all environments (up to 3 million individuals per square metre of soil), are of considerable ecological importance. How do these huge populations react to the use of fertilizers, pesticides, atmospheric pollution, climate change, and so forth? Which species are declining and which are proliferating? We have no idea. Moreover, it would appear that huge populations of unique invertebrates inhabit the depths of the sea – from the dark bed up to the sunlit zone, where small amounts of light penetrate (around 200 metres deep). Once again, we know virtually nothing about the species found here and even less about their conservation status.

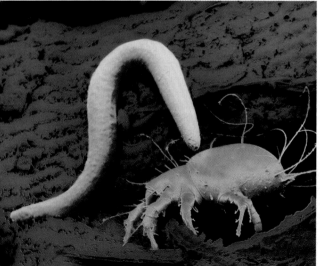

Acarids and nematode worms, which dominate the subsoil fauna, are still very poorly known. These minute organisms play a crucial role in fertilizing the soil.

The enigma of micro-organisms

Our ignorance of the world of micro-organisms – in other words, single-celled organisms – is even greater. Around 4,000 species of microscopic fungi have been described, whilst in reality there must be around one or two million. Their ecological role, especially in the carbon cycle, is extremely important. Another example is all oceanic organisms between 0.2 and 2 micrometres in size (a micrometre is a thousandth of a millimetre). These are classified as picoplankton. Picoplankton generally contains chlorophyll, and thus synthesizes enormous quantities of oxygen. It forms the basis of food for larger types of plankton and, in certain ocean zones, accounts for 80% of the biomass. However, less than 30 species of picoplankton have been described to date. The oceanographers' task is made all the more difficult since most of these organisms are very hard to tell apart, even with the most powerful of microscopes.

Under this carpet of dead leaves one gram of humus contains up to ten billion bacteria and a whole host of other tiny organisms that recycle organic matter, breaking it down into small molecules which can be reabsorbed as nutrients by the trees.

What is a microbe species?

It is not easy to talk about species in the universe of micro-organisms. A species is generally defined as a group of similar organisms which are able to interbreed and produce viable, fertile offspring. However, in single-celled organisms, many individuals multiply using asexual reproduction or exchange small fragments of genetic material in unusual ways.

Nevertheless, they possess certain biological features (reaction to different molecules, reaction to light, optimum temperature, etc) that clearly show they are all very different from one another. A similar problem occurs with bacteria, which can be found everywhere, since each one of us has around 250 million on his or her skin alone: only 4,000 out of a possible one million species of bacteria have been described. And we should not forget the viruses (3,500 types identified), of which there are probably around 500,000 on the planet.

Which species are endangered? **95**

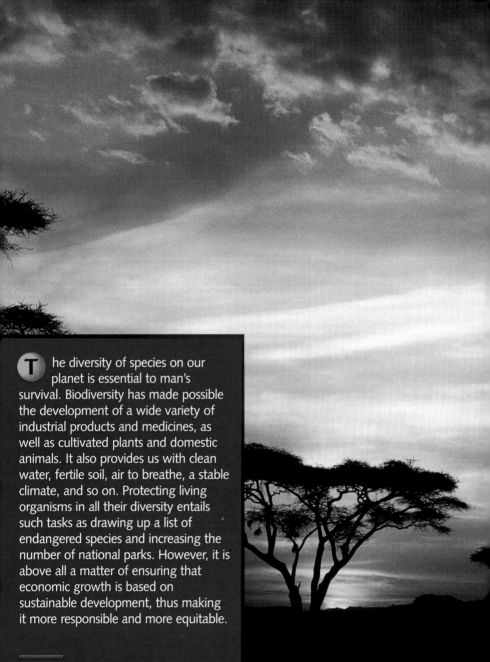

T he diversity of species on our planet is essential to man's survival. Biodiversity has made possible the development of a wide variety of industrial products and medicines, as well as cultivated plants and domestic animals. It also provides us with clean water, fertile soil, air to breathe, a stable climate, and so on. Protecting living organisms in all their diversity entails such tasks as drawing up a list of endangered species and increasing the number of national parks. However, it is above all a matter of ensuring that economic growth is based on sustainable development, thus making it more responsible and more equitable.

Today, habitat conservation, as in the Serengeti National Park, Tanzania, is a matter of high priority

Sustainable action
and conservation

Why should species be protected?

The need to maintain biodiversity is supported by substantial ecological and economic arguments. However, we also have a moral duty to conserve living organisms.

The disappearance of natural environments brings a whole host of extinctions in its wake: the deforestation of tropical environments will sound the death knell for tree-dwelling spider monkeys like this one.

Conflict of interests

Inevitably, practical efforts to conserve species come up against conflicts of interest. Depriving poor populations of a natural resource, whether overexploited or not, can constitute a real threat to their wellbeing – especially where certain forms of hunting, fishing, collecting, firewood gathering or farming are forbidden. In the absence of compensatory measures, prohibitions of this kind can have drastic consequences.

More often, conservation gets in the way of private interests that have no vital social dimension. Forceful economic arguments are then put forward to defend these private enterprises. Those in favour of a new dam will point out the advantages of cheap water and energy; those who want to set up mines or factories will highlight the jobs and wealth they will create; those who champion pesticides and fertilizers will talk of the threat of reduced crop yields. The authorities are, on the whole, far more receptive to these arguments than to those of environmentalists, who are often seen as idealists with their heads in the clouds. However, healthy ecosystems provide a wealth of free, natural resources that are essential for human communities; the cost of replacing these resources would be astronomical.

A natural drinking-water factory

A water purification plant capable of supplying the city of New York with drinking water would cost US$6—8 billion. The city chose instead to spend US$1.5 billion on protecting the Catskill and Delaware water tables, which have provided the city with naturally purified drinking water for decades, against urban development. This is an outstanding example of the economic benefits to be gained from the protection of natural ecosystems.

Carbon storage

Large, complex ecosystems such as the oceans or the soil/subsoil complex play an essential role in storing carbon – a waste product we generate in enormous quantities in the form of carbon dioxide – and in transforming it (by photosynthesis, for example). Each year, the world's forests are responsible for fixing over 100 billion tonnes of carbon dioxide. If the populations of all these ecosystems – whose species composition is still poorly recorded – lose some of their species, their ability to carry out this task might be compromised, and this would speed up global warming.

The importance of the water cycle

The water cycle, which is central to all life, is also highly dependent on natural ecosystems. Forests help to prevent flooding, stop groundwater (and thus rivers) from periodically drying up and can

Many mangrove swamps have been destroyed and turned into fish farms or even seaside resorts and marinas. This is a catastrophe for the countless aquatic organisms that breed in these habitats.

also guard against soil erosion and landslides. Deforestation generally leads to floods, soil loss and a drier climate. The disappearance of wetlands has an equally detrimental effect on the water cycle. Other major biological cycles such as the oxygen and nitrogen cycles are also dependent on living organisms and their diversity. Oxygen is produced by plants – mainly large forests – which release almost 100 billion tonnes of this gas into the atmosphere each year. The nitrogen cycle, meanwhile, is particularly dependent on certain species of plants and bacteria.

> **Map** (following pages)
>
> Zoos are fast becoming places of refuge for endangered species. However, the conservation of animals and plants depends above all on the creation of protected areas. Most of the 4,500 protected areas in the world are too small to guarantee the long-term survival of the species found there. The few reserves that are large enough to conserve entire ecosystems are located in zones with very low population density (polar regions) and not in areas with high biological diversity (tropical rainforests).

The world's protected areas

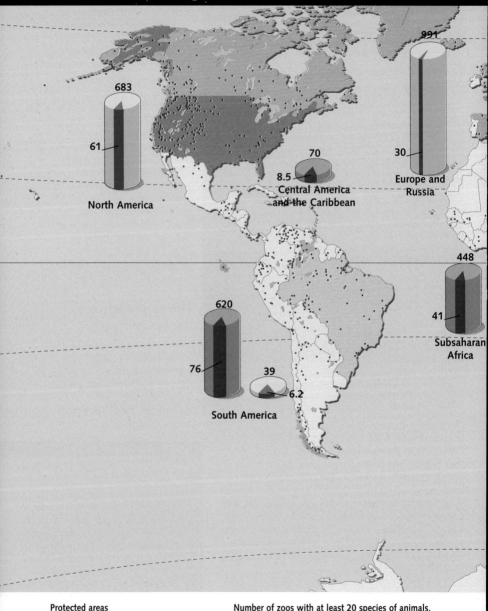

683
61
North America

991
30
Europe and Russia

70
8.5
Central America and the Caribbean

448
41
Subsaharan Africa

620
76
South America

39
6.2

Protected areas

over one million hectares
over 100,000 hectares

Number of zoos with at least 20 species of animals, birds or fish in 2001

over 100 zoos
31–100

11–30
fewer than 11

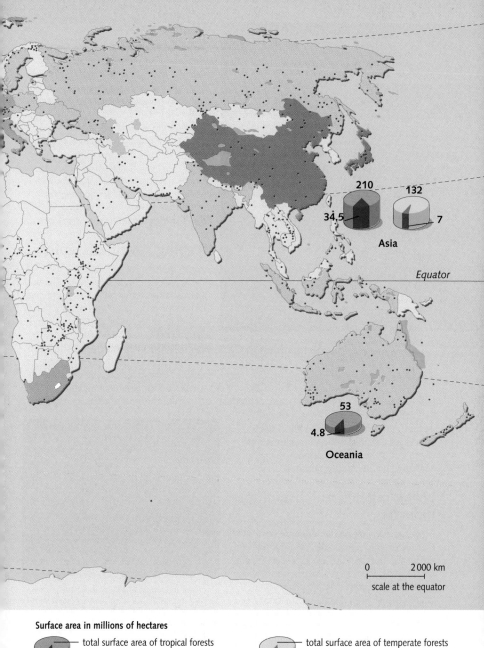

210

132

34,5

7

Asia

Equator

53

4.8

Oceania

0   2 000 km

scale at the equator

Surface area in millions of hectares

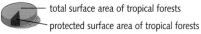
total surface area of tropical forests
protected surface area of tropical forests

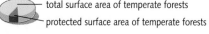
total surface area of temperate forests
protected surface area of temperate forests

This rare tree, the triangle palm (*Neodypsis decaryi*), part of the world's natural heritage, benefits from a reserve specially created for the species in south-east Madagascar.

Waste removal

Natural ecosystems also eliminate a substantial proportion of our waste products. Many relatively toxic substances which are released into rivers are consumed or recycled by living organisms and are absorbed by the forests growing alongside the watercourses. This 'purification' is effective, even if limited. The sludge from sewage treatment plants, once it has been dispersed by nature or spread on fields, is likewise transformed into living matter. When microbic and invertebrate animals are disturbed, these processes slow down or even stop.

Keeping agriculture going

Farming is the human activity most closely linked to living organisms. The wild 'cousins' of both our cultivated plants and our livestock constitute a gene pool that is and will be essential for improving and adapting agricultural production, especially if climate change leads to a rise in temperatures or an increase in the aridity of certain regions. Moreover, plant growth and development rely on pollinating animals (bees, bumblebees, butterflies and even bats in some latitudes), animals that break up and aerate the soil (moles, worms) and decomposers (bacteria, fungi, insects, etc). If any of these organisms were wiped out, it would have terrible consequences for food production.

Living organisms – useful for industry

Industry also uses products derived from living organisms: cotton, wool, silk, rape (for fuel and lubricants), leather, latex, wood, and many others still to be discovered. Similarly, 40–70% of all medicines produced by the pharmaceutical industry derive from natural substances. Scientists at the world's largest cancer research institution, the American National Cancer Institute,

The red jungle fowl (*Gallus bankiva*) from India, the wild ancestor of most of our domestic chickens, constitutes an indispensable gene pool for improving domestic breeds.

have been studying plants for decades in order to try to develop new anti-cancer drugs. Over 35,000 extracts have already been tested, leading to the discovery of over 800 active molecules. The anti-cancer molecule Taxol, for example, was originally isolated from the bark of the Pacific yew (*Taxus brevifolia*) from western North America. Today, 40 years after its discovery, Taxol is still a best-seller for the multinational company that manufactures and markets it.

The moral dilemma

However, over and above the ecological and economic reasons already mentioned, living organisms should be protected for ethical reasons. Living forms are a valuable commodity in themselves and are sometimes described as our 'natural heritage'. 'Usefulness' is not everything. Would we knock down a 500-year-old cathedral to make room for a supermarket? The latter would no doubt be more frequently visited and thus be more profitable. Just like our historical heritage, our natural heritage deserves to be protected. We have inherited from our ancestors a planet with an extraordinary wealth of natural organisms. Do we have the right to pass on a dirty, impoverished planet to our children?

Many plants (including many cultivated species) cannot live without insects, especially bees, which pollinate their flowers.

Zoos and botanical gardens

The inexorable disappearance of habitats presents us with the problem of having to keep certain species in captivity while they wait to be reintroduced into the environment (with no guarantee of success).

Conservation tools

Concern for the future of many species of animals and plants has altered the philosophy and status of zoos and animal parks. These institutions have partly become conservation tools or sanctuaries for species that are extinct in the wild (currently estimated at around 60 species). The first institution to assume such a role was Warsaw Zoo in 1923, when it was discovered that the last wild herd of European bison (*Bison bonasus*), which lived in Poland, had not survived World War I. The zoo's authorities made a list of all the European establishments that housed European bisons and launched a programme to rebuild the population based on 54 individuals. The programme worked well and, since then, the animals have been reintroduced successfully into several sites with suitable environments, notably the primary forest of Bialowieza in Poland.

Today, around 3,000 European bison survive thanks to Warsaw Zoo's initiative in 1923, when they decided to save the species by rebuilding it from captive animals.

The golden lion tamarin (*Leontopithecus rosalia*, on the right) and the hyacinth macaw (*Anodorhynchus hyacinthinus*, on the left) breed in captivity. But their survival in the wild hangs in the balance.

Modern Noah's Arks

Today, many organizations devote themselves to the difficult task of conservation. Complex laboratory techniques (artificial insemination, in vitro fertilization and the conservation of embryos at extremely low temperatures) are used to breed some of the most endangered species. Animals' living quarters have been considerably improved and some animals are even removed from public view during breeding periods. Zoos, animal parks and aquariums are often organized in networks in order to share scientific expertise and to avoid inbreeding depression (a decrease of vigour or yield due to inbreeding) when crossbreeding animals. However, these zoos and parks, of which there are far too few, can only play a very minor role in conserving living things. Only 25 species close to extinction have been saved in this way. These include the above-mentioned European bison, Przewalski's horse, Père David's deer, the Arabian oryx and the California condor. The reason these institutions cannot do more is that they have neither the space nor the means to cope with all animals that are at risk (probably around 2,000 vertebrates).

The Sumatran rhinoceros

The Sumatran rhinoceros (*Dicerorhinus sumatrensis*) is one of the most highly threatened species of mammal on the planet – it is currently classified as critically endangered by the IUCN. There are only around 150–300 individuals left, living in their forest habitat (an ecosystem which is in rapid decline). In spite of great efforts, it has not been possible to breed it in captivity. Another possible solution would have been to spend the money used for trying to breed this rhinoceros in captivity on saving its natural habitat.

The limitations of zoos

Keeping animals in captivity brings with it a large number of specific problems created by a lack of space, unsuitable temperatures, artificial social conditions (with solitary animals being kept in groups and sociable animals being isolated) and the constant presence of humans. Captivity generates stress, which can produce endocrine disorders, ulcers (frequent in captivity), reproductive problems (spontaneous abortions) and behavioural disorders (mechanical rocking of the body or the head, walking round in circles, etc).

Costly and difficult reintroductions

It is unrealistic to think we can recreate a Noah's Ark to save endangered species, especially if we have allowed their habitats to disappear. There is no point carrying out captive conservation if it does not lead to the successful reintroduction of the captive-bred species into its natural environment. Reintroductions of this kind are extremely costly operations and particularly difficult. They presuppose the existence (or creation) of a suitable environment into which the animals can be released – an ecosystem from which the factor that led the animal to become extinct in the first place has been removed. If, for example, poaching was the cause, it is absurd to reintroduce the species before this threat has been eliminated. The recreated populations then need to be monitored for many months or even years.

The example of the Arabian oryx (*Oryx leucoryx*) is instructive. In the 1980s, this antelope was on the verge of extinction. The last individuals living in the wild were captured and placed in a special reserve. A semi-captive breeding programme was started, which produced very good results. Oryx were released into the desert in Oman. In 1997, the population of this single herd of wild Arabian oryx was estimated at 400 individuals. Two years later its numbers had dropped to

The reintroduction of captive-bred animals (here orangutans on Sumatra) often requires a long supportive feeding regime before the animals become self-reliant. And success is not guaranteed.

Feeding protected species, such as these storks, eliminates the animals' natural fear of humans, thereby causing many problems.

fewer than 100. The return of poaching and illegal hunting, aimed at supplying the private collections of rich emirs in the Gulf, had wiped out years of work.

Changes in behaviour

Certain types of natural behaviour, linked to life in the wild, are lost when animals are held in captivity. Hunting techniques, ways of escaping from predators, how to make shelters, nests and dens – these are not written in the genes, but have to be learnt from an animal's parents or the rest of its group, at least in the case of mammals and birds. Once these habits are lost, trying to recreate them is a long, laborious process, in which humans often have to compensate for the lack of a proper social group (for example, by artificial feeding or by eliminating predators).

A weakened gene pool

The appearance of a certain amount of inbreeding can seldom be avoided in captive-bred populations, which by their nature are small. However, when close relatives are crossed, juvenile mortality is 33% higher than in young animals with non-related parents.

This phenomenon, known as 'inbreeding depression', also causes a reduction in fertility, growth imbalances and an increased vulnerability to disease. Unfavourable genes, which would have been eliminated naturally in the wild, can also spread in captivity, where animals are cared for and fed by humans. There is a risk that features which favour captivity and handicap life in the wild will become established: fearful animals, subjected to stress, will have a harder time surviving in a zoo than those that are less wary. Eventually, the less wary animals will become more numerous in the population. Then, when the time comes to reintroduce the species, there is a high risk that its ability to survive in the wild will be impaired.

And what about plants?

Initially designed to supply medicinal plants and introduce exotic species, botanical gardens today are geared towards species conservation. Unfortunately, botanical gardens are far more numerous in the northern hemisphere (540 in Europe and 290 in North America) than in the southern hemisphere, where biodiversity is concentrated. There are fewer than 100 in the whole of South America, where over 90,000 species of plants are to be found. Gene banks are also widespread. These focus on agriculture, where seeds and cellular cultures of a wide variety of plants are kept, particularly those of endangered species. However, such facilities are costly, especially since it is necessary from time to time to cultivate plants again from scratch because the stored samples can lose their germinating power after a certain time. According to the FAO, the funding granted to these institutions is decreasing worldwide, despite an increased need for this kind of conservation work.

Protecting wildlife and wilderness

The current priority is the creation of a network of protected areas, especially in the 'hotspots', with significant funding and support from local populations.

In-depth studies, carried out in the Amboseli Game Reserve in Kenya, have thrown light on the subtle social relationships among savanna elephants.

'Umbrella' species

By selecting emblematic species, especially large animals, useful protection can be obtained for the ecosystems they inhabit, and this in turn safeguards a number of smaller, less prestigious species. For example, the Atlantic salmon (*Salmo salar*) and the Danube salmon (*Hucho hucho*) benefit from EC funding which has made it possible to build fish ladders and passages on previously insurmountable dams. When well built, these ladders and passages are also used by dozens of other species of fish, whose chances of survival

Breeding animals in protected areas

Protected areas are often the location for interesting initiatives such as local 'farms' for highly prized animals, from crocodiles to birds and butterflies. These farms, located in the middle of protected areas, favour the multiplication of the target species. Only a fraction of the population is removed for commercial purposes, leaving the rest of the animals protected.

108

Programmes to reintroduce the Alpine ibex (*Capra ibex*) have been successfully implemented in several countries.

are thus enhanced. Improvements in the water quality, made to help the salmon, also benefit other species. Similarly, recent measures to protect the eastern imperial eagle (*Aquila heliaca*) in Hungary have also helped to conserve the brown hare and some of the small carnivores that the eagles feed on by helping to limit the impact of industrial agriculture.

Too few protected areas

It is only possible to protect species if the ecosystems to which they are intimately linked are protected as well, so as to conserve the as yet uninvestigated (or simply less recognizable) organisms of the living world. Created in the USA in 1872, Yellowstone was the world's first national park. Today, there are over 13,000 protected areas worldwide, ranging in size from several hectares to tens of thousands of square kilometres. Taken together, the world's protected areas represent 3.5% of the total surface of the globe, spread out over 4,500 sites. Although that might seem a high number, in reality our natural heritage still does not enjoy sufficient protection. Firstly, many reserves are too small, at least for large animals, or they do not cater for all the requirements of the species that live there. Secondly, these areas are more numerous in temperate zones (in industrial countries) than in tropical ones, yet tropical zones are the parts of the planet that are of crucial importance because of their high degree of biodiversity.

Lastly, even in rich countries, protected areas are often located in sparsely populated regions. France is a good example of this. Lagging far behind in nature protection (the first national park was not created until 1963), today France has seven national parks, five of which are situated in mountainous regions – areas that are certainly spectacular, but that are sparsely populated. The biodiversity is relatively low, even if it is more fragile than elsewhere. On the other hand, in the Mediterranean region of France, which has a higher biodiversity and a larger number of endemic species, there is only one national park, the tiny island of Port-Cros (700 hectares). This problem can be found all over the world: the percentage of protected areas that are deserts (arid or frozen) or mountainous regions is far higher than is justified by their biological value.

Breeding crocodiles for their skin and meat illustrates the possibility of combining economic development and the protection of natural areas, while reducing the pressure exerted on wild species by hunting.

Sustainable action and conservation **109**

Paying the price of conservation

Half of the protected areas in the world are only protected on paper, and the percentage of these 'paper parks' is higher in poor regions such as tropical zones. Of the 'protected' areas in South-East Asia, only three are considered to be reasonably well managed. The number of scientists and other staff, as well as the amount of equipment available, is extremely low. Furthermore, these parks are not supported by local populations, to say the least. The latter often have to suffer inconvenience for the sake of this biodiversity conservation: certain areas are closed off to them, they are prevented from hunting some of the animals and from collecting certain plants, and they generally receive nothing in return. With the money it generates, 'green' tourism can be an excellent source of motivation as long as the profits do actually reach these rural populations. Of course, local people should also be educated in the importance of conserving species. But this can only be done at a price, and the developed countries need to take part in this process, or even take full responsibility for the costs if the country in question has insufficient means to do so.

By printing bank notes that proudly display its wild animals, a country like Namibia shows that it has understood what it can gain from this natural resource in terms of the money generated by ecotourism.

Setting up networks of protected areas

The creation of a protected area does not mean that the rest of the surrounding land should be ignored. There are numerous examples of national parks that have diverted attention from the destruction of rich habitats nearby. First conceived by UNESCO's Man and Biosphere (MAB) Programme in 1974, biosphere reserves were created to preserve areas that represented terrestrial ecosystems, conserved biodiversity, promoted economic development and maintained cultural values.

Each of these reserves (today there are a total of 300 throughout the world) has a central core area which is legally protected

More marine reserves are needed

At present, most of the areas that have been protected are terrestrial. Marine environments are increasingly in need of conservation, and there is an urgent need to increase the number of marine reserves. In 2002, the Australian government took a positive step in this direction by creating a 6.5 million hectare reserve in the Indian Ocean sector of the Southern Ocean. This makes the Heard Island and McDonald Islands Marine Reserve the largest area on Earth to be protected from all commercial species removal.

Plant corridors linking reserves allow animals to range over far larger areas. Gallery forests, which form a corridor of trees along river valleys, perform this role by helping to connect animal populations.

and devoted to conservation. This is surrounded by a buffer zone, where human activities compatible with conservation, such as tourism, take place. Finally, there is a transition area, where sustainable resource management practices, which respect the environment, are promoted and developed. In addition to conserving species and natural habitats, these reserves allow scientists to measure precisely the impact of human activities on the environment. Conservation experts believe it is essential that gene exchange should occur in the protected areas (and thus that it be possible for animals to circulate freely). There should in fact be 'corridors' joining these zones, which would be nodal points in a 'natural network'. This structure would make it easier for species to resist the onslaught of human activity and the global changes that it brings about. However, this worldwide network remains for the moment a decidedly long-term objective.

Sustainable development

How can three-quarters of the human race improve their underdeveloped economies without overburdening the planet's natural ecosystems? Perhaps by creating an entirely new type of economy.

The concept of sustainable development

There is definitely an urgent need to increase the number of protected areas on our planet and to improve the way they function. However, preserving a few strips of land while nearby habitats and ecosystems are being destroyed is not a viable long-term solution. The thinking behind the way human societies work needs to be redirected along less destructive lines. Born out of this need, sustainable development has been defined as 'development which meets the needs of the present without compromising the ability of future generations to meet their own needs'. Ever since this term first appeared in an official report in 1987, the concept has become extremely popular.

The explosive, anarchic development of cities such as Lagos (Nigeria) is a real test for the surrounding natural areas. Planned urban development, respectful of the environment, is possible … but at a price.

Contrived unanimity

However, although the concept has unanimous backing, real progress towards sustainable development has been negligible. Part of the explanation for this lies in the vagueness of the term. Thus, multinational companies have embraced the concept of sustainable development because they are attracted above all by the idea of 'development', which they interpret as increased production that will continue on a sustainable basis. Conversely, there is a current of thought among some members of the environmental protection organizations – admittedly the minority – that the main concern is to protect ecosystems and that the improvement of the fate of human populations is secondary. Others interpret 'development' as meaning improved hygiene, culture, social links, democracy, and so on, but not necessarily greater material production, or at least only within certain limits.

The 'precautionary principle'

The same ambiguity attaches to the 'precautionary principle', which is part and parcel of sustainable development. This principle lays down that, in situations of scientific uncertainty, the authorities should take all possible precautionary measures where there is a risk of serious harm

Biopiracy

The abusive exploitation of countries in the southern hemisphere by industrial firms in the north is called biopiracy. The rosy periwinkle (*Catharanthus roseus*), which is endemic to Madagascar, is at the centre of a shocking scandal. This rare plant contains compounds that have been used to develop two anti-cancer drugs, vincristine and vinblastine. The pharmaceutical group that markets them makes around US$100 million a year from these alkaloids, but the poor of Madagascar have received nothing in return. Furthermore, the intensive collecting of this plant has brought it to the brink of extinction. The pharmaceutical and cosmetic industries, among others, shamelessly harvest the fruits of biodiversity, which earn them US$600 to US$900 billion a year.

being done to human beings, natural resources or the environment. This principle is important because it moves the burden of proof from the victims and back onto those who are damaging the environment. It is up to the latter to prove that any given activity is compatible with the environment and not up to environmentalists to prove that serious damage is being caused. Despite the fact that a large number of countries have accepted this idea, the hope that the precautionary principle will be properly applied is, in general, just wishful thinking.

In certain reserves in Kenya, the herding of domestic animals by local tribes is allowed: the coexistence of man and nature need not be a contradiction in terms.

Sustainable action and conservation **113**

The planetary ecosystem has a limited capacity for absorbing waste, so the richest countries should limit their consumption of natural resources in order to ensure that the world remains a safe and clean place for everyone. Would such restrictions make people any less happy?

Sustainable technology

Sustainable development entails thinking about the long-term consequences of human activity with regard to the conservation of both natural resources and ecosystems. Scientists provide definitions of sustainable fishing, forestry, agriculture, transport systems and industry. They work out techniques, indicators and thresholds which will take into account the needs of future generations. It is already possible to predict whether a fish factory or a forestry company's activities will allow for the renewal of the resources they exploit. International certification organizations dedicated to promoting the appropriate management of natural resources – such as the Marine Stewardship Council (MSC) and the Forest Stewardship Council (FSC) – have logos which guarantee that the products carrying them have been created without contributing to the depletion of valuable natural resources.

Not only a technical problem

Solutions for achieving sustainability currently exist, or are within our reach. However, they incur additional costs: a 'sustainable' product is thus more expensive than its 'non-sustainable' competitors.

114

In a globalized economy based on competition, industrialists making sustainable products are at a disadvantage. Sustainability regulations for everyone to abide by would be a possibility, but in the absence of international laws all we can do is sign multilateral agreements, which are particularly hard to formulate, never mind apply. These issues are made even more complicated by the astounding inequalities which characterize the world we live in today. The difference between the standard of living of a senior executive in the West and that of a poor farmer in Bangladesh exceeds anything seen before in the history of the human race. The difficult matter of improving the standard of living of three-quarters of humanity – without compromising the future of the planet and its ecosystems in the process – needs to be resolved. It appears inevitable that the richest countries will have to make a relative 'sacrifice' in their standards of living, since the Earth cannot supply enough water, energy and other resources for the whole of humanity to enjoy the lifestyle currently enjoyed by the West.

Changing our economy and our values

A great change in our way of life and in the global economy is required. Our economic system continues to embrace values opposed to sustainable development: short-term profits, individualism, irresponsibility, absence of solidarity with other peoples or future generations, and so on. By tackling society's frantic consumerism and various forms of selfish behaviour, and by utilizing science and technology in the interests of humanity, it will no doubt still be possible for man to assume the role he should rightly play – that of custodian of the biosphere.

Eliminating overpopulation by development

Because of their rapid population growth, the inhabitants of developing countries are often 'accused' of causing habitat loss. Human pressure on ecosystems has definitely reached breaking point. However, in developing countries, having a large family is often the only way of ensuring you are cared for in case of illness or accident and in old age. And yet, within just one or two generations, economic and cultural development can lead to a sharp drop in the birth rate. Helping countries in the south develop, even if this is costly, is the only efficient and acceptable way of solving the problem of overpopulation.

Sustainable action and conservation

How should large carnivores be managed?

Large carnivores attract the attention of the public and conservationists alike. But how should their protection be balanced with the problems of farmers who regularly lose livestock to these same carnivores? There are fierce arguments over how carnivore populations should be maintained and what role the state should play.

Animals and humans – living together

In the countryside, there is often conflict between farmers, who must protect their livestock and crops, and wild animals, who see farms as a ready source of food for themselves. There are plenty of petty thieves likely to drive farmers to despair: many birds are very fond of seeds and grains; a number of large herbivores (deer in Europe, elephants in Africa, kangaroos in Australia) graze in fields and pastures or trample on crops; small carnivores (mammals such as the fox and mongoose, or large lizards such as the Tejus from Central America and the West Indies) are quick to take advantage of unsecured hen-coops to make a meal of the poultry. Although all of these animals can cause considerable damage, some of the greatest tension between man and nature occurs in farmers' relationships with large carnivores such as the lion or leopard in Africa, the tiger in Asia, the puma in America and the lynx

and wolf in Europe. In addition to these mammals, carnivorous reptiles such as crocodiles and large snakes can cause similar problems in some countries.

They may cause damage, but are they dangerous?

Large carnivores can inflict real damage on the livelihoods of sheep farmers (in the case of the wolf) and cattle farmers (in the case of the lion or tiger), but the problem goes beyond actual physical destruction. The perceived threat that these animals present to livestock and property provokes sufficient fear and concern that, over time, man's

The lynx, too small to attack humans, generally only takes sheep. Because each individual occupies a vast territory, the damage is limited.

strong feelings about them have given rise to numerous myths and legends. The danger that carnivores really present to man is exaggerated by such folklore. The danger presented by wolves, for example, is relatively minor – not a single attack on a human has been recorded for decades anywhere in the world. Although it is true that bears can be dangerous, only a few attacks have occurred in the whole of Europe over the last decade. In most cases, this was due to the victims' lack of common sense – a Finnish walker, for example, was seriously injured because he had come across fresh bear tracks in the snow and decided out of curiosity to follow the trail. Tigers and crocodiles, on the other hand, are distinctly more dangerous. Injured, sick or old tigers sometimes attack humans because they are easier to catch than the animals' usual prey. In India, people quite regularly fall victim to tiger attacks. In Africa, crocodiles often attack people who venture too close to rivers. Some reports indicate that during the rainy season in Malawi, two people are killed each day by crocodiles. These deaths may be linked to the decline in fish (the crocodiles' normal diet) that has resulted from man's pollution of the rivers.

The brown bear is an opportunistic, intelligent omnivore and, under certain conditions, it can lose its fear of humans. When this happens, it can be extremely dangerous.

Demon or animal?

Throughout history, the high level of intelligence displayed by large carnivores has proved surprising to humans. The sophisticated hunting strategy of the wolf – an animal that shares out tasks within the pack – is impressive, and it is often depicted as an intelligent and cunning hunter (typified by the big, bad wolf in *Little Red Riding Hood*). Bears are credited with similar qualities. One female brown bear in Austria is reported to have learned to open the sluice gates of the ponds in a fish farm, in order to feed on the fish. Apparently this bear would also come running – even from far away – whenever she heard a gunshot, in the hope of finding a dead roe deer or wild boar before the hunter who had fired the gun could get to his kill. Although such stories sound unlikely they have led people to conjure up a humanized, evil or even demonized image of these animals, something often seen in mythology. Many myths personalize animals, giving them names and endowing them with magical powers and malicious intentions. In reality, predators' cognitive skills may be explained quite simply by the fact that any animal at the top of the food chain must have developed a relatively large brain. Despite this logical explanation, the abilities of these large carnivores can appear amazing, and it is understandable that some legends have been created around them.

Belief in legends such as these tends to be more widespread in rural areas. City-dwellers, on the other hand, often view the same animals quite differently, with an equally unrealistic view that sometimes seems to have come straight out of a Hollywood film. From this perspective, carnivores are seen as beautiful, proud, free and even noble animals (note the anthropomorphism of this terminology) that only kill to eat, and almost appear to regret having to do so. Once again, this is a distortion of reality. Carnivores have a very strong predatory instinct, essential for their survival. A wolf finding itself in a flock of sheep will not only kill to eat, but in the panic and excitement caused by the prey's desperate attempts to escape, it may well kill significantly more animals than it can eat. Similarly, foxes may kill all the hens in a coop in a single night.

These two opposing views of nature (even if they are not always as extreme as portrayed here) are at the heart of the increasingly frequent conflicts between farmers and large carnivores.

The accursed wolf

As a result of effective conservation measures and the exodus of rural populations to the cities, the number of large predators in Europe and the United States is on the increase. Wolves are found in considerable numbers in Spain, Portugal and Italy, and are gradually migrating across the Alps into Switzerland and France, where they have been extinct for more than 60 years. From Eastern Europe, they are moving into Germany, and from the former Soviet Union into Scandinavia. Despite the protection that this species should receive, wolves are still poisoned illegally in some countries. Their real ecological impact is, however, very low: since 1993 wolves have killed around 7,000 sheep in the Alps, compared with the 150,000 killed each year by stray dogs, brucellosis and various types of accident.

Under European legislation, governments are required to investigate the possibility of reintroducing indigenous but now extinct species. The last wolf in Scotland was shot around 1743, and it has been suggested that wolves should be reintroduced to the Highlands.

The puma is a powerful, formidably armed feline. Nevertheless, it can be kept away from herds of cattle by protecting the latter with guard dogs.

Predators: what good do they do?

Many farming communities across the world are hostile to carnivores, and critical of the environmental laws that force them to coexist with these predators in order to fulfill a view of what wild countryside 'should' be like. Farmers may question the necessity of protecting wolves or brown bears – after all, these animals are almost never seen, so what difference does it make if they are there or not? Most farmers regard carnivores as pests, just like rats, cockroaches or the Colorado Beetle. To them, the idea of the noble predator is simply a fantasy.

The question of the value of biodiversity is brought into sharp focus here. The ecological value of predators, as represented in environmental awareness campaigns, is often seen by rural inhabitants as something irrelevant to their lives, provoking such questions as 'Is there anything wrong with nature in countries where the wolf (or the brown bear) has died out? Is nature any less beautiful there? If not, then why should we protect these animals?'

The ecologists' argument

Anyone concerned about environmental conservation would argue that the existence of complete ecosystems that include predators is far preferable to biologically impoverished environments without them. Predators help to maintain the biological equilibrium by preventing the proliferation of herbivores, which would be harmful in a different way. For example, in Scotland there are currently estimated to be around 300,000 red deer, which, despite extensive culling, cause considerable damage to native trees. The proposed reintroduction of wolves would keep the numbers of deer in check. Additionally, by getting rid of sick or weak individuals, predators ensure the populations of their prey species remain healthier. It is generally accepted that ecosystems are better able to cope with traumatic events if they

The wolf is a carnivore that hunts in a pack, in which tasks are sometimes shared out between individuals in a remarkably sophisticated fashion. The wolf is unrivalled at avoiding any traps that are set for it.

have a high level of biodiversity than if they are impoverished. Such events include both 'natural' disasters such as floods, fires and diseases, and those caused by man, such as pollution and damage due by excessive extraction of natural resources. Furthermore, there is the issue of preventing species from extinction, a responsibility we owe to future generations. Obviously, the fate of a species cannot simply be determined by the 'value' man currently places on it. The notion that a 'useful' species has to be protected and a 'harmful' species needs to be eliminated is far too simplistic, since the judgement of which category is appropriate for any particular species will vary with time and place.

But keeping ecosystems intact comes at a price, and it would be unfair if this had to be paid by farmers alone. If society as a whole, out of concern for biological diversity, is in favour of protecting and reintroducing large predators, it should collectively help rural communities cope with the impact of these animals. However, the form this help should take is a matter for debate. Compensating the victims of the damage caused by the large carnivores may be one solution. Farmers could be paid a certain amount of money for each animal that is killed. This practice, although it has never made livestock owners sympathetic to predators, is sometimes enough to defuse their aggression.

However, such a system can cause problems. Refunding the loss of a sheep or a cow is one thing, but how do you measure the impact of the stress inflicted on the rest of the herd? The constant presence of predators creates continual stress for herbivores, stops them putting on weight and causes sheep to have miscarriages. How can this damage be assessed in financial terms?

Moreover, compensating farmers for animals killed by large carnivores can have the undesirable effect of encouraging unscrupulous farmers to be less vigilant in protecting their animals. Protection entails the use of various techniques (human surveillance, guard dogs, rounding the animals up at night), which involves extra expense and effort. With a compensation scheme, farmers who have made the effort to protect their herds are in danger of receiving less money than their more careless colleagues.

Providing a fixed subsidy for all the farmers in a high-risk zone may be a fairer and more satisfactory solution. The risks must of course be very carefully defined, because those who do not raise livestock in the high-risk areas will inevitably complain of unfair competition from their neighbours who do. Furthermore, the size of this subsidy will be difficult to judge, to ensure that farmers cannot make a better living from collecting subsidies that from careful husbandry.

Raising public awareness

In order to promote the coexistence of man with the large carnivores, public awareness campaigns are essential and, when carried out properly, can be most efficient. Rural populations do not, of course, consist exclusively of livestock farmers; other social groups can have less clear-cut views and may be more likely to support the protection of predators. This is due in part to the perceived benefits of increased tourism which may result from the enhancement of natural surroundings, as well as to the respect and admiration that many people generally hold for nature.

Glossary

[Acarids]
These animals are ticks and mites related to spiders, and are generally very small. The soil is teeming with numerous acarid species and they play an extremely important ecological role in recycling nutrients.

[Allopatric speciation]
The creation of new species from populations separated geographically by natural obstacles (river, mountain range, creek etc), with the result that interbreeding between the resulting populations is prevented.

[Arboreal]
This adjective is used to describe animals that live in trees (monkeys, frogs, squirrels, etc).

[Arthropoda]
Arthropoda is considered to be the largest phylum in the animal kingdom, containing over one million species. All arthropods have a segmented, rigid exoskeleton – which supports the musculature and protects the animal – and jointed appendages such as legs or mouthparts. The Arthropoda include the arachnids (spiders and scorpions), insects, millipedes and crustaceans.

[Bacteria]
Bacteria are prokaryotes – simple living organisms made up of a single cell with no nucleus. Bacteria come in a large variety of shapes and have adapted to many different environments.

[Biodiversity]
Biodiversity is a measure of the variety of all the genomes, species and ecosystems occurring in a specific area. The term comes from the two words 'biological' and 'diversity'.

[Biomass]
Biomass is the term used to describe the total mass of living organisms in a specific ecosystem, population or other unit area at a given moment.

[Canopy]
The canopy is a tropical forest environment, situated 50m above the ground and made up of the tops of tall trees. It forms an ecosystem which is home to a large number of different species.

[CITES]
Signed in Washington DC in 1973 by various governments, the Convention on International Trade in Endangered Species of Wild Fauna and Flora, more commonly known as CITES, came into force in 1975. It regulates international trade in over 30,000 species of plants and animals. The species covered by CITES are listed in three Appendices according to the degree of protection they need. These lists are regularly updated.

[Cloning]
Cloning refers to the reproduction of several specimens of genetically identical organisms, in particular when this is carried out using artificial methods.

[Coleoptera]
A vast order of insects, which contains over 350,000 species (beetles, ladybirds, weevils, glowworms, etc).

[Deciduous forest]
This is a forest dominated by broad-leaved trees (which lose their leaves in winter) as opposed to conifers.

[Decomposers]
Those small organisms found in the soil which break down dead organic matter (carcasses, plant debris, etc) into smaller molecules that can be reused by plants.

[Division]
Groups of species with similar structure (molluscs, arthropods, vertebrates, vascular plants, etc) are said to belong to the same division (plants) or phylum (animals).

[DNA (Deoxyribonucleic acid)]
DNA is a large organic molecule in the form of a double helix, found in the nucleus of cells. It stores genetic information and conveys it from one generation to the next.

[Ecoregion]
The Earth is considered to have a total of 200 terrestrial and marine ecoregions. These are regions with ecosystems that are particularly rich in species. These ecoregions harbour the greatest biodiversity and are thus the traditional targets for conservation. The WWF defines them as 'large units of

land or water which contain a geographically distinct assemblage of species, natural communities and environmental conditions'.

[Ecosystem]
An ecosystem is a community of organisms (plant, animal and other living forms), together with their environment (or biotope), functioning as a unit.

[Endemic]
An endemic species is one that only occurs in a particular geographical region and is believed to have evolved there.

[Epiphyte]
An epiphyte is a plant that grows on another plant for support, but which is not parasitic on it (epiphytic plants include lianas and orchids).

[Gene]
A gene is a sequence of DNA which allows living organisms to build the proteins they need.

[Genome]
A genome is an entire set of genes carried by an individual or shared by the members of a reproductive unit such as a population or a species. A genome contains the instructions required to build and develop a living being and to allow it to function.

[Groundwater]
Groundwater is water beneath the surface of the earth resulting from the infiltration of rainwater. It is the source of water for wells and springs. The upper surface of the groundwater is called the water table.

[Hotspot]
This is the term for each of the 25 regions that constitute the richest – and most threatened – reservoirs of plant and animal life on Earth.

[Humus]
Humus is organic matter resulting from the decomposition of dead organisms and plants.

[Invertebrate]
An invertebrate is an animal without a backbone. This group includes animals such as worms, insects, molluscs, sea urchins, crustaceans and spiders.

[IUCN]
Founded in 1948, the International Union for the Conservation of Nature, whose official name was changed to 'IUCN – The World Conservation Union' in 1990, brings together several dozen research and nature conservation organizations, states, government agencies, NGOs (non-governmental organizations) and scholars in a unique partnership. With the aim of conserving the integrity and diversity of nature, it also puts together and regularly updates the 'Red List' of the world's threatened species.

[Mangrove swamp]
A mangrove swamp is a forest community made up of any of several species of salt-tolerant tropical and subtropical mangrove trees, which can grow partially submerged in water. Mangrove swamps are found in salt marshes and on mudflats along tropical coasts on both sides of the equator.

[Marine regression]
The retreat of the sea and a drop in the sea level, causing shallow seas situated on the edges of continents to disappear and with them the numerous species that lived there.

[Mutation]
A permanent structural alteration in DNA that can be transmitted from one generation to the next. Changes in DNA usually either have no effect or cause harm. Occasionally, a mutation can improve an organism's chance of surviving and passing the beneficial change on to its descendants.

[Neurotoxic]
This adjective is used to describe a substance that can adversely affect the nervous system.

[Open habitat]
An open habitat is an expanse of open land, such as a natural grassland, steppe or scrub area, which is treeless or has very few trees.

[Overgrazing]
Overgrazing occurs when land is overexploited by livestock to such an extent that the vegetation and soil are significantly degraded.

[Pampas]
A vast, grassy, treeless plain found in southern South America.

[Pathogenic]
This adjective is used to describe any micro-organism that can cause disease in a living organism. These micro-organisms include viruses, bacteria and fungi.

[Pesticide]
A chemical substance (for example, an insecticide or fungicide) that kills harmful organisms and is used to control pests such as insects, weeds or micro-organisms. Pesticides are commonly used in agriculture.

[Photosynthesis]
This is a natural biochemical process whereby green plants manufacture carbohydrates using the light energy from the sun (trapped by the pigment chlorophyll), carbon dioxide from the air, and water. Oxygen is released in the process.

[Phylum]
Groups of species with the same structure (molluscs, arthropods, vertebrates, vascular plants, etc) are said to belong to the same phylum (animals) or division (plants).

[Plankton]
A collection of microscopic plants (phytoplankton) and animals (zooplankton) that floats passively or drifts with the current in the surface waters of seas and lakes.

[Prairie]
A large, open expanse of flat or rolling natural grassland, generally without trees. Prairies are found in both temperate and cold regions.

[Primary forest]
This term is used to refer to pristine forests that exist in their original state. These are forests that have never been touched by humans, or have been relatively unaffected by human activity.

[Red Queen effect]
In Lewis Carroll's *Alice Through the Looking Glass*, the Red Queen runs without actually moving forward because everything around her is also moving and keeping pace with her. This analogy describes the situation in which organisms are forced to adapt constantly in order to 'stay in the race' and maintain their status quo.

[Sahel]
A sub-desert zone on the southern fringes of the Sahara Desert.

[Salinization]
Salinization often occurs in warm, dry locations with desert or steppe climates. This term refers to the process in which soluble salts precipitate from water and build up in the upper layer of the soil, making it unsuitable for cultivation. Salinization is caused by the overexploitation of groundwater.

[Savanna]
An open habitat typical of tropical and subtropical regions, made up of vast expanses of level grasslands. A savanna is either treeless or dotted with bushes and trees.

[Species]
A group of organisms all of which have a high degree of physical and genetic similarity and in which the individuals are able to interbreed and produce viable, fertile offspring.

[Steppe]
A steppe is an extensive, grassy and usually treeless plain found in both temperate and cold regions.

[Sympatric speciation]
This occurs when two populations physically in contact with one another become genetically isolated, for example when their reproductive cycles no longer coincide.

[Tundra]
Any of the vast, relatively treeless areas in cold regions, characterized by very low temperatures, low precipitation and an abundance of lichens.

[Ungulate]
A hoofed, herbivorous mammal such as an antelope or giraffe.

[Vertebrate]
Any animal with a backbone consisting of bony or cartilaginous vertebrae enclosing a spinal cord.

[WWF]
The World Wide Fund for Nature is an international nature conservation organization, founded in 1961. WWF originally stood for 'World Wildlife Fund' before the name was changed in 1986. However, the USA and Canada have retained the old name. The WWF collects funds and finances many programmes to protect species that are most at risk.

Useful addresses and websites

Biodiversity World Map
http://www.nhm.ac.uk/science/projects/worldmap

Carnivore conservation
http://www.carnivoreconservation.org
Portal with links to many other sites related to carnivore conservation.

Committee on Recently Extinct Organisms
CREO: Committee on Recently Extinct Organisms c/o Department of Ichthyology, American Museum of Natural History, Central Park West at 79th Street, New York, NY 10024, USA
http://creo.amnh.org

Conservation International
1919 M Street, NW Suite 600 Washington, DC 20036, USA
http://www.conservation.org

Convention on Global Biodiversity
393 St Jacques Street, Office 300, Montreal, Quebec, Canada H2Y 1N9
http://www.biodiv.org

Convention on International Trade in Endangered Species (CITES)
UK contact:
Department for Environment, Food and Rural Affairs (DEFRA), Global Wildlife Division, 1st Floor, Temple Quay House, 2 The Square, Temple Quay, Bristol BS1 6EB, UK
http://www.ukcites.gov.uk

Convention on Migratory Species
UNEP/CMS Secretariat, United Nations Premises in Bonn, Martin-Luther-King-Str. 8, D-53175 Bonn, Germany
http://www.wcmc.org.uk/cms/

Food and Agriculture Organisation (FAO)
Viale delle Terme di Caracalla, 00100 Rome, Italy
http://www.fao.org

Friends of the Earth
26-28 Underwood Street, London N1 7JQ, UK
http://www.foe.co.uk

Greenpeace International
Ottho Heldringstraat 5, 1066 AZ Amsterdam, The Netherlands
http://www.greenpeace.org

International Whaling Commission
The Red House, 135 Station Road, Impington, Cambridge CB4 9NP, UK
http://www.iwcoffice.org

IUCN – The World Conservation Union
Rue Mauverney 28, Gland, 1196, Switzerland
http://iucn.org

IUCN Red List of threatened species
http://www.redlist.org

Marine Mammal Center
The Marine Mammal Center, Marin Headlands, 1065 Fort Cronkhite, Sausalito, CA 94965, USA
http://www.marinemammalcenter.org

TRAFFIC International
219a Huntingdon Rd, Cambridge, CB3 ODL, UK
http://www.traffic.org
Concerned with trade in endangered species.

United Nations Environment Programme (UNEP)
United Nations Avenue, Gigiri, PO Box 30552, Nairobi, Kenya
http://www.unep.org

World Conservation Monitoring Centre (UNEP-WCMC)
Information Office, UNEP-WCMC, 219 Huntingdon Road, Cambridge CB3 ODL, UK
http://www.unep-wcmc.org
Helpful information and maps.

World Resources Institute
10 G Street, NE (Suite 800), Washington, DC 20002, USA
http://www.wri.org

WWF (World Wide Fund for Nature)
WWF-UK, Panda House Weyside Park, Godalming, Surrey GU7 1XR, UK
http://www.panda.org

Suggestions for further reading

Burton, J (ed), *The Atlas of Endangered Species*, Apple Press, London, 2000

Fossey, D, *Gorillas in the Mist: A Remarkable Story of Thirteen Years Spent Living with the Greatest of the Great Apes*, Phoenix, London, 2001

Fry, S, *Rescuing the Spectacled Bear*, Hutchison, London, 2002

Gorke, M, *The Death of Our Planet's Species: A Challenge to Ecology and Ethics*, translated by Patricia Nevers, Island Press, Washington, DC, 2003

Green, I, *Wild Tigers of Bandhavgarh: Encounters in a Fragile Forest*, Tiger Books, Tunbridge Wells, 2002

Mackay, R, *The Atlas of Endangered Species: Threatened Plants and Animals of the World*, Earthscan, London, 2002

Reeve, R, *Policing International Trade in Endangered Species: the CITES Treaty and Compliance*, Royal Institute of International Affairs and Earthscan, London, 2002

Wolfe, A et al, *The Living Wild*, The Harvill Press, London, 2000

Index

Page numbers in *italics* refer to illustrations. **Bold** type indicates pages where the topic is dealt with in some detail.

Illustration credits

Photographs

Drawings and computer graphics